ETHNIC IDENTITY

Ethnic Identity

STRATEGIES OF DIVERSITY

Anya Peterson Royce

Indiana University Press • Bloomington

For Elizabeth Colson

First Midland Book Edition 1982

Manufactured in the United States of America

Library of Congress Cataloging in Publication Data

Royce, Anya Peterson.
Ethnic identity.

Bibliography: P.
Includes index.
1. Ethnicity.   I. Title.
GN495.6.R68   305.8   81-47168
ISBN 0-253-31035-0   AACR2
ISBN 0-253-20279-5 (pbk.)

1   2   3   4   5   86   85   84   83   82

Contents

Acknowledgments

It is impossible to date the beginning of this book. For as long as I can remember I have been fascinated by the question of identity. In the course of accumulating experiences, doing research, and, finally, writing, I have incurred many debts.

To few am I indebted as much as to Elizabeth Colson. Her own awesome scholarship sets a standard that is always there as a measure. Moreover, she taught me a respect for the craft of anthropology, without which no amount of experience will produce anything of value. Her foundation in both American and British anthropology gave me the broadest context in which to set the issue of ethnic identity. I am grateful for the extensive comments she made on several drafts of this book. Some of the chapters were changed substantially, and where I followed my original outline, my thoughts have been clarified by her questions. It is with great respect and affection that this book is dedicated to her.

Many colleagues gave fully of their time in reading and commenting. Not all of them agree with the concept of ethnic identity, but they were generous with suggestions nonetheless. At Indiana University they include William Cohen, Della Collins Cook, Raymond DeMallie, Ivan Karp, Irving Katz, John Lombardi, the late Alan Merriam, Harold Schneider, and James Vaughan. Elsewhere, George De Vos commented on the original prospectus, and several anonymous reviewers were helpful with drafts in various stages. Abner Cohen read the next-to-final draft, and I must thank him for his perceptive comments, which occasioned some final changes and clarifications.

Many helpful discussions and arguments were generated in the course I offer on ethnic identity. Successive classes were uniformly helpful, and I thank all those students who were part of the process that produced this book. Some must be singled out—Paméla Dorn, Alan Goldberg, Kent Maynard, Roberta Singer, and Gloria Young.

My debt to the people of Juchitán is enormous. As exemplars of a proud and successful ethnic identity within the overwhelmingly non-Indian population of Mexico, they, more than any other factor, are responsible for my essentially positive view of ethnic identity. Over the last thirteen years I have come to appreciate what it means to be Zapotec, and I thank all those Juchitecos who have helped me reach that understanding.

A variety of sources have funded my research in Juchitán, beginning in 1967 with a Ford Foundation scholarship and a training grant from NIMH in 1971-72. Since then Indiana University, through its several small grants programs, has made it possible for me to return frequently to Juchitán. These sources include the Biomedical Research Small Grants program, Grants-in-Aid of Faculty Research, and The President's Council on International Programs.

Indiana University has provided other kinds of support. A faculty study in the library continues to be a haven without distractions. Rita Brown, with diligence and good cheer, typed and retyped several portions of the manuscript.

As always, my parents must be acknowledged. They gave me that security without which one does not dare venture into new territory. Sometimes the ventures have caused them distress, but their love and support have been constant.

My husband, Ronald R. Royce, is one of the few people who understand and tolerate my passion for learning from experience and ventures into new territory. For that alone, I owe him much. His contributions to this book, however, are tangible and substantial—from making the index, to suggesting valuable references, to correcting some of my excesses, to goading me on when I wanted to rest after each minor hurdle. There is something to be said for being married to one's best critic. Thank you now and always.

Introduction

THERE ARE ADVANTAGES AND disadvantages to writing about ethnic identity, and they stem from the same characteristic: ethnic identity is a powerful phenomenon. It is powerful both at the affective level, where it touches us in ways mysterious and frequently unconscious, and at the level of strategy, where we consciously manipulate it. Its power is also perceived and interpreted differently by individuals and groups, whether they are users of ethnicity, observers of ethnicity, or analysts of ethnicity. Presenting a coherent view of a field that revolves around such a phenomenon is a difficult, often frustrating, always exciting task. One would like to be fair. That is difficult because even scholars, who are, after all, human, are not neutral about ethnic identity. One attempts a broad coverage both geographic and temporal. Yet selections have to be made or the task would be impossible. Competing theories and perspectives ought to be presented, yet too much coverage results in a potpourri that might be heady but lacks the strength and coherence of a unified approach. Finally, one wants to look at ethnic identity in ways that are meaningful to those who use ethnicity or are confronted with it in their daily lives as well as to the students of ethnic identity, to whom it is a phenomenon that characterizes the contemporary world.

Ethnic identity is one of many identities available to people. It is developed, displayed, manipulated, or ignored in accordance with the demands of particular situations. Human beings are aware of their surroundings and manipulate other individuals or situations in order to achieve what they perceive to be a more desirable context for themselves. While this view is dynamic and somewhat interactionist, it is not wildly so. People being what they are, some consistency and structure must characterize everyday life or we would be unable to cope with it. George De Vos puts this statement nicely: "Ethnic identity requires the maintenance of sufficiently consistent behavior to enable others to place an individual or a group in some given social category, thus permitting appropriate interactive behavior" (1975:374).

But what shapes the consistent behavior? The answers to this question range from institutions to past experience in interaction. The first half of this book is devoted to some of the larger institutional contexts that affect ethnic behavior. Contexts such as colonialism, nationalism, immigration, and internal migration affect the experience of ethnic identity at a level beyond the control of the individual. The second half of the book considers ethnicity primarily from the individual point of view, exploring motivation and the construction of symbols, tactics, and strategies. These are the major emphases that shape the two halves of the book. That does not mean that the first half looks only from an institutional point of view, nor that the second considers only the personal level. The discussion of colonialism, nationalism, and immigration, while focusing on institutions and larger contexts, also considers the response of the individual. The discussion of tactics and symbols in the second half, of necessity, includes institutional forces.

Some readers will note the de-emphasis on two possible ways of approaching ethnic identity. The first, the neo-Marxist approach, characterizes some studies of ethnicity and identity primarily at the institutional level. The second, the psychoanalytic approach, occurs at the level of the individual. Omitting these two perspectives from this book was a deliberate choice dictated in large part by the limitations of time and space. Moreover, there exist other sources devoted to these approaches. The psychoanalytic approach to ethnic identity is used fruitfully by scholars such as De Vos and George Devereux (1975). Or we have, in the case of Dominique Mannoni's *Prospero and Caliban* (1956), a penetrating analysis of colonialism from the point of view of psychology. I have incorporated some of that perspective in places where not using it would have meant distorting or missing some crucial aspect of the point at hand. To have incorporated it throughout would have made the book much too long and fragmented. Likewise, some scholars have used the neo-Marxist approach well, particularly in the relationship between class and ethnic identity.

There are two problems with a neo-Marxist approach to ethnicity. First, it has been used in an ideological sense by nations such as the Soviet Union and China as a way of ignoring the problems of ethnic minorities within their boundaries. If the problems of these groups derive from their class standing and limited access to resources, as is argued, then ethnicity has no relevance and need not be considered as part of any solution proposed. (Similar arguments have been made for indigenous groups within Latin American countries.) Second, a neo-Marxist approach has little empirical value in most of the situations of ethnic interaction in the contemporary world. As will be apparent in the examples presented later in the book, there has not been a unidirectional shift from ethnic identity to class consciousness. Neither does the use of one strategy preclude the use of the other at another time.

In addition to the very general assumption that individuals, within certain constraints, will use ethnic identity how and when it suits them, some specific themes are developed in the course of this book. One revolves around the three factors of power, perception, and purpose. It is possible to view any inter-ethnic situation in terms of these three factors. Aside from the fact that they are universally applicable, these factors are also analytically useful because they apply equally to ethnic and nonethnic, dominant and subordinate, participant and observer. Using them we may analyze motives, tactics, and even analyses, scholarly and otherwise.

Of the three, power is perhaps primary. If one has the power to impose one's definition of any situation, one will normally do so, and considerations of perception and purpose will be secondary. A corollary of this proposition is that everyone in a subordinate position is potentially an ethnic, it being the privilege of the dominant group to assign roles and lay down rules. Dominant groups rarely define themselves as ethnics.

Power is usually derived from a combination of material and ideological resources and may have an historical component as well. Subordinates, by definition, have less power. However, they do have access to certain kinds of power that dominants ignore or overlook. Even if one does not have the resources to define a situation positively, one may still have the power to define it negatively. Individuals and groups can and do resist. They sometimes simply refuse to abide by others' rules, or they may accept them on the surface but resist them on a deeper level. Sometimes subordinate groups have been able to use the fact of their subordination as a weapon in interactions with guilt-ridden members of dominant groups. This strategy is becoming more and more frequent. Subordinate groups derive a certain power as well from the fact that they generally view situations in all their complexity rather than in simple black and white terms. They are aware of subleties of meaning that may appear to dominants as simple statements. For subordinates, this skill is necessary if they are to make the best of their situation. A recent study by Lorand B. Szlazay and James Deese, based on associative meanings of words and subjective culture, uses materials collected from different ethnic and national groups. One analysis illustrates the difference in awareness on the part of dominants and subordinates. Black students were "less likely to think about their own ethnicity and that of others in terms of simple oppositional dichotomies, with all their ambiguity, negative affect, and potential for oversimplification" (1978:64–65). Further, "Blacks were more aware of Whites than the White students were themselves . . . the Black students were self-consciously aware of themselves as a minority, whereas the White students hardly ever had to think of themselves as distinctly White" (ibid.:72).

Very simply, if you control society long enough, you begin to assume that your power is the natural state of affairs. You do not need to be aware of the complexities of the situation under your dominance because you control it by fiat and superior power. The view from below is quite different—to survive at all, to get ahead, requires knowledge of the subtleties of institutional structure as well as knowledge of the thoughts and values of the dominant group.

I have been speaking above of the kind of long-term power that is typical of stratified societies. There are also more-equitable situations in which power is negotiated and renegotiated frequently between individuals or groups who are more or less equals. Or power may cease to be an overriding concern, as in the case of mutual interest.

Perception is a second factor that must be considered in any interethnic interaction, whether long term or situational. How do members of different groups perceive themselves and the others? How do they view the society as a whole? How do they perceive each situation? We rarely perceive anything or anyone in an unbiased fashion. We tend to see what we have been socialized to expect, and are blind to the unexpected. Few empirical studies have been done on the development of perceptions about identity. One of the few is Ann Beuf's (1977) research on the acquisition of ethnic imagery among American Indian and Anglo children. Using the techniques of game playing and storytelling, Beuf elicits data that indicate clear-cut perceptions of "differentness" in children by the age of 5. Moreover, for the Indian children, their differentness was negatively valued. More positively, she presents some evidence to suggest that this negative evaluation reverses itself as the child matures.

Perceptions take concrete form as symbols and stereotypes. Symbol construction and stereotype building are not unidirectional processes, nor do they occur in isolation. Like everything else having to do with ethnic identity, the presence of "others" stimulates, molds, inspires. The process may become fixed at any point; it may be in a constant state of flux; it may reverse itself; it may be perversely negative or blatantly self-congratulatory. Perceptions and their material manifestations may be firmly fixed in reality, but just as often they choose to operate on the basis of myth. And then there is the middle ground, which is so seductive because it hints of reality but offers at the same time the fantasy of myth. Because the human mind is endlessly inventive, weaving realities for itself out of bits and pieces, one can safely posit only limited stability; and one has to anticipate responses with the understanding that one may, at any point, be wrong.

It is basic to human nature to attempt to improve one's lot at least some of the time. In this tactical process, one must have a purpose even if it is not conscious. Purpose is easier to detect and isolate in the frameworks of of colonialism, nationalism, and immigration. Often, in the case of the first two, purpose is stated explicitly, frequently becoming a banner behind which one may rally supporters. Of course the stated purpose may not be the same as the underlying motivation. Britain may have claimed to be colonizing East Africa to rid the world of the menace of the slave trade, but at the same time she was enjoying the economic benefits. Similarly, since a lust for gold and spices is more difficult to justify than the saving of thousands of heathen souls by conversion, the rallying symbol used is religion. There may be many purposes, and their ranking may vary considerably from individual to individual within the group.

Purpose is quite apparent in long-term identity switching or "passing," when individuals or groups who feel that they are in an inferior position seek to improve their situation. "Inferior" may refer to a negative image forced upon the subordinate group, to a less-favorable economic situation, or, often, to a combination of these factors.

Short-term or situational selection of identity is sometimes more difficult to attribute to one purpose as opposed to another. Any situation may be perceived in terms of its economic, status, and dominance implications, or simply as a challenge to create or manipulate an identity. (While "getting ahead" is a serious business, human beings are also wont to play, and sometimes they play with identity.)

Readers are encouraged to assess theories and examples presented in the following pages in light of power, perception, and purpose. In addition to this schema, important oppositions appear throughout the book. They cannot be so conveniently or mellifluously catalogued, but they are crucial nonetheless. The most obvious and therefore perhaps the best choice to begin with is the contrast between institutions and individuals. It may be that ethnic identity, more than most subjects, is equally divided between these two ends of a continuum. Surely, where ethnic identity is concerned, the interaction between institutions and individuals creates a case that amounts to more than the sum of its parts. The two halves of this book reflect this dichotomy, the first being devoted primarily to institutions and the second to what individuals do. Obviously, there is a relationship between the two—just as institutions derive their shape and color from the actions of individuals so do individuals shape their actions on the basis of the institutions of their society. The term "institution" here also refers to the ethnic group. Persons make choices as individuals but if they are to have any saliency in an ethnic identity they must have an ethnic group as a referent. Certain obligations accompany the benefits of group membership, and, in some instances, individual preference may be overridden in favor of group coherence.

A second contrast occurs with regard to ethnic content as opposed to ethnic boundary. Again, there is a relationship between the two, and neither can be fully understood without reference to the other. Sometimes, for purposes of analysis and clarity of thought, we separate them but we are in error if we fail to put them together again. In earlier studies what frequently served as "content" were little more than laundry lists of ethnic traits by which we thought we could identify any particular group. A turning point was reached in 1969 with the publication of Fredrik Barth's *Ethnic Groups and Boundaries*, a collection of essays that focused on the boundaries between groups rather than on the internal construction or content of particular groups. Since then, we have seen numerous books, articles, and collections of papers devoted to boundaries at the expense of content. Barth takes the reasonable position that one cannot know an ethnic group by its content alone; therefore we should pay attention to its behavior, particularly its boundary-maintaining behavior. This idea was taken by many to mean that content was out and boundaries were in. It is time to return to a middle ground for the simple reason that one cannot understand let alone explain ethnic behavior without reference to both content and boundary, symbols and behavior.

Let me list briefly some of the interconnections that will be elaborated in the body of the book. No ethnic group can maintain a believable (viable) identity without signs, symbols, and underlying values that point to a distinctive identity. However, those signs and symbols are products of interaction with other groups, and part of the viability of the identity depends on the comprehensibility of the ethnic content and its manipulation so as to present a positive image across boundaries. Furthermore, contents change as situations change and in response to the larger society. Some symbols are relevant specifically to inter-ethnic boundaries. Others are used to differentiate within groups and may have no relevance whatsoever to nonmembers. The two systems may interact, and there may be some bleeding across boundaries; but they may also function as separate systems with their own patterns of response and rates of change. The ability of an ethnic group to maintain boundaries, hence survive as a distinct entity, may depend on its ability to marshall an impressive array of symbols. Conversely, a symbol system without boundaries cannot continue to exist.

Martin Doornbos, in a provocative article on conceptual problems with ethnicity in integration analysis (1972), suggests that individuals take their identity from two different sources, one being the ethnic group itself, the other the sense of solidarity that devolves upon groups that find themselves different from other groups or cut off from society. It seems to me that the first focuses on those items that define the group to itself, while the second stresses the contrast between groups epitomized by boundaries.

Regardless of the larger framework or the situation, there is a continuous interaction between contents and boundaries. If we are to
understand ethnic behavior without shutting our eyes to its complexity
and ambiguity, we must pay equal attention to the two contrasting
features.

A third dichotomy exists between the material and the ideological.
This contrast is first raised in chapter 1, on definitions, which refers to
objective versus subjective definitions of ethnic identity. Objective
definitions require material demonstration of ethnic identity—language, phenotype, dress, dance, religious belief, foods. Subjective
definitions revolve around ideological positions—"I am an X because I
identify with other X's." The chapter concludes that the only satisfactory definition for the participant in ethnic encounters as well as for the
analyst is a combination of these two. The groups that survive and
thrive have defined themselves in this combined way.

Groups will demand some concrete evidence of ethnic identity from
members and potential members, especially if they are threatened in
their status by outsiders. The Lumbee of North Carolina, a group that
is threatened, pose a threat to other American Indians. While they claim
an identity as Lumbee, American Indians, they have very little in the
way of material resources to support their claim—no Lumbee language, no coherent tribal history or homeland, and no ceremonies
specific to the group; and their phenotype can be labeled Black, White,
or Indian because it is so variable (See Blu 1980).

Material and ideological resources also become important in settings
in which the survival of the group is problematic—colonialism, conquest, nationhood, immigration. Here, material resources include access
to a means of subsistence, geographic location that will slow down the
process of conquest, a political organization that will allow concerted
resistance or offensive strategy. The ideology, of course, must also be
present or there will be no reason or will to maintain a separate identity.

The same pair occurs in the construction of symbols and stereotypes
and characterizes ethnic interaction, whether long term or situational.
Material traits and resources change just like ideologies, and there is
some evidence to suggest that they are quicker to change than
ideologies. As a corollary, it is also probably true that there is more
borrowing and exchanging of material items than of ideologies. However, as Abner Cohen points out in *Two-Dimensional Man*, ideologies
often take on identities of their own, at which point they may be

adopted wholesale by an interest group rather than the group's developing an ideology of its own (1974:82). At some point there must be an
attempt to bring the two into line. That happens most often when there
is a loss of group cohesiveness or stability. It is precisely at these points
that it is easiest to see what are the combined resources of the group.
But only if we are looking for two kinds of resources. For this reason it
is important that we always keep both ends of this particular continuum
in mind.

The question of persistence versus change is another important contrast. Barth (1969) raises it as an issue in speaking of definitions of
ethnic identity and ethnic groups. How much change is allowable in the
signs and symbols of a group identity before we must speak of the
group as something else? If we tie a definition of an ethnic group to X
language, X style of dress, X religion, is it the same group when it has
Y language, Y style of dress, and Y religion? Barth raises this point as a
way of indicating that we must consider other defining factors, but it
also is linked to old ways of thinking about "tradition."

For many scholars in the past (fewer today, one hopes), the hallmark
of an ethnic group was its adherence to "tradition," by which they
meant that the group maintained old customs, old symbols, and old
modes of behavior, which were passed down from time immemorial.
Some ultimate beginning was posited and the customs were inherited
unchanged by each generation. Once change was introduced, tradition
was somehow diminished. This view probably never corresponded
very closely to reality. Humans constantly acquire new traits, change
and rework old ones, abandon some features altogether. Because a
plastic jug replaces a pottery jug does not necessarily mean that the
function or symbolism of the jug has changed. Western society does not
work that way. Why should we assume that non-Western societies do?
Or is it that there is some romance attached to thinking that there exist
marvelous, unchanged, conservative traditionalists? Elsewhere (Royce
1975) I have proposed the term "style" to replace "tradition," and I use
"style" in that sense throughout this work. Style assumes choice and
allows for change. It is not burdened with the cultural connotations that
we unconsciously attach to the term "tradition" and is therefore more
appropriate for describing ethnic groups.

We have examples in the contemporary world of groups that have
gone back and recreated an ethnic style after not using that style or their
ethnic identity for generations. There was a period when to be an ethnic

was to be undesirable, and many individuals and groups played down their ethnicity. But today, an ethnic identity is becoming an asset and an essential part of peoples' repertoires of identities. If a number of generations have passed since a group's ethnic features have been used, recreating symbols and customs and reestablishing a viable identity can be a difficult task. It has not daunted the determined groups who search out genealogical records, histories, ethnographic descriptions, and old people who still remember. How do we classify groups like these in terms of identity? Persistence? Were they always ethnic even when there were no outward and visible signs? Are they now the same ethnics they once were? These bothersome problems tend to disappear when one is dealing with empirical rather than hypothetical situations.

Up to now we have been speaking primarily about change. There must also be some attention paid to persistence and constancy. In real-life strategies, it is easier for an ethnic group to use ethnicity as a basis for tactics if the group has an historical tradition that contains some elements of long standing. To be effective, this past must be acknowledged by other groups, and acknowledgment comes more easily if people can recognize some relatively constant features. There is also a sense of assurance people derive from the knowledge that their roots go far back in time.

Yet another important contrast is that between cognition and behavior. It is a commonplace that people do not always do what they say they do. It is a commonplace that people hold to a particular set of values or a particular mental view of the world and then belie that set or view in their behavior. All human behavior and interaction should be regarded with this principle in mind, but ethnic behavior is perhaps even more crucially affected by the contrast possible between cognition and behavior.

In examining the relationship between cognition and behavior, we must also be aware of the distinction between the individual and the group. There are values shared by group members and behaviors that characterize all group members in response to particular situations. When threatened from the outside, for example, an ethnic group will tend to present a unanimity of thought and behavior, but that does not mean that all the members of a group have the same ideas about their ethnicity or that they will always behave in similar ways. There may be a great deal of variation within a group, sometimes to the extent of developing factions. It is easier for us to see and understand variations in behavior than differences in thoughts and values. Somehow we regard those value systems as being basic and unchanging and held in common. Individual behaviors that vary are simply epiphenomena. This view is held by both insiders and outsiders—persons viewing their own groups and persons viewing another group from the outside. The emphasis on behavior is understandable. It is a tangible sign of ethnic identity. By regulating behavior, we think that we can regulate ethnicity. In the chapters to follow there are examples of such attempts at regulation. Dominant groups trying to enforce a kind of uniform assimilation will often prohibit the use of a native language, native dress, or ritual. The dominant groups often assume that behavioral compliance with these strictures means a corresponding cognitive shift and compliance. They are assuming a one-to-one relationship between objective indicators and subjective identification. That assumption is contradicted by any number of examples in which groups have maintained a distinct value system based on their difference and opposition but show no outward sign of their difference.

Few studies have explored the relationship between cognition and behavior in any systematic fashion (two exceptions are J.C. Mitchell in Cohen 1969 and Norman Whitten in his book on ethnicity in Ecuador 1976). A useful observation was made by Tamatsu Shibutani and Kian M. Kwan (1965) about the difficulty of assessing mental compliance. They argue that when behavioral conformity is enforced by law or social consensus one must look at the *style* of the compliance. Individuals may be forced to behave in certain ways. Do they do so willingly? Grudgingly? Graciously? This kind of analysis and assessment is important in looking at the tactical use of ethnicity. Both Elizabeth Colson, writing about the Makah (1953), and Edward Spicer, dealing with persistent identity systems (1971), isolate an area of intergroup interaction that revolves around a set of values and ideas. They suggest that groups may persist for long periods with ethnic consensus and cohesiveness occurring only in this realm. The present book does not pretend to analyze the relationship between cognition and behavior based on any single ethnographic example. It suggests, first, that these two categories do exist and that there is a relationship between them, and, second, that there are important implications for the use and study of ethnic-based action deriving from this pairing.

The title of the last chapter is another dichotomy, this time between myth and reality. One does not have to read widely or deeply about ethnic identity to confront this opposition. Neither scholars nor lay persons are neutral about ethnic identity, hence the elaboration of myth to support one's particular view. In a sense, this dichotomy is false—myth implies the opposite of reality; reality implies something that has a concrete, immutable existence. In truth, it is almost impossible to separate them into neat, non-overlapping categories. One person's myth is another's reality and vice versa. Furthermore, if people plan their actions on the basis of an assumption, it matters little whether that assumption is myth or reality. Stereotypes are perhaps the best example of the ability of the human mind to believe fiercely in whatever it wants to believe even when one can demonstrate empirically that the belief is inaccurate. Recent studies of stereotypes and political behavior showed people believing firmly that certain white ethnics were politically conservative, even though all the figures on actual voting behavior indicated otherwise. No amount of empirical data would change the minds of most of those respondents, and they will plan and behave on the basis of their inaccurate assumptions.

This fact can be frustrating for the students of ethnic identity if they have mental constructs that correspond to "myth" and "reality." On the other hand, if one views these contradictions as an eminently human characteristic, the frustration becomes enjoyment and fascination. The ground beneath ethnic identity shifts constantly, and one has to be ready to make the mental leaps to more solid ground or to ignore the temporary unease of standing in shifting sands.

The final and probably most important contrast is between "us" and "them." Without this contrast, ethnic identity does not exist. The hypothetical group on an island with no knowledge of others is not an ethnic group; it does not have an ethnic identity; it does not have strategies based on ethnicity. We define ourselves in large measure in terms of what we are not, and that derives from our experience of what others are and how we differ.

"Us" and "them" exist for scholars too. We define ourselves theoretically and methodologically by contrast with others. Frequently we build rather solid myths to support our particular stance and deny the reality or validity of other views. I cannot claim immunity from this basic human pattern. This book is written in the firm conviction that humans are adaptable and will usually employ and change strategies in order to improve their lot. I do not credit humans with always behaving rationally or in their best interests, for there are too many examples that contradict that assumption. In choosing and developing this basic conviction, I stand in contrast to those who see humans primarily as subordinate to institutions and to those who view human behavior as essentially programmed and immutable.

My aim in this book is to present theories and analyses that reflect the eclecticism and contrasts that characterize the phenomenon of ethnic identity itself. The reader will be forced to engage in creative reflection and analysis and to tolerate what will sometimes appear as contradictions. But it is the only way to dramatize the complexity, contrariness, and infinitely exciting variety of those human behaviors, thoughts, and values that we define as "ethnic."

Definitional Debates and
Theoretical Backgrounds

PART ONE

"Neither Christian
nor Jewish . . ."

I

Nature of Definitions

THERE ARE MANY CONCEPTS for which definitions are problematical. "Ethnic identity," "ethnic group," and "ethnicity" are three such. There is always a temptation to create watertight definitions with neat boundaries, thereby eliminating the possibility of confusion with neighboring concepts. In an essay on comparative aesthetics, John Ladd follows Wittgenstein in commenting on this tendency and in reiterating the necessity of distinguishing different orders of phenomena:

> Inexact, fuzzy concepts are different from scientific concepts or other kinds of concepts that are susceptible of exact definition. Wittgenstein compares the attempt to define such concepts with the attempt to "draw a sharp picture corresponding to a blurred one. . . . Anything—and nothing—is right." [1975:417]

This does not mean that we should abandon attempts to define inexact concepts; rather, we must be content with elastic definitions that approximate what we wish to define. Moreover, we must not agonize over our inability to reconcile exceptions and contradictions. "Ethnic identity," "ethnic group," and "ethnicity" are concepts that take their form and content from the give and take of human behavior, from shaping actions and from being acted upon. There is the same continuity and change about them as there is about human behavior.

In this spirit, I offer the following definitions. An "ethnic group" is a reference group invoked by people who share a common historical style (which may be only assumed), based on overt features and values, and who, through the process of interaction with others, identify themselves as sharing that style. "Ethnic identity" is the sum total of feelings on the part of group members about those values, symbols, and common histories that identify them as a distinct group. "Ethnicity" is simply ethnic-based action. These definitions are sufficiently specific to mark off a category we may call "ethnic," and at the same time they are flexible enough to allow for change. The history of thinking about ethnic identity and related phenomena has not always been characterized by such flexibility. That brings us to the definition of "ethnic" that provides the title of this chapter and that will serve as an appropriate point of departure for discussions of definitional debates.

> **ethnic 1:** neither Christian nor Jewish: HEATHEN 2: of or relating to races or large groups of people classed according to common traits and customs [*Webster's 7th Collegiate Dictionary*]

This definition is a useful pedagogical device for two reasons. First, it supplies two unambiguous definitions that represent much of the early thinking about ethnic groups and ethnic identity. Second, it brings home to us the fact that it is precisely these kinds of definitions that provide the basis from which most people derive their ideas about appropriate attitudes and behavior toward others.

The first definition, "neither Christian nor Jewish: HEATHEN," is, in fact, a nondefinition. We are told what ethnic is not and then given a label that, in Frederick Gearing's terms (1970), resorts to the notion of character. "Heathen," as it refers to the heathen character of acting consistently in describable heathen ways, allows us to sort and summarize a mass of facts. It is an undemanding and undiscriminating process. After all, we know the characteristics of heathens. Further, we assume that all heathens share the same characteristics. Further still, we hold that someone born a heathen will always be a heathen. We do not have to consider the heathen who converts to Christianity for the simple fact that the individual heathen convert is no longer an ethnic because he is a Christian.

The key words and phrases in the second definition that epitomize early ideas about ethnic identity are "races," "groups," "classed," and "common traits and customs." Those who hold this kind of definition assume certain features to be true of those classified as ethnic. Their overriding assumption is that an ethnic identity is one into which one is born, that it is as immutable as race, and that there is an entity in the real world corresponding to our phrase "ethnic group" all of whose members share common traits and customs. Again, this kind of unambiguous definition is a source of comfort because it allows us to impose order on an otherwise complex and confusing phenomenal world. We can identify ethnics by certain traits, genetically inherited or otherwise, and they will always be the same ethnics.

Attempts by earlier anthropologists and sociologists to define "ethnic" share many characteristics with the Webster definitions. These scholars believed in the distinctiveness and immutability of ethnic groups, a view that is not surprising in light of the general emphasis in the social sciences on social institutions, equilibrium, and the analogy that society, like all organisms, made sense; that is, it was an internally consistent system. Ethnic groups were seen as another kind of social institution that fit into the larger society in certain ways and that maintained a conservative equilibrium. The ways in which analysts saw ethnic groups relating to the larger society are treated in chapter 2. Let us now turn our attention to ethnic groups as institutions.

If ethnic groups are real, we must be able to point to tangible evidence of their reality. Wsevolod Isajiw (1974) reviews definitions of ethnicity and lists attributes of ethnic groups that appeared in 27 definitions. He abstracted a total of twelve characteristics. The five that appeared most often were, in descending order of frequency, common ancestral origin, same culture or customs, religion, race or physical characteristics, and language. They are attributes that are immediately apparent or easily checked for presence or absence. The remaining attributes include many based on feelings or status, such as sense of peoplehood, common values or ethos, and *Gemeinschaft* relations. Because they are less visible, they are less useful for quickly categorizing individuals or groups. Many people assume that a person acquires all these characteristics and learns the meaning of symbols and values by virtue of being born into an ethnic group. "A person does not belong to an ethnic group category by choice. He is born into it and becomes related to it through emotional and symbolic ties" (Breton and Pinard 1960).

Objective Definitions

Definitions based primarily on traits or combinations of traits and feeling-states fall into the category of objective definitions, according to Isajiw (1974). But overt traits do not retain the same form throughout all time. Not only do they change but quite often they do not grow exclusively out of the traditions of the group that displays them. How does one know at what point a particular group really was that particular group? For example, if a group defines itself by the circumstance that its members speak a language different from that of the larger society or surrounding groups, what happens when that language ceases to be spoken or changes? Now that the Makah Indians of the Northwest Coast speak English, wear the same clothing as the larger white society, and celebrate Christmas instead of having potlatches, are they no longer Makah? On the basis of observable criteria, we would probably not call them Makah. They are Makah, however, by virtue of self-definition based, in part, on common values that apply to areas of Makah-Makah interaction that are not shared with Anglos and that do not govern Anglo-Makah interaction. This self-definition is buttressed by the fact that the United States government recognizes them as American Indians of the Makah tribe.

The Waswahili of eastern Africa offer another example of the insufficiency of purely objective definitions. The only overt feature they shared was the Swahili language, but Swahili is a lingua franca for East Africa and, as such, is spoken by a great many people who are not Waswahili. As William Arens notes, definitions based on overt features are useless for this particular group:

> Such a typology leaves few, if any, of the residents of East Africa out of the picture. On this basis a Mswahili [singular] could be a Christian, Muslim, or Pagan; dress in an Arabian, European, or traditional style, and live in a town or in the scattered hamlets of the interior — just to mention a few of the possibilities. In effect, the cultural characteristics are extremely diverse and infinite and there is no reason for assuming that this should not be the case. It does not seem profitable, therefore, to pursue a definition in terms of cultural phenomena since the use of a common language appears to be the only constant. [1975:429]

Boundaries vs. Cultural Features

Fredrik Barth's call for attention to the boundaries of ethnic groups as the important defining features, rather than the cultural stuff enclosed by the boundaries, is probably the most significant attempt to articulate the problems of making objective definitions of ethnic groups:[1]

> [T]he cultural features that signal the boundary may change, and the cultural characteristics of the members may likewise be transformed, indeed even the organizational form of the group may change—yet the fact of continuing dichotomization between members and outsiders allows us to specify the nature of continuity, and investigate the changing cultural form and content. [1969:14]

Barth seems to be saying that we cannot define ethnicity solely on the basis of overt cultural features. This position is perfectly logical and acceptable.

The response to Barth, however, brought social scientists to the opposite, equally narrow position. Individuals took only the first part of Barth's prescription, ignoring or overlooking the important phrase "allows us to . . . investigate the changing cultural form and content." With this new charter, they embarked upon studies of interaction and boundary maintenance to the virtual exclusion of discussions of cultural features. Cultural features, in fact, become crucial in the strategies of identity selection and management (see chapter 7).

Subjective Definitions

There are other ways of defining ethnic groups. The opposite of an objective definition is one that is subjective. Isajiw defines the subjective approach as one that

> defines ethnicity as a process by which individuals either identify themselves as being different from others or belonging to a different group or are identified as different by others, or both identify themselves and are identified as different by others. [1974: 115]

---

1. Arens (1975), quoted above, is an excellent example of the application of some of Barth's distinctions to a specific case.

It is a process of self and other ascription. The subjective kind of definition seems to have been preferred by sociologists and by those concerned with the United States and the immigrants to the United States. Although objective features are not usually mentioned in the definition as important criteria, they are assumed to be the basis for the ascriptive identification. Two definitions should make this approach clear. Max Weber speaks about objective criteria and, at the same time, rejects them as being unimportant:

> We shall call "ethnic groups" those human groups that entertain a subjective belief in their common descent—because of similarities of physical type or of customs or both, or because of memories of colonization and emigration—in such a way that this belief is important for the continuation of nonkinship communal relationships . . . regardless of whether an objective blood relationship exists or not. [1947:306]

Nathan Glazer and Daniel P. Moynihan adopted a subjective definition, confronted as they were with the realities of ethnic pluralism in New York City:

> [A]s the groups were transformed by influences in American society, stripped of their original attributes, they were recreated as something new, but still as identifiable groups. Concretely, persons think of themselves as members of that group, with that name; they are thought of by others as members of that group, with that name; and most significantly, they are linked to other members of the group by new attributes that the original immigrants would never have recognized as identifying their group, but which nevertheless serve to mark them off, by more than simply name and association, in the third generation and even beyond. [1963:13]

Continuing that kind of subjective definition, Glazer and Moynihan discuss the fate of the original cultural features of immigrant groups to New York. Distinctive language, culture, and customs and even biological distinctiveness are lost, largely in the second generation and even more so in the third. Yet groups persist in a sense of distinctiveness:

> In the third generation, the descendants of the immigrants confronted each other, and knew they were both Americans, in the same dress, with the same language, using the same artifacts, troubled by the same thing, but they voted differently, had different ideas about edu-

cation and sex, and were still, in many essential ways, as different from one another as their grandfathers had been. [Ibid.: 14]

These observations are very much in accord with what we have noted about cultural features. Features change, but frequently not at the same pace as the changing self-concept of the group. The differential rates of change of objective cues and subjective states is a valuable area of research. In the past this issue has generated less interest than have many other aspects of ethnic identity, but it makes a powerful argument for retaining some notion of observable features in a definition of ethnic group or identity.

Composite Definitions

Extreme subjectivity in a definition is not very useful to people involved in interacting on the basis of ethnic identity or to the analyst who wants to make cross-cultural comparisons and ultimately reach a point where generalizations about ethnic identity are possible. Most contemporary definitions of ethnic groups and associated phenomena are composed of both objective and subjective criteria. In the past we also had composite definitions, such as the following two:

> When I use the term "ethnic group," then, to refer to a type of group contained within the national boundaries of America, I shall mean by it any group which is defined or set off by race, religion, or national origin, or some combination of these categories . . . all of these categories have a common social-psychological referent, in that all of them serve to create, through common historical circumstances, a sense of peoplehood for groups within the United States. [Gordon 1964:27–28]

> An ethnic group consists of people who conceive of themselves as being of a kind. They are united by emotional bonds and concerned with the preservation of their type. With very few exceptions they speak the same language, or their speech is at least intelligible to each other, and they share a common cultural heritage. Since those who form such units are usually endogamous, they tend to look alike. Far more important, however, is their belief that they are of common descent, a belief usually supported by myths or a partly fictitious history. [Shibutani and Kwan 1965:40–41]

These definitions are different from contemporary definitions. They are irrevocably linked to past ideas about ethnicity by their emphasis on the immutability of the group. If we assume that ethnic groups are corporate in nature, we tend to assume that the ethnic group is an ever-present feature in every group member's life, whether or not its presence is advantageous. Earlier observations in non-Western societies and more recent observations in the United States have gradually led social scientists to the conclusion that ethnic groups are simply another kind of reference group that individuals may choose to invoke, ignore, or oscillate between depending on their perception of the situation.

Features of Contemporary Definitions

In 1973, a symposium was held under the auspices of the Social Science Research Council on the theme of ethnic identity. One of the goals of the meeting was to agree on at least a working definition of terms such as "ethnic group" and "ethnicity." The six criteria of the final ssrc working definition include all the significant features of most contemporary definitions. For the scholars in the symposium, ethnicity seemed to involve:

1. a past-oriented group identification emphasizing origins
2. some conception of cultural and social distinctiveness
3. relationship of the ethnic group to a component unit in a broader system of social relations
4. the fact that ethnic groups are larger than kin or locality groups and transcend face-to-face interaction
5. different meanings for ethnic categories both in different social settings and for different individuals
6. the assumption that ethnic categories are emblematic, having names with meaning both for members and for analysts.

There are many familiar characteristics in this list. The first criterion has appeared under the various guises of "national origin," "common descent," "common ancestral origin," and "common cultural heritage." Some definitions that include this characteristic also indicate that the common heritage may not be demonstrable but that belief in it is sufficient (see Weber 1947; Glazer and Moynihan 1963; Royce 1977).

Others maintain that the past, if not readily demonstrable, may be shored up by myths or a partly fictitious history (see Shibutani and Kwan 1965).

The second SSRC criterion includes two different orders. The first refers to a people's sense of distinctiveness, the second more specifically to characteristics on which the sense of distinctiveness is built. As we have seen, the characteristics that can be invoked to convey ethnic distinctiveness include such things as differences in physical type, language, dress, religion, music, dance, and other forms of expressive behavior.

The third item speaks to the fact that ethnic groups are set within a broader system of social relations. This idea is implicit, if not explicitly stated, in definitions that refer to immigrant groups in the United States. Otherwise, this notion of interaction within a larger setting is a recent one (see Barth 1969 and Spicer 1971). Building on the work of these two scholars, Abner Cohen provides an operational definition of ethnic group in which the interactive process features prominently:

> a collectivity of people who (a) share some patterns of normative behavior and (b) form a part of a larger population interacting with people from other collectivities within the framework of a social system. [1974:ix]

The notion that interaction is essential for ethnic identity to be felt or maintained was not included in many early studies of rural indigenous populations, especially where the influx of outsiders had occurred in the long-distant past.

The fourth criterion is necessary for distinguishing ethnicity from other determinants of group formation such as kinship and locale. It also stipulates that ethnic identity has to go beyond mere face-to-face interaction. The fact that the members of the symposium felt it necessary to emphasize this point reflects the continuing tendency of social scientists to think in terms of groups rather than individuals. Unlike the rest of the SSRC criteria, this one is not usually included in contemporary definitions, particularly those that view ethnicity as a strategy. A more useful way of distinguishing ethnic groups from kinship or locale was proposed by Max Weber (1947). His distinction also predates by many years the recent stress on the frequently noncorporate nature of ethnic groups.

The ethnic group differs from the kinship community precisely in being a group (which believes in its common descent) but not a community, unlike the kinship group, which is characterized by actual communal action. In our present sense, the ethnic community itself is not a community; it only facilitates and promotes all types of communal relationships, particularly in the political sphere. On the other hand, it is primarily the political community, no matter how artificial, that inspires the belief in common ethnicity. This belief tends to persist even after the disintegration of the political community, unless drastic differences in the custom, physical type, or, above all, language exist among its members. [1947:306]

The fifth criterion, that ethnic categories have different meanings in different social settings and for different individuals, reflects a recent view of ethnicity as a strategy adopted to fit a particular situation. It speaks as well to the possibility of very different individual interpretations of displays of ethnic identity both within an ethnic group and between groups. Situational use of ethnicity implies a number of things: (1) that individuals can choose, within certain constraints, between a variety of identities; (2) that individuals will maximize the options available to them and will use ethnic identity if they perceive an advantage in so doing; (3) that individuals have to contend, in this process, with other individuals engaged in the same process whose interests and perceptions may be quite different. In other words, the use of ethnic identity is fluid and flexible (see Nagata 1974).

The last SSRC criterion focuses on the symbolic nature of ethnic categories, saying that they have meaningful names for both members and analysts. It, too, speaks for the necessity of including cultural features in any definition of ethnic group. Names of ethnic groups by themselves are powerful symbols around which the negotiation of identity takes place. Names with negative implications can be used to impose a sense of inferiority on groups or may be used to define a dominant-subordinate relationship. For example, in Mexico the term *indio* has negative connotations; *indios* are backward, illiterate, and obstacles to progress, and most indigenous groups never use this term in referring to themselves. The few groups that are aggressive in their self-identification as indigenous peoples use a specific tribal name. Two who do so effectively are the Yaqui of northwest Mexico and the Zapotec of the Isthmus of Tehuantepec. That Mexicans enjoy the dominant role is implicit in the term *indio* and even more so in its diminutive form, *indito*. *Inditos* have to be taken care of and brought into the Mexican nation gradually. In this respect, along with women, children, and the mentally deficient, they have had a special status within the Mexican constitution.

Groups concerned with changing their status or image will often change the name by which they are known. Thus, the designation "Negro" was replaced by "Black Americans," and the politically active segment of the Mexican-American population now identify themselves as "Chicano." Puerto Ricans in New York City have become the Nyoriqueños, a name symbolic of their special status apart from both New Yorkers and Puerto Ricans.

Names of ethnic categories also provide individuals with something to invoke when they have no other immediate indicators of ethnic identity. A name serves as a rallying point, and a tangible one, around which an identity can be rebuilt. Glazer and Moynihan see that happening in New York: "The mere existence of a name itself is perhaps sufficient to form group character in new situations, for the name associates an individual, who actually can be anything, with a certain past, country, race" (1963:17).

Although the SSRC criteria give us important guidelines for talking about ethnic identity and ethnic groups, taken together they make an unwieldy definition. The definition of ethnic group offered at the beginning of this chapter eliminates many of the redundancies in the SSRC guidelines and in other definitions, combines both objective and subjective criteria, and stresses the flexibility of an identity based on ethnic criteria. To repeat that definition, an ethnic group is a reference group invoked by people who share a common historical style (which may only be assumed), based on overt features and values, and who, through the process of interaction with others, identify themselves as sharing that style.

Style

In this kind of definition we have come a long way from Webster's and Webster-like definitions that viewed ethnic groups as monolithic stitutions whose individual members were members from birth to death, and whose individual fortunes were irrevocably linked to the fortunes of the group. The emphasis now, in contrast, is on the personal rather than the institutional level and on the individual as a choice-maker; on process rather than on equilibrium. The idea of continual change, on the one hand, and choice, on the other, is evidenced by the use of the term "style" rather than "tradition." "Tradition," the descriptive term most frequently applied to ethnic groups and identity, has too often implied something conservative and unchanging, something that is passed on from generation to generation in its original form. But that does not account for the facts of most situations. "Style," though a venerable term, does not have these conservative implications. On the contrary, it often implies the opposite, as in the phrase "changing styles." I use it to refer to a complex of symbols, forms, and value orientations that, when applied to ethnic groups, signals both the overt cultural contents and the underlying subjective values and standards by which performance is judged (Royce 1975). "Style" also implies that individuals have a choice in selecting appropriate styles, a feature defined by Alfred L. Kroeber: "There must be alternative choices, though actually they may never be elected. Where compulsion or physiological necessity reign, there is no room for style" (1963:150).

While the general reaction against the conservative institutional view has led to a much-needed emphasis on change and choice, it has also generated much debate over the necessity of admitting tangible evidence of ethnic identities as part of our definitions. The alternative, proposed by some, is that self-ascription is sufficient or, at least, most important, in the situational selection of ethnic identity. Part of the reason for the unhappiness with using cultural features as diagnostic of identity, as has been stated earlier, is that those who took an essentially institutional view of ethnic groups applied the same conservative, monolithic approach to the cultural features. When viewed in this light inventories of cultural features are of very little use and, in fact, cast ethnic groups into a somewhat negative light. This need not be the case. We can apply the same ideas about dynamics, choice, and situational use to cultural features as we do to the fact of self-identification. To my mind, not to do so and to ignore observable traits is to explain only part of ethnic-based behavior.[2]

---

2. Mine is not the only voice in support of definitions that incorporate both objective and subjective criteria. Pierre Van den Berghe leaves no doubt about his position on this

Double Boundaries

One of the ways in which this debate might be approached is from the concept of boundaries. Barth called for closer attention to the boundaries that signal ethnic dichotomies, but we can go further and speak of double boundaries; that is, the boundary maintained from within, and the boundary imposed from outside, which results from the process of interaction with others. Individuals enclosed by the inner boundary share a common cultural knowledge; hence, their interaction may be varied and complex and tolerate a great deal of ambiguity. Interaction across the outer boundary is much more limited because of the lack of shared knowledge. If all cultural knowledge were the property of all groups, boundaries would be blurred and eventually disappear. Where these boundaries exist, groups tend to limit the circumstances in which they are willing to interact to those that do not threaten their cultural integrity. In that sense, the economic sphere is often regarded as "safe."

Sydelle Levy, in an article on the Lubovitch Hassidim of Brooklyn, discusses the different behaviors associated with inner and outer boundaries. Outsiders see the Lubovitch Hassidim as one homogeneous group sharing the same traits and values, but within the group there are many behavioral alternatives implying great heterogeneity. The Lubovitch Hassidim comprise four distinct categories based on degree of orthodoxy. The four categories are set off by symbols and cultural forms immediately recognizable to insiders but nonexistent for outsiders, for whom all Lubovitchers are more or less the same. "[T]he criteria for ethnic group membership defined by the Lubovitchers themselves was significantly different from the way in which members of the larger society defined the Lubovitchers" (1975:27). Levy attributes this difference in part to the fact that the standards for success within the group are different from those in the larger society. The use

subject: "[I]t is clear that I reject both the old ethnographic conception that an ethnic group is simply a set of people who share a certain language, customs, and so on, and the newly fashionable notion that an ethnic group exists whenever someone says it does" (1976:242). However, no one has yet given adequate reasons for paying attention to both aspects of ethnic identity. As I see it, ethnic identities do not exist in a vacuum but provide one kind of social strategy. To use ethnic identity and maneuver within it one must perform adequately—that is, display certain features and behaviors successfully. At the same time, the decision to choose ethnicity as a strategy is a subjective one.

that an individual Lubovitcher makes of the ethnic charter must be viewed in light of this double purpose—the need to succeed within and the need to succeed without.

Barth: Ascription vs. Performance

Perceptions of and judgments about ethnic identity vary radically depending on which boundary is relevant. The relative importances of cultural features and self-ascription also vary accordingly. Both Barth and George Devereux have made distinctions that may elucidate the problem of categorization and standards of performance. Barth divides the cultural contents of ethnic dichotomies into two orders:

> (i) overt signals or signs—the diacritical features that people look for and exhibit to show identity, often such features as dress, language, house-form, or general style of life, and (ii) basic value orientations: the standards of morality and excellence by which performance is judged. [1969:14]

Barth further states that belonging to an ethnic category implies the claim to be judged and to judge oneself by standards relevant to that category. He also makes the distinction between ascription and performance:

> [A]scription is not conditional on the control of any specific assets, but rests on criteria of origin and commitment; whereas *performance* in the status, the adequate acting out of the roles required to realize the identity, in many systems does require such assets. [Ibid.:28]

If we recognize that there is a greater complexity of shared knowledge within groups than between groups, where interaction is restricted to certain structured situations, then it follows that performance becomes important within the inner boundary. It is there that individuals are judged on the extent of their cultural knowledge. Their claims to membership in the group are judged on their ability to behave adequately in the role rather than on identity based on ascription.

What takes place between groups is more a process of self- and other-ascription than judgments about performance. Since relatively little cultural knowledge is shared, ascription occurs on the basis of a few mutually intelligble symbols of identity. Because these symbols are standardized so as to be understood, they tend to be the most immediately recognizable and unambiguous symbols of identity (the range of symbols that function in this way will be discussed in more detail in chapter 6). The process can best be described as "labeling." We attach a label to people demonstrating certain diagnostic features and rarely look beyond them at performance.

Devereux: Ascription vs. Performance

Devereux makes almost exactly the same distinction as Barth. His term "ethnic identity" is simply a sorting device for oneself and for others. It is a label that refers to an all-or-nothing proposition. In Devereux's terms, either one was a Spartan or one was not. In other words, the sorting categories are purely ascriptive. His term "ethnic personality," in contrast, implies judgments about adequacy of ethnic performance derived inductively from concrete data that include both directly observed distinctive behavior and verbal behavior consisting of generalizations about standards of performance (cf. Devereux 1975).

Cultural Features and Underlying Values

Whether one is ascribing or judging within an ethnic group, some reference must be made to both the cultural features and the underlying values. Because of their limited knowledge individuals outside the group usually rely on cultural features only, and even more narrowly on those features about which they have some knowledge, in order to assign other individuals to their proper category. This difference is cru-cial to our understanding how different interpretations of ethnic identity may be held even though they are supposedly based on the same ob-servable cultural contents. A group may maintain an identity, although to the outside observer it has no features that set it off from the larger society. In such a case, we must look to subjective features, standards of morality, and values to explain what otherwise is inexplicable.

Several writers have discussed this point, but two stand out for the clarity with which they present the concept. Spicer (1971) speaks of persistent identity systems—cultural systems that have demonstrated a high potential for survival in changing situations—and sets out certain areas of participation necessary for the maintenance of these systems: (a) communication through language; (b) sharing of moral values (guid-ance in the realities of opposition. The meanings of symbols include ideal behaviors relative to opposing peoples and stereotypes of the behavior of those people); and (c) political organization for achieving the objectives of group policy. The three areas of participation are related, and when activity in one is intense, activity in the others may be less so. Activity in any one of these areas seems to be sufficient to allow the system to persist. Areas (a) and (c) consist of observable behavior on which outsiders make their assessments of group identity. Outsiders hardly ever have access to knowledge of area (b), the moral sphere, and so it does not enter into their categorizations. That has led to frequent surprises for opposing peoples, who take a lack of overt activity as evidence of a loss or disintegration of identity.

Elizabeth Colson (1953) distinguishes between a moral sphere, which she calls "sanctioned idea patterns," and formal behavior. In her description of the Makah Indians, very little in the way of formal behavior distinguishes the Makah from the Anglos living on the reservation or interacting with them in other ways. This lack of distinction has largely resulted from an enforced educational system, which teaches Anglo behaviors and values, and the small size and concentration of the population, which has restricted traditional Makah behavior. However, the Makah have not become Anglo in Makah-Makah interactions governed by sanctioned idea patterns related to traditional Makah culture. Colson stresses that a program for assimilation such as that imposed on the Makah can deal directly with formal behavior only. One cannot posit that a change in form always signals a change in underlying assumptions. There is no way of judging conformity except by its outward manifestations.

Conclusions

The individuals enclosed in the inner boundary use one set of standards, while those outside that boundary are limited to standards based on overt behavior and thus qualitatively different from the first set. The existence of two sets of standards has many implications for perception of identity and statements about ethnic groups. It explains the debate between those who maintain that ethnic groups have no existence except as referents to be invoked when needed and those who hold that a certain minimal consistency of behavior is necessary for interaction to be possible. Subjective self-ascription may be sufficient for a member of an ethnic group to identify him- or herself. It is not sufficient for those outside the group to make identifications. George De Vos states this proposition rather nicely:

> Ethnic identity, like any form of identity, is not only a question of knowing who one is subjectively, but also of how one is seen from the outside. Ethnic identity requires the maintenance of sufficiently consistent behavior to enable others to place an individual or a group in some given social category, thus permitting appropriate interactive behavior. [1975:374]

In light of the preceding discussion, we are led to the conclusion that any definition of ethnic group or ethnic identity must be composed of both subjective and objective components and must also support the notion that ethnic groups are eminently mutable, providing yet another reference group with which individuals can vary their social strategies.

From Conflict
to Opposition

2

THE CIRCUMSTANCES IN WHICH ethnic identity may be manifested, maintained, or lost is a popular topic among researchers and writers. The title of this chapter reflects the chronology, or at least the two end points, in theories about possible responses of ethnic groups to the larger social context in which they find themselves. In this sense, conflict and opposition are not at all synonymous.

Conflict Approaches

As Donald E. Gelfand (1973) has observed, early sociological studies were hampered by attempts to remain apolitical. They avoided questioning, let alone criticizing, the major institutions of the dominant society and viewed ethnically plural situations and interactions as being basically antagonistic and full of conflict. Many contemporary social scientists also hold this conflict interpretation of heterogenous societies. The crucial difference is that early theorists saw conflict as being bad while contemporary theorists regard it as basic, and therefore normal, to all social interaction. So while both groups might agree with the statement that man's life in the company of his fellow men is nasty, brutish, and not short enough, given all the unpleasantness, they would disagree in their moral judgments about the state of conflict. The first might respond that that kind of life is abnormal and is the result of people's having strayed from the proper healthy state of equilibrium.

The second would argue that that is the way society works, for better or for worse.

Equilibrium is one of the key concepts in understanding the older studies of ethnic identity that espoused a conflict approach. It best describes the way society was viewed: as a self-contained and self-regulating organism all of whose constituent parts worked together and contributed toward maintaining the whole organism in a harmonious state. Conflict, friction, and sources thereof were threats to society and had to be eliminated or, at the very least, regulated.

Three Ways of Controlling Conflict

One prime source of conflict is the existence of a group whose members do not know or share the goals of the larger society. They cannot be counted on to support society, especially when it demands something that runs counter to the interests or values of the group. In a nation like the United States, the many ethnic enclaves were viewed as time bombs that had to be defused or somehow brought under control. A variety of approaches was tried. One was to limit immigration drastically, in particular, the immigration of those who had shown themselves too different to be able to accommodate, assuming that they were willing, to dominant American society. A quite different attitude was shown toward model immigrant groups like the "Jenny Lind Swedes," who not only held many of the same values as did the dominant group but also had the means and the energy to make honorable lives for themselves (see Coleman 1973).

A second method of controlling conflict was to allow groups that could not or would not assimilate to exist within their own cultural shells in return for performing certain services for the larger society that were necessary but illegal or otherwise unappetizing. Francis Ianni (1974) makes the point that organized crime, by and large, is run by the newest ethnic group with an undesirable image. When and if the group's image changes because its members have been able to work their way into another economic niche, the group ceases its unsavory activities. They are taken over by members of a newer group who have no alternatives. Society allows ethnic groups engaged in illegal activities to retain as many of their cultural features as they wish as long as the groups are inward-focused and police themselves. As soon as they look beyond the confines of their own ethnic enclave and their ways impinge upon the dominant group, society tries to find some way to regulate them.

A third way of minimizing the conflict inherent in a plural setting is the tactic of isolating ethnic groups from society altogether. In the United States, Indians were removed to reservations. In their case, and probably in other instances as well, this strategy was adopted because neither of the others was feasible. American Indians, except in individual hard-won cases, were not regarded as good material for assimilation into mainstream United States. Unlike the Swedes, they did not look like members of the dominant white society. In addition, some had demonstrated their unwillingness to accept white values by long and bitter resistance. Even those who were spoken of as the "civilized tribes" (Cherokee, Creek, Choctaw, etc.) were driven west of the Mississippi in one of the big land grabs of the nineteenth century. The second way of defusing ethnic groups by limiting them to the illegal and the unacceptable was also not feasible in the case of American Indians. Even if they had desired them, these unsavory jobs were preempted by wave after wave of immigrants who settled in the urban areas where those activities flourished.

In many ways, the early conflict theorists were only voicing what was in the minds of many citizens of the United States, namely, fear and suspicion of anyone who did not subscribe to the one-nation-united-in-purpose goal. That might seem rather strange for a nation founded by immigrants with a heritage of undeniable heterogeneity. It is not so strange in light of the American concept of "nation" (which is essentially the same as the English and the French): a political state where one language and, implicitly, the culture that goes along with it, will dominate. This meaning contrasts quite strikingly with the European notion of nationalism that arose out of the German school of Romanticism: a nation is not an artificially created political entity that imposes uniformity on its inhabitants but a natural creation, a people with a God-given culture that lasts through time and has its own destiny. Weber is an articulate spokesman for this view:

> In the sense of those using the term at a given time, the concept [nation] undoubtedly means, above all, that one may exact from certain groups of men a specific sentiment of solidarity in the face of other groups. [1977:18]

> One might well define the concept of nation in the following way: a nation is a community of sentiment which would adequately manifest itself in a state of its own. [Ibid.:20]

The influence of this European view of nationalism came into anthropology through the work of Franz Boas, who saw each culture as a unique occurrence resulting from historical and environmental factors that mandated its unfolding. However, this kind of cultural relativism did not characterize sociological writing of the day, which was more firmly in the American mold.

In this light, it is not surprising to find American writers regarding nonconformity as a threat to the status quo, with conflict the logical consequence. The terminology in early studies indicates the attitude of the dominant society and the theorists. We find such terms as "prejudice," "discrimination," "race," "minority-majority," "alien," and "persecution," and such titles as "The Problem of Minority Groups" (Wirth 1944).

Early Conflict Theories: Summary

In the philosophy of these early writers, the ideal, hence normal, state of society was one of equilibrium. In order to maintain that equilibrium, all society's constituent parts had to contribute to that goal. Finally, groups that did not share that goal could only be a threat to the larger society. The attitudes toward assimilation held by American sociologists, as described by Paul Metzger, illustrate nicely the feelings the average American held about cultural pluralism:

> Sociologists, by and large, have accepted the image of Horatio Alger in the Melting Pot as the ideal definition of American Society. Although they have repeatedly documented the discrepancy between social reality and cultural myth in America, they have also taken the view that the incorporation of America's ethnic and racial groups into the mainstream culture is virtually inevitable. . . . Successful assimilation, moreover, has been viewed as synonymous with equality of opportunity and upward mobility for the members of minority groups; "opportunity," in this system, is the opportunity to discard one's ethnicity and to partake fully in the "American Way of Life"; in this sense, assimilation is viewed as the embodiment of the democratic ethos." [1971:628–629]

Isolationist Approaches

In what could be termed an "isolationist" approach, some scholars felt that ethnic identity could persist only in the absence of interaction. Like the older, conflict theorists, they reasoned that ethnic groups who were able would adopt the ways of the dominant society and cease to be ethnics; and those that did not assimilate but did not actively resist the dominant society would persist in their own cultural ways and thus isolate themselves artificially from the rest of society, that is, create ghettos for themselves. The isolationists assumed that those who resisted would either cease to exist in the struggle or would be forcibly isolated from society.

Once research spread beyond the borders of the United States, an isolationist, conflict-is-bad approach to ethnicity became more and more untenable. There were too many instances that did not fit this particular model. However, one area of study outside the United States that continued in the older mold for a considerable period of time was the ethnographic research done in Mexico from the late 1920s to the 1940s. During this period there were a number of studies of single communities that were described as indigenous and having had little or no contact with the Mexican nation. They were located in remote areas and had no access to the outer world by means of roads or radios. The rest of the studies focused on what were called peasant communities, which were no longer indigenous because, by definition, peasant society was a part of and dependent on the larger society, or Great Tradition, for its survival. It was assumed that with contact inevitably comes change and loss of traditions. Robert Redfield, in describing the folk-urban continuum (1941), posited that the greater the distance from the urban centers the less acculturated the population would be.

In actuality, very few groups in Mexico are isolated. Before the Spanish Conquest in 1521, over 200 different groups (based on linguistic criteria) lived and died in isolation. (Between 10 and 20 million formed part of the Aztec empire in the latter part of the fifteenth century.) After Conquest, few groups escaped the Spanish influence, either military or ecclesiastical. All these groups are different from whatever they may have been originally. Some are indistinguishable from the *mestizo*, who constitute 85% of the Mexican population. Some groups actively maintain traditions that for them and for the Mexican nation are distinctive and described as indigenous. We cannot explain this complex situation, however, by invoking isolation and lack of contact or by measuring distance from urban centers.

Why, then, did the isolationist explanation persist? It persisted primarily because researchers were viewing communities as if they *did* exist in isolation from each other and from the nation. The studies were synchronic and bounded by the geographic confines of the community itself, and the researchers were using the basic model of society as an integrated organism characterized by an overall state of equilibrium. Explanation was geared toward describing how all the parts functioned to maintain the whole. There was little, if any, use of historical materials, at least for the purpose of discovering factors contributing to the persistence or loss of a distinctive identity. In Mexico, as in the United States, there was a dominant society which was viewed as the ideal state toward which all subordinate groups were striving. It was bad to be an Indian; it was good to be a Mexican. These factors help us understand the preference for isolationist explanations of ethnic identity that characterized early Mexican ethnography.[1]

Interactionist Approaches

Research in non-Western countries undergoing rapid development and urbanization, especially Africa, proved fatal to analyses that relied on isolation and conflict as the primary explanations of ethnic identity. Interaction was now seen as the crucial factor in creating and maintaining ethnic identity. One of the most significant of these studies was done by A.L. Epstein (1958) on the Copperbelt region of Rhodesia, an area that was developed at a dizzying rate. Copper mines opened one after the other, giving the region its new name. Towns sprang up overnight to service mine owners, engineers, and laborers. The last

---

1. The Mexican case stands in sharp contrast to the situation in most of Africa. Dominant in the Mexican population were the *mestizos*, the mixed-blood product of Europeans and Indians brought about by the simultaneous decline in the indigenous population and the increase of European colonists. In much of Africa, the indigenous peoples remained numerically dominant and separate. The British were not interested in making the Africans in their colonies British, but were content to have a heterogeneous mix ruled by a small British elite.

group from all parts of Rhodesia and representing a myriad tribal groups, poured into the Copperbelt. Tribesmen who had formerly been separated by as much as the width or length of the country now came into contact with one another. Epstein observed that, contrary to predictions based on the older model, the different tribes did not meld to become homogeneous citizens of the Copperbelt. Rather, what occurred was a process of retribalization in which tribal identities were sharpened. According to Epstein, the tribesmen gained a sense of who they were by being exposed to others who held different customs and values.

Two years earlier, Mitchell (1956) had described similar behavior on the part of members of the Kalela dance group, again in the urban Copperbelt. In the context of African-African interaction in which Europeans were absent, tribal affiliations were stressed. Bisa tribesmen, for example, would sing songs praising the virtues of the Bisa and making fun of other tribes. Outside of this leisure-time setting, however, the Bisa and the others would temporarily ignore their differences and present a united front to the Europeans.

What both Mitchell and Epstein emphasize is that interaction and contact with others who are different often prompt a strengthening of each group's identity. They also present information on the situational use of identity. Cohen articulates these two ideas even more strongly in speaking of retribalization:

> It is the result, not of ethnic groupings disengaging themselves from one another, but of increasing interaction between them, within the context of new political situations. It is the outcome, not of conservatism, but of a dynamic sociocultural change brought about by new cleavages and new alignments of power. It is a process by which a group from one ethnic category, whose members are involved in a struggle for power and privilege with the members of a group from another ethnic category, within the framework of a formal political system, manipulate some customs, values, myths, symbols, and ceremonies from their cultural tradition in order to articulate an informal political organization which is used as a weapon in that struggle. [1969:2]

In other words ethnic identity is more often the product of increasing interaction between groups than the negative result of isolation.

Researchers in other areas were also coming to similar conclusions about the nature of ethnic identity and cultural persistence. They described situations in the Scandinavian countries, Burma, southern Mexico, Afghanistan, and Malaya that could only be explained on the basis of interaction. The best-known and most frequently cited derives from Barth's research in Afghanistan. In the introduction to a collection of articles on ethnic groups, Barth points to the major role of interaction and contact in determining ethnic identity:

> Categorical ethnic distinctions do not depend on an absence of mobility, contact, and information, but do entail social processes of exclusion and incorporation whereby discrete categories are maintained despite changing participation . . . one finds that stable, persisting, and often vitally important social relations are maintained across such boundaries, and are frequently based on the dichotomized ethnic statuses. In other words, ethnic distinctions do not depend on an absence of social interaction and acceptance, but are quite to the contrary often the very foundations on which embracing social systems are built. Interaction in such social systems does not lead to its liquidation through change and acculturation; cultural differences can persist despite inter-ethnic contact and interdependence. [1969:9–10]

This shifting of emphasis away from isolation reflects changes in the field of anthropology in general. Perhaps the major change was from an emphasis on equilibrium to a concern with process. This shift had a number of repercussions. Instead of studying artificially bounded units as they existed at a particular time, anthropologists began looking at change, regarding societies as being continuously influenced by forces beyond their own boundaries. The image of conflict as something unnatural and therefore evil underwent a reversal. Conflict came to be regarded as inescapable, an essential as well as functional feature of social life. Gelfand (1973), in discussing ethnic relations and social research, explicates the switch from functional theories to conflict theories in sociology. Much of the impetus for the change, he argues, came from criticisms of the functionalist model. It was condemned for being too conservative because it held that equilibrium was a societal goal arising from consensus based on institutionalized values. One of the earliest sociologists to deal with this problem was Lewis Coser. In 1956, he tried to unite the two perspectives, showing that conflict was functional and therefore fit into the pattern of forces that bind a social system together. Max Gluckman and Meyer Fortes, two British social anthropologists, had made much the same argument a few years earlier. Gelfand reasons that uniting the two approaches was important because it enabled people to view conflict as something nonthreatening. It also gave conflict theory a better name as far as the functionalists were concerned.

Gelfand claims that the revival of conflict theory in its new form in the late 1950s and 1960s was linked to political developments such as the rise of the civil rights movement in the United States. This kind of reaction would follow logically from the earlier assimilationist view, which argued the inherent evils of diversity and conflict. When a large number of subordinate groups begin to demand the same rights that are guaranteed to members of the dominant group and are able to capture enough important supporters, ideas about conflict and diversity must somehow change to bring them into accord with reality.

R.A. Schermerhorn (1974) concurs in relating theory to social developments in his discussion of events and the state of society that led to the crisis of the 1960s. He notes that before the Black civil rights movement, while European ethnic groups made small but solid economic gains that enabled them to move into better neighborhoods and educate their children, only a tiny Black elite advanced, while Blacks living below the poverty line had lower incomes in the 1950s than in the 1930s. During this period European ethnics were referred to as "nationality groups," and assimilation was the desired goal. Blacks had no place in this scheme, since they were not a nationality group nor were they easily assimilated, according to the views of the day. All these factors gave rise to the civil rights movement. Attainment of some measure of equality by Blacks seriously threatened white ethnics. They resented Blacks' moving into their neighborhoods and the increased federal funding being allocated to Blacks. Their indignation led to what Schermerhorn calls the rise of the white ethnics, in which pluralism and separatism have become the order of the day. Social theory in this case followed social fact.

In views such as those of Coser, Gluckman, and Fortes, equilibrium was still the ideal. The incorporation of conflict into functionalism was a little like wanting to have your cake and eat it too. For contemporary theorists, conflict is a given. Sometimes it contributes to the maintenance of society; sometimes it disrupts society; sometimes it creates new societies.[2] The potential for conflict is higher in heterogeneous

---

2. These manifestations may still be classed under the broad rubric of functionalism. The neo-Marxist approaches to ethnicity based on coercion rather than conflict differ in this respect.

societies, and it takes different forms in ethnically heterogeneous societies than in societies whose heterogeneity is based on other criteria.[3]

> It seems necessary . . . in a discussion of ethnicity, to start from a theoretical position that regards some form of conflict as a normal or chronic condition in a pluralistic society. Such social tensions, however, are manifested differently in pluralistic societies than they are in stratified societies composed principally of an ethnically homogenous populace. [De Vos 1975:56]

Oppositional Approach

Along with the changing image of the role of conflict in society came a subtle change in studies of ethnic identity—from those that claimed that interaction was a factor in creating and maintaining identity to those that went further and said that opposition was a prime factor in persistent identity. At first glance, it might not appear that these two concepts are so different, but if we compare Spicer's remarks about the oppositional process and Barth's statements about interaction, we will see that they are speaking about two different processes.

> Tentatively . . . it appears that the oppositional process is the essential factor in the formation and development of the persistent identity system. . . . The oppositional process frequently produces intense collective consciousness and a high degree of internal solidarity. [Spicer 1971:797,799]

Spicer's view differs greatly in degree from Barth's, in spite of the use of the word "tentatively." Barth maintains that social interaction and acceptance are often the foundations on which ethnic distinctions are built and that cultural differences can persist *despite* inter-ethnic contact. In contrast, Spicer argues that the oppositional process is the *essential factor* in ethnic persistence.

---

3. Weber presents a different view, although he is talking about more than just conflict: "There is no difference between the ethnically relevant customs and customs in general, as far as their effect is concerned. The belief in affiliation of descent [*Abstammungsverwandtschaft*] in combination with a similarity of customs, is likely to promote the diffusion of communal action among those allied by ethnic ties, because 'imitation' is generally encouraged by the consciousness of community. . . . The content of communal action that is possible on an ethnic basis remains indefinite" (1947:251).

In evaluating the intent of these two models, we must consider the sort of case to which each approach applies. Barth's statement about the importance of interaction is applicable to a wide range of situations, while Spicer speaks about specific types of situations that the concept of opposition is able to explain. So, we might fairly say that Barth's interaction is more generally useful, but, for those instances of persistent identity systems, it explains less than does Spicer's opposition. It might well be the case, however, that the seeming specificity of Spicer's concept is due more to the fact that few people have used it than to any limitations inherent in the concept. The lack of application of the Spicer model, as I see it, is due to its essentially diachronic, historical, and ethnohistorical character. While Barth, on the other hand, might invoke historical factors, he never considers them crucial to what is primarily a synchronic explanatory mode. It is only very recently that historically oriented ethnography has once again become popular.

Spicer Model

Persistent Identity System

The Spicer model offers a better explanation of some situations than does any other approach, and it may prove even more applicable as more diachronic studies are done. Two concepts are central to Spicer's thesis—the persistent identity system and the oppositional process. Spicer uses the first to refer to cultural systems that have demonstrated their ability to survive over long periods of time in different cultural environments. His examples include the Jews, Basques, Irish, Welsh, Catalans, Maya, Yaqui, and Navajo. They share the following conditions: (1) each group has outlived two or more kinds of state organizations into which it has been incorporated (with the exception of the Navajo); (2) each has had pressure applied for economic, political, or religious incorporation into the larger organizations; (3) each has resisted these pressures; and (4) each has developed well-defined symbols of identity differentiating it from other groups or the larger society. It should be obvious that not all ethnic groups constitute persistent identity systems.

Three aspects of Spicer's approach to persistent identity systems make his model both different and more useful than many others. It is valuable to discuss, as Spicer does, how they are related to and how they differ from Kroeber's concept of systemic patterns. Kroeber's use of the alphabet as an example of a systemic pattern has become a classic. It illustrates features that Spicer takes to be diagnostic of the Kroeberian concept; that is, it is an example of the persistence of a stable form in sharply contrasting cultural environments (Spicer 1971:795).

As the first feature of his approach, Spicer retains the aspect of systemic patterning in contrasting environments but finds that stability of form does not aid in the delineation of process. He describes his own concept as having certain advantages not apparent in the Kroeber formulation. The essential feature of any identity system is "an individual's belief in his personal affiliation with certain symbols, or more accurately, with what certain symbols stand for" (ibid.: 795–796). In other words, Spicer posits a relationship between human beings and their cultural artifacts. The social aspect—the fact that artifacts have meaning for their creators and users—is missing from the systemic pattern of Kroeber. The meaning may remain the same in the sense of systemic patterning, while the outward form may change.

Spicer's second distinct feature is his view of history. Spicer is concerned with history "as people believe it to have taken place. . . . It is history with a special meaning for the particular people who believe it" (ibid.:796). Thus the significant history for a people may vary from textbook accounts. He contends that we must consider the cumulative character of culture.

Third, Spicer's persistent identity system view allows us to include individual motivation in our analyses. Motivation to continue the identity system comes from people's cumulative image expressed in symbols meaningful to those who identify with a particular historical experience.

Spicer's ideas about the persistent identity system are different not only from Kroeber's but also from much previous theory-building. Spicer argues against cataloguing forms apart from their proper context, which is in a meaningful relationship with human beings. This argument runs counter to many definitions of ethnic identity that relied almost totally on lists of traits. It does not, however, say that traits are not important, as do many of the purely subjective definitions of ethnic identity. It is, rather, a sensible approach, which says that one must look at cultural artifacts as having meaning for the people who use them.

Spicer is committed to the kind of explanation that springs from a concern with historical process, but, again, a history that is meaningful for those who ascribe to it. This aspect differs from many descriptions of ethnic groups and ethnicity that are synchronic. Spicer also differs from those analysts who agree that history is important but who fail to distinguish between history as recorded by an outside observer and history that is personally meaningful to the individual or group. What is important for a group's persistence is an interpretation of historical events that is culturally meaningful, even though this interpretation does not coincide with the views of official historians. For example, the Yaqui Indians of northern Mexico maintain that they have always been an autonomous nation. This view of history has allowed the Yaqui to survive the many larger social organizations that attempted to incorporate them. It is also an interpretation that would find little support from historians, and it maddened all the various social entities that sought Yaqui allegiance. In the negotiation of identities a group's historical charter may be challenged, and demonstrability becomes important. Note that Spicer does make this contrast between kinds of historical interpretation.

Oppositional Process

It is his second concept, the oppositional process, that sets Spicer apart from others who deal with ethnic identity. All the persistent identity systems he lists are the result of continued opposition, throughout their histories, to attempts to incorporate or assimilate the groups into the larger whole. The conflicts have varied from open warfare to silent resistance, but the one constant is firm opposition to the idea of incorporation. Without this kind of antagonism, persistent identity systems would fail to develop. It is important to assess the larger society's resources in the struggle to incorporate smaller groups as well as those available to the smaller groups for resisting. In the case of the Yaqui, several conditions enabled them to resist effectively: their geographic situation permitted them to defend themselves militarily; their land was relatively undesirable, having few natural resources attractive to outsiders; because of their limited contact with outsiders they avoided many of the diseases that proved disastrous to other, less-favorably located groups; and they were economically independent because they were never alienated from their land. None of these circumstances were shared by the adjacent Mayo Indians, and today, it is clear that the Yaqui have persisted in maintaining their identity whereas most Mayo, for all intents and purposes, have become Mexicans.

The kinds of resources mentioned above do not represent the sum total available to persistent identity systems. Of equal importance, as Spicer maintains, are the moral resources gained from a sharing of meaningful symbols, which is generated and maintained by the oppositional process.

> The oppositional process frequently produces intense collective consciousness and a high degree of internal solidarity. This is accompanied by a motivation for individuals to continue the kind of experience that is "stored" in the identity system in symbolic form. [Spicer 1971:799]

Symbols of Identity Systems

Let us now consider the characteristic symbols of identity systems and some mechanisms for the maintenance of these systems. The one characteristic that seems to dominate both symbolic content and mechanisms for persistence is flexibility. Since persistent identity systems develop as a response to attempts at incorporation by outside forces, flexibility is as understandable as it is necessary. There is a dynamic relationship between identity systems and the larger society. As changes occur in one system, corresponding changes appear in the other.

Keeping this dynamic quality in mind, let us look at the symbolic content of systems. Spicer posits that the set of symbols chosen to represent a persistent identity system is "necessarily characterized by some combination of land and language elements" (ibid.:798), which he sees as being a distinctive feature of this kind of system as opposed to other systems. The form in which these two elements may appear is variable. The peoples concerned may in fact control an area of land or share a language that is both vibrant and viable. Equally effective for generating an identity, however, may be the sense of attachment to a land that once was held or to a language that may have been lost and recreated or that exists in the form of only a few words. Other common symbols of identity systems are music, dance, and heroes. The emphasis on one or another of these elements varies from system to system, and, within a system, it varies over time. Again, we must look to the oppositional process for much of the explanation. As Spicer comments, meaningful symbols arise in areas where pressure is concentrated, and the symbols will change in response to changing interests on the part of the dominant peoples. What ties the whole system of symbols together and allows continuity and persistence is that they fit into a complex that has meaning for the people involved.

> The meanings amount to a self-definition and an image of themselves as they have performed in the course of their history. The selection of cultural elements for symbolic references goes on in terms of the character of this image; the frequent shifts in emphasis are part of the process of maintenance in response to alterations in the environment. [Ibid.:798]

Several examples of persistent symbol systems will be documented in later chapters. At this point, it is sufficient to note that Spicer's emphasis on the responsiveness of systems to their environment is precisely what gives them their ability to persist.

Three Areas of Participation

Spicer sees three areas of participation that are necessary for the persistence of identity systems. As outlined in chapter 1, they are communication through language, the sharing of moral values, and political organization for achieving the objectives of group policy. They are also characterized by flexibility and shifting emphasis in response to environment: "There can be no identity system without common participation in all of the spheres but fluctuation in participation is characteristic" (ibid.:799).

Spicer sees the symbolic content of identity systems resulting from a process that is distinct from the one that maintains a total culture pattern and distinct from the persistence of a particular set of culture traits. Similarly, he finds that these areas of participation are different when they deal with the mechanics of identity systems and when they are simply part of the general cultural process. For example, in the area of language, a specialized vocabulary is used to articulate the features of the oppositional process. It includes words for self-identification and reference and for defining the opposition. Language is thus a way of creating unity within the identity system as well as a means of maintaining the boundaries between the system and the others; "the specialized vocabulary is a vital part of the mechanism of social separation" (ibid.:799). The sharing of moral values, to Spicer, means using the specialized part of the moral world that deals with inter-ethnic interaction and opposition. It provides prescriptions for dealing with others based in large part on stereotypes of character and behavior. Similarly, political participation means political activity and organization for the purpose of maintaining the identity system in the face of opposition.

Although participation in all three areas is necessary for the survival of the group, the intensity of participation in each sphere varies. It may well be that political activity at one point is not feasible, and so the moral and language areas carry on the system until political activity is possible. This important point is sometimes overlooked by those who see ethnicity as a purely political phenomenon.

Spicer Model: Summary

Spicer's theories do not account for every inter-ethnic situation. His persistent identity systems may include many instances of ethnic identity, but his concept applies more specifically to systems that have endured over time in radically different environments. In those cases it provides a powerful explanatory model that works better than more-general interaction-based models of ethnic identity. Even when we are trying to explain situations in which ethnic identity is not synonymous with identity systems, many features of Spicer's model can help sharpen our perceptions and our ways of considering behavior. His emphasis on flexibility and responsiveness to environment, both physical and social, is one we would do well to imitate. It may be that identity systems that persist demonstrate more flexibility and responsiveness than others, but all human interaction relies on a certain degree of choice-making and flexibility. This view is assuredly more realistic than a previous one that regarded human beings as essentially captives of the institutions they create. Spicer's emphasis on identity development and persistence has much to offer those who study systems that, by definition, rely on some assumption of historical charter. Further, Spicer's notion of opposition as healthy is in itself a healthy step toward viewing situations of ethnic-based behavior as they really are. Finally, his concept of symbol systems as dynamic and meaningful to the human beings who create and use them is a powerful antidote to those who would take symbols out of context for analysis as well as those who would ignore symbol systems altogether.

Conclusions

In this chapter we have examined some of the models and theories proposed to explain the response of ethnic groups to the larger social setting. We have seen in them a gradual progression from those that assumed that inter-ethnic contact would bring either assimilation or conflict to that proposed by Spicer, which sees the oppositional process as an essential part of the formation and persistence of identity systems. In between those two views lay the school of thought that regarded conflict as an integral feature of social life and viewed inter-ethnic interaction as supporting ethnic differences. We have tried to show how these models and theories were related to trends in the social sciences in general. Moreover, through the examples in the United States, Mexico, and Africa, we demonstrated the relationship between theory-building and the situations in which theorists are working.

In the next two chapters, we shall see how identities are created, persist, or fade away within the framework of the larger political entity, be it empire or nation, and consider ethnic groups within the context of immigration and internal migration. We shall follow Spicer's admonition that every ethnic group or identity system is responsive to and reflective of the larger social context in which it finds itself.

Frameworks of
Tolerance and Denial

PART TWO

Ethnic Groups and the Colonial Experience

3

THE COLONIAL SITUATION is one of the larger settings in which ethnic groups may find themselves embedded willingly or otherwise. However benign the brand of colonialism, the world is no longer the same for the indigenous peoples. Perceptions, knowledge, and behavior change as the ways of the empire make themselves felt.

Contact Situations

One of the early statements about contact situations (primarily those brought about by colonialism) was formulated by Bronislaw Malinowski. He voiced the opinion of many social scientists of his day when he argued that the elements in contact situations should be kept totally separate from each other in analyses. He said, moreover, that we should focus on the traditional cultures having change imposed on them since change "is the result of an impact of a higher, active culture upon a simpler, more passive one" (1945:12). Malinowski enunciated a rigid assimilation or conflict attitude that should be familiar to us. In his view, when the higher, active culture came into contact with the lower, passive one there could only be two results. If interests differed, there would be conflict. If mutual interests were involved, the lower, passive culture would make the necessary adjustments and change would come about. Change, in other words, was unidirectional in this view of the world.

Immanuel Wallerstein speaks of a related way of viewing contact situations, which was prevalent in the first third of the twentieth century. He explains the attraction for anthropologists of tightly bounded social groups sharing a common culture on the basis of their own intellectual tradition, which made the existence of a common culture the defining feature of a social group.

In these terms then the only coherent social groups were the traditional units indigenous to the situation. Even if the colonial administrators were regarded as a coherent group, they were not viewed as objects for study in their own right, not even in the areas where they impinged upon the indigenous peoples. Social scientists and colonial administrators were even more reluctant to admit that there might be something like a "colony" with a structure and rules of its own. Wallerstein argues that it is the colony and not the traditional unit that should be the focus if we define a society "not as a unit which shares common culture but one which shares at the very minimum a common authority capable of maintaining itself and propagating its values and whose legitimacy is recognized by peer authorities elsewhere" (1966.:2).

Malinowski framed part of his argument as criticism of such writers as Isaac Schapera, Meyer Fortes, and Max Gluckman, who insisted on regarding contact situations as social fields rather than as segmented units. Moreover, Gluckman argued that it was indeed proper to study the colonial administrators as well as the tribal headman, the doctor as well as the medicine man, and even more important to look at the relationship between them as it developed in the colonial situation.

Balandier and the Colonial Equation

George Balandier articulated the most-productive approach to colonial situations, though his argument is implicit in the work of Fortes and of Gluckman. In his article on theoretical approaches to colonial situations, Balandier argues that our focus should be the complex he calls the colonial situation, if, in fact, we are concerned with understanding conditions as they are, "not sacrificing facts for the convenience of some dogmatic schematization" (1951:35). He sees three parts to the equation: the indigenous society, the foreign minority, and the colonial situation. They are all intimately related, so that no change can occur in one without having some effect on the others. Other writers have discussed the foreign minority, but it is Balandier who speaks with precision about the third element, the colonial situation.

Balandier enumerates five characteristics of the colonial situation. (1) Domination is imposed by a foreign minority on an indigenous population that is numerically superior but is viewed as materially inferior.

(2) The domination links the two groups in a special kind of relationship. (3) The two components of the relationship are an industrialized, economically powerful society with a Christian background contrasted with a nonindustrialized, "backward" society that is non-Christian. (4) The relationship is basically antagonistic, since the colonial people are regarded as "instruments" of the colonial power. (5) In order to maintain its dominance, the colonial power uses not only force but a whole system of justifications and stereotypes (ibid.:54–55).

Totality of the Contact Situation

Although there are three parts to the colonial equation, let us remember that it is the totality and the oneness of the situation that are important. Balandier questions the reality of the "groups" constituting the "global society" or the colony. In so doing, he criticizes, in ways paralleling the criticisms made by Wallerstein of Malinowski, the early writers on acculturation and culture contact. Specifically, he objects to the simplistic and arbitrary division of "contact" into stages: the phases of conflict, adjustment, syncretism, and assimilation (or a counteracculturation reaction).

We might summarize the current thinking about contact and change with particular reference to colonial situations by stressing, as does Balandier, that the parts of the colonial equation have no reality apart from the total environment in which they function. Further, we might emphasize that, while there are similarities, the colonial situation itself has distinctive qualities and features shared by no other contact situation.

In empires around the world and in various eras, ethnic groups have responded to the colonial situation in a variety of ways. At least three factors shape the direction that responses will take: power, perception, and purpose. For the sake of clarity, we will first treat these factors as if they were independent of one another, even though in most situations, they are related in ways crucial to the shaping of the response.

Power

In a sense, power is the primary factor. Simply by its presence or absence, it frequently dictates the situation or sets the course that will be taken before perceptions solidify into bases for action or before the purpose of colonization is considered. However much it may be regretted at some later point, the temptation to use power when available to expedite matters is irresistible. In most colonial situations, the invading people have the power to impose their definition of the situation, and more often than not, the kind of power available to the invaded is the ability to resist. In other cases, two different definitions of the situation may exist at the same time. In the case of the Yaqui, for example, the Spanish defined their part of the New World as belonging, both lands and inhabitants, to the Crown of Castile, and called it, with the arrogance of conquerors, New Spain. The Yaqui defined themselves as an independent nation. Each group dealt with the other more or less harmoniously according to its own definition.

A third possibility is that the invaders find themselves gradually defined out of existence. China had been ruled by invaders from Mongolia and Manchuria. Yet after each conquest, the prestige of Chinese culture remained high, with the Chinese defining their rulers as "barbarians." One by one the invaders and conquerors were absorbed into the general population (Shibutani and Kwan 1965:471). Owen Lattimore offers an ecological explanation for this kind of response. He argues that one environment favored mobility while the other favored the accumulation of wealth. As the Mongolians and other mobile peoples invaded China, they of necessity lost mobility, became entangled in the Chinese bureaucracy, acquired wealth, and were assimilated (1940:76-77).

Bases of Power

How do colonial powers impose their definition of the situation, or from what base do they derive their power? Military superiority is most often the answer. The advance guard of empires is almost always outnumbered by the colonists-to-be, so superior weaponry is the decisive factor. Also important is the ability to win allies among a heterogeneous indigenous population. Even superior weaponry is not sufficient without manpower and a source of supplies. Competing indigenous groups have often used invaders as a means of shifting the balance of power in their favor. That was certainly the attitude of the Tlaxcalans, Mixtec, and Zapotec, who resented Aztec attempts to incorporate all of indigenous Mexico into its empire. These three strong powers, as well as others, offered their services to the Spanish conquistadores in return for the overthrow of the Aztec. Needless to say, in their eagerness to be rid of the Aztec menace, they did not foresee the even more effective domination of the Spanish.

This reception provided the conquistadores with a mandate for disregarding the sovereignty of another country. In Spanish eyes, the Aztec were evil tyrants who were making the lives of their subjects miserable. The Spanish would liberate all the groups subservient to the Aztec and rule them in an enlightened and benign fashion. To make their raw use of military power even more palatable, the conquistadores had the further justification of faith. By bringing Christianity to the New World, they would save thousands of souls from heathenish lives and, worse, from heathenish deaths.

Some individuals or groups within the colonized land often gain or consolidate positions as a result of the imposition of rule by an outside power. The Tlaxcalans improved their lot in three ways: they were essentially granted autonomy from Spanish control; their rivals the Aztec had been broken; and they established trade relations with the conquistadores, handling products introduced by the Spanish and finding a new market for their own goods.

Thus far, we have spoken about the colonial situation primarily in terms of power available to the colonizers, specifically, the power of force supported by justifications on the basis of improving the lot of the colonized—in some instances saving them from the tyranny of oppressors and in all cases bringing them the benefits of civilization. What about the kinds of power available to the beneficiaries of these noble efforts, who, in their ingratitude, just as often as not persisted in a preference for things the way they were?

Resources to Resist Domination: Material and Ideological

The superiority of force the newcomers were able to muster was often not available for indigenous groups. Although the weight of numbers was frequently on their side, in most cases they could not mobilize their troops for long enough to defeat and subjugate the Europeans. Disease was one reason for their inability to organize an effective defense. Yet there are many instances where ethnic groups have successfully resisted incorporation in all but a nominal sense.

The resources for resistance can be divided into the material and the ideological. In the first category fall such items as an independent means of subsistence and economic stability, population of sufficient size and density to allow for persistence, geographic factors that allow a certain amount of local autonomy, and an organization capable of rallying the group. The ideological category consists largely of a sense of people-hood arising from a shared history, which can be the basis for a spirit of resistance. Just as we concluded in the discussion of definitions, it is also necessary to think in terms of both the material and the ideological in explaining successful persistence of identities. Thus, a group may possess all the appropriate material means to resist incorporation successfully but, without the commitment to do so, incorporation will result. Similarly, a group may have a strong ideology of opposition, but without material resources it cannot maintain effective opposition for very long.

Material Resources

The most important material resource for gaining a livelihood is a land base—either to work oneself or to rent to others—the income from which provides the means of subsistence. Sometimes subsistence is derived from a symbiotic economic arrangement (which frequently occurs in regions where the terrain is diverse). In Manchuria the Tungus and the Cossacks each exploited a different ecological niche, thereby allowing each to contribute necessary items to the other's subsistence. Along with this material reliance on each other went a mutual respect. Such an inherently delicate situation is easily upset by conquest if existing allegiances are broken. The patron-client ties between the Hutu and Tutsi of Burundi—the former were agriculturalists while the latter were pastoralists—constituted one of the forces uniting the two groups before Burundi became a Belgian mandate. Instead of emphasizing the symbiotic nature of the situation, the Belgians stressed the ethnic differences by the simple act of placing rule in Tutsi hands. The ethnic differences thus loomed larger and larger and ties based on other than ethnic factors became less and less able to bind the diverse groups within Burundi when the country became independent. Ethnic genocide was the result.

The more economically independent the groups involved are the better their chances for resistance unless opposition encourages an alliance. When a people no longer controls its own subsistence base, it also loses the means for an effective independent identity; for when the livelihood is provided by outsiders, the group's allegiance and goals become those of the providers. Psychologically, being dependent weighs negatively on resistance. However, if a group has demonstrated the ability to resist, periods of dependence may be less damaging and may even be turned to the group's advantage.

Yaqui guerrillas holding out in the Bacatete Mountains and making periodic devastating raids on the Mexicans were supported largely by the earnings of Yaqui working on Mexican haciendas. It is doubtful that the guerrillas would have resisted in this manner had they not already had the commitment to a land and a system of political organization that together made up the essence of Yaqui character. Many indigenous groups persisted in Mexico for at least 300 years after the Spanish Conquest because of communal landholdings granted to groups of Indians from which non-Indians were specifically excluded. With the Land Reform Law of 1857, which was aimed at breaking up the extensive landholdings of the Church but which was worded so as to apply to all communal land, many of the hitherto corporate Indian communities were fragmented. With that breakup of an economic base came a gradual loss of a distinctive Indian identity.

A certain size and stability of population is required for the persistence of a people. Despite many similarities of history and geography, the Yaqui persisted as Yaqui while the Mayo gradually became integrated into the Mexican nation. The Mayo population was drastically reduced by waves of epidemics, but the Yaqui, being further from Spanish and Mexican influences, escaped the ravages of disease for the most part. By the time the Yaqui population in Sonora was reduced by deportation to Yucatan, a tradition of resistance and persistence had already been firmly established.

Density works in different ways. For the Yaqui a concentrated population was effective in mounting an active defense. However, another Mexican Indian group, the Tarahumara, survived, partly because they were scattered over the countryside in a manner that made control difficult if not impossible. Sheer numbers and density worked in favor of the Chinese and against their would-be conquerors, like the Mongols and the Manchurians, who were gradually absorbed into the Chinese masses.

Spicer states that opposition quite often generates identity systems, particularly in colonial situations, but that opposition must be manageable, or potential identity systems will be opposed out of existence before they have time to develop. One essential feature of successful identity systems directly related to this point is local autonomy. In most cases, geographic isolation determines how much autonomy a group will have. Unless there are other, overriding concerns, such as valuable mineral deposits in the area, difficulty of access seems to dampen the enthusiasm of colonial powers for incorporating isolated groups.

Robert B. Ekvall (1939) describes different responses along the Chinese-Tibetan border that are shaped by the terrain. The region of the Koko Nor, which is relatively easy of access and has fertile lands, has been extensively colonized by Chinese who have preempted the land from the Tibetan tribes. In other regions, where the terrain is forbidding, the Tibetans have successfully resisted the advances of the Chinese.

Pre-existing social structures, often related to geographic isolation, also affect the fate of indigenous groups. Many colonial systems had policies of indirect rule. In 1897, Captain Thruston, a British administrator in Uganda, explained what was implied by indirect rule, namely that England ruled through native administrators. Its effect was that non-leaders and originally subordinate groups had little or no direct contact with the colonial powers. Rather, the word of the outsiders was filtered through their familiar superiors.

Local autonomy is also affected by the new masters' perceptions of indigenous groups. In Spain's colonies, for example, the native population fell into three categories: those who were fit, as they were, for incorporation into the bosom of Spain; those who had the potential, as yet undeveloped, to become adequate citizens of the world; and those who exhibited none of the necessary human qualities for this educational process. Groups of the third type enjoyed more autonomy than those in the other two categories.

The following example demonstrates how local autonomy can result from difficulty of access and pre-existing structures. The Isthmus Zapotec colony of Juchitán was founded in 1486 as a military outpost of the Zapotec kingdom, which was ruled from the center in Tehuantepec. At the time of the Spanish Conquest in 1521, Juchitán was still an insignificant village with no attractions to lure strangers into the searing heat and dust—that part of the Isthmus is inland from the Pacific but not yet in the highlands. Tehuantepec was a big city, prettily situated and cooled by ocean breezes, and was made the seat of the Bishop of Tehuantepec. Tehuantepec and its inhabitants identified themselves with the outside world, with their identification as citizens of Tehuantepec being secondary. Juchitán from the beginning was fiercely inward in its loyalties, and it enjoyed the autonomy to maintain and strengthen that view. By the time Juchitán surpassed Tehuantepec in size, the Juchitecos were already totally committed to local nationalism.

The last type of resource critical to the persistence of groups within the larger colonial system is, like Spicer's third area of participation, political. A group must have some kind of organization capable of rallying its members to fend off attempts at incorporation. It may be an indigenous structure or one imposed on the group by early invaders. In many cases, the imposed structure is much more efficient and effective than the indigenous organization, thus enabling the group to resist later invaders with a greater chance of success.

Many examples from North America and Africa demonstrate that indigenous groups with a form of political organization recognizable to dominant outsiders could count on at least some minimal understanding in their interactions. By this means, they were frequently able to resist total incorporation. In some cases, the Iroquois nation, for example, the indigenous group was viewed as having a structure equal to that of the outside group, even if separate.

Ideological Resources

Any group that could claim most or all of the features discussed above had at least the material means with which to remain a system unto itself. Whether it would choose to do so was largely the result of the presence of another kind of component, the ideological one. In order for an ideology of resistance to incorporation to develop, a people have to be bound by strong ties of history reinforced by shared values and goals. Frequently even that is not enough if the identity of the group cannot compare favorably with that of the outsiders. People on the whole do not like to continue a performance that is patently inadequate in comparison with other available identities. Barth speaks to this point rather succinctly, saying that adherence to the basic value standards of an ethnic identity will not be retained when an individual's "comparative performance is utterly inadequate" (1969:25).

In the Roman Empire, Roman identity was so desirable that many groups clamored for citizenship. They considered all other identities inadequate when compared to being a Roman. In contrast, although some Australian aborigines sought recognition from the British and were repelled, others did not rush to adopt the traits and values of the colonizers of their country. The aboriginal philosophical systems gave far more meaning to their lives than the Europeans seemed to derive from their own moral philosophy. The lives led by the white frontiersmen were certainly comprehensible to but not desirable for the aborigines, and the missionaries' behavior gave a constant lie to the Christian doctrine they preached. In short, for the aborigines, there was no more-attractive alternative and few that seemed as good (see Tonkinson 1974).

An identity can be satisfying to those who claim it in several ways. The longer its history the more attractive the identity will be. We can see how important the time depth is when we look at many of the revivals of identity that have recently occurred. William Bittle (1962) documents the Kiowa Apache revival of a society and dance that were unknown to almost all contemporary tribal members. Their reconstruction was a collaborative effort on the part of old tribal members and anthropologists, past and present. The choice of this society to revive was partially based on the fact of its antiquity. The search for roots in Africa by American Blacks can be partially explained by the importance of history. The sense of past is satisfying because it lends continuity to one's life. In the case of ethnic groups, it can mitigate against the choice of a new identity.

The pervasiveness of an identity is also significant. One that reaches out and touches all aspects of an individual's life, integrating it, giving it a consistency and unity, has a higher potential for survival than one that, by its fragmentary nature, forces individuals into behavior that seems inconsistent either to themselves or to others. The various philosophical systems of the Australian aborigines are bases for identities that are integrated wholes, that make sense. That is, they provide charters for satisfying identities as long as they form bases for action. We can point to cases in which the philosophical base has been retained solely in the form of rituals that are performed periodically. In these instances it is no longer an active, meaningful force, and therefore more easily abandoned, and, with it, the distinctively aboriginal way of life (Tonkinson 1974).

Whether or not an identity will be retained also depends on the distinctiveness and cost of its characteristic features. One that is impressive enough to compete with alternative identities is more likely to be retained than one that seems cheap or inadequate. The fact that it costs as much or more to maintain an Isthmus Zapotec identity as it does to be a Mexican of the same class is undoubtedly a major contributor to the vitality of Zapotec identity. It is much more difficult to apply disparaging terms to someone wearing $5,000 worth of gold and a $900 embroidered costume and who has a sleek and affluent manner than someone whose affluence is not so apparent.

Any group that has an ideological component made up of a sense of common history plus the motivation to dramatize an identity through an integrated, distinctive, and attractive style has a good chance for survival in situations that threaten incorporation.

Finally, there are identities based on an ideology of oppression. Persecution or oppression over long periods of time should not be underestimated as a motivating force behind the persistence of an identity.

Perception

Perception colors the ways in which power is employed and frequently determines the effectiveness with which it is wielded. From the point of view of would-be colonial powers, two areas of perception seem to shape the way the contact situation develops: how the colonists view the indigenous populations and what they think is the nature of the pre-contact situation.

Cultural Bases of Perception

All human beings are raised with certain kinds of culturally based suppositions about the world and its people. We are never free from this kind of cultural baggage; the best we can do is recognize that it is there. We carry it with us wherever we go, and it colors the way we perceive any situation. People who are part of efforts to dominate other peoples are no exception. They come to the situation with ideas about the way the world works and about the kinds of people who are in it. These ideas are tenacious and persist in spite of evidence to the contrary.

One might reasonably ask, for example, how the Spanish could feel justified in claiming, without recompense, an area of the world that contained at least two high civilizations at the time of Spain's appearance on the scene? As it happened, they had a charter for this action. It said that any land not governed by a Christian prince was available to any Christian prince who wished to claim it. In the world view of the Spaniard of the sixteenth century, "Christian" was equated with "civilized." By extension, anything or anyone not Christian was not civilized and hence had no voice in the council of civilized men. So they confronted the wonders of Aztec and Inca civilizations and proclaimed the Indians, at best, barbarians (when admiring their architecture and gold work) and, at worst, savages (when some conquistadores had their hearts torn out and offered to inadmissible gods).

The fact that the Spanish recognized three categories of people had a profound effect on the relationship between them and the indigenous population of the New World. The natives who were ready for civilization were allowed to govern their people in the name of the Spanish Crown and were later educated in the Spanish system. Those who had the potential were gradually converted to Christianity, taught new trades and new farming techniques and crops, and introduced to animal husbandry. Those considered less than human were put to work on plantations and in mines. The native priests who refused to abandon their beliefs and embrace Christianity were regarded as incorrigible and were put to death.

The English brought to their colonies a different but equally tenacious view of the world. Geoffrey Gorer describes what was perhaps the cornerstone of that view, those who are like us and those who are not.

> The upper middle class administrators were notably uncorrupt, just, and considerate for all under their administrations, provided the administered did not claim social equality. When equality was claimed it was callously resisted—"Dogs and Chinamen not admitted." The private clubs, centers of all social life in the tropical empire, for example, excluded not only "the natives," but all other Englishmen ˙ı lower social classes. . . . One of the things which was most wounding to many of the excluded lower middle class is that this exclusion treated them and "the natives" alike. [1975:167–168]

For the British, the apex of civilization was, of course, Britain. So, just as the Spanish ignored the remarkable achievements of the New World civilizations because they were created by non-Christians, the British ignored the accomplishments of the Ashante, Benin, and Ife kingdoms of West Africa because they were produced by people of color.

The attitudes of the French toward most of the peoples they administered was very different from either the Spanish or the British view. In Africa and in Southeast Asia, their goal seemed to be to turn their colonies into a part of France and to make the colonized people French. Similarly, Alexander the Great strived to create a fusion of the Greek and Asiatic peoples. After his victory over the Iranians in 329 B.C. he promoted the adoption of Persian dress and court etiquette. Not only did he have natives trained in the Macedonian army but he left many of the native rulers in their places of authority. He took a Persian woman as wife and encouraged his officers and men to follow his example. Eighty officers and 10,000 soldiers did so.

Perceptions of Relationships

Perceptions of other peoples seem to fall into three categories depending on the relative positions of the groups in stratified systems. There are a limited number of relationships possible. Groups may be perceived as being stratified with some dominant and others subordinate; they may be viewed as being in opposition to one another; and they may be perceived as sharing a cooperative or symbiotic relationship. People behave in certain ways toward other people depending on which of these relationships is thought to characterize the situation.

Relationships of Stratification

From the perspective of the colonials, in most cases the relationship is considered to be of the first, stratified, kind. Any demonstration on the part of the indigenous people that would indicate their nonacceptance of a subordinate position leads to a characterization of the situation as one of opposition. Rarely do colonial powers regard the situation as a symbiotic one, though it may actually be one of cooperation. The way the relationships are perceived provides a charter for action. Perceiving a group as inferior implies certain kinds of policies and behaviors. One can afford to be tolerant and benevolent toward inferiors. In much of British colonial policy, a dedication to improving the natives' lives was mandatory. If a group is perceived as so inferior it is not to be admitted to the category of human being, then almost any kind of treatment is justifiable. Slavery and worse are frequently the result of this kind of perception.

Religion also contributes to the perception of a group as inferior. Throughout history, being of another faith has been as disastrous as being considered subhuman. Those who would impose their religion on others frequently allow only one response — conversion. People who are not willing to convert must suffer the fate of unbelievers. At first perceived as inferiors who were unfortunate enough not to have been exposed to the true faith but who could now rectify that omission, the impenitent nonconverts now become characterized as the opposition and are regarded as threats.

Religion has not been a monolithic evil, however, in the history of colonial expansion. In many cases, it has been the agent of change in improving the quality of people's lives. The Jesuits in Mexico, for example, measurably improved the lot of the indigenous populations by introducing new technologies, crops, and animals as well as by providing schools and medical aid. They also fought to maintain the integrity of Indian communities against the encroachment of the conquistadores and the ever-growing *mestizo* population.

Relationships of Opposition

Quite another response is generated by the perception of opposition—feelings of frustration and fear. Benevolence and tolerance no longer apply when it is a question of your existence or theirs. The Brazilian Indians who attacked prospectors and rubber gatherers encroaching on their territory were tracked down and eliminated. Similarly, in South Africa, starting in the seventeenth century, when Blacks began attacking Boers, they were systematically exterminated or driven beyond the frontier. If, however, a group projects an image of invulnerability coupled with an aggressive fighting nature, that is sometimes sufficient to discourage attempts to control them. The Yaqui of Mexico bought some years of peace in this manner.

Relationships of Cooperation

People rarely perceive cooperation as existing in the colonial situation. To see the relationship in this way would be to admit equality for the groups involved. In the case of Alexander, the cooperation took the form of borrowing certain items in the Persian cultural inventory, such as dress and food, and encouraging intermarriage between Greeks and Persians. Some sort of cooperative spirit also existed between the Spanish and the Tlaxcalans during the first century after the Conquest of Mexico. Tlaxcala had proved to be a valuable ally for Spain, and Spain rewarded her by offering the Tlaxcalans positions in the colonial administration and by exempting them from the otherwise ubiquitous tribute levies.

Ethel Lindgren, in her article on the relationship between the Tungus and the Cossacks in Manchuria (1938), cites their mutual respect as a crucial factor in the excellent relations between the two groups. Each possesses attributes that elicit the respect of the other, so that a weakness in one sphere is balanced by a strength in another. For example, the Cossacks are literate while the Tungus are not. The Tungus, however, are better linguists, having command of both Tungus and Russian. Lindgren supports her argument that mutual respect is necessary for cooperative relationships to develop by citing the results of psychological experiment; in one case 33% of the subjects believed that cooperation would be impossible between groups having a marked difference in IQ. That attitude would certainly seem to apply to inter-ethnic contract as well as to the colonial situation.

As groups learn more about each other, they change their perceptions, sometimes drastically. Perception is responsive to reality, albeit the response is sometimes long in coming. Policy, being based on perception, is also responsive to change.

Change in Perception

Between 1850 and 1890, the Bakweri in the interior of the German colony of West Cameroon grew very wealthy. They had great success with their cocoyam crops, the related raising of livestock, and trade with coastal settlements, which brought them commerical goods and guns. As their affluence increased, they began raiding: and, even though their forays were on a small scale, they were perceived by the Germans as a threat. This belief was reinforced when a Bakweri village defeated a German expedition in 1891. The Bakweri correctly appraised the relative invulnerability of their mountainous position as well as the relative poverty of German colonial coffers at the time. Having learned from the 1891 encounter, the Germans mounted their 1894 expedition with a careful eye toward eliminating the Bakweri threat. What should the German commander, Von Stetten, find but a rather timid group of people living in scattered huts in the forest raising cocoyams and pigs. Recovering from his shock and disbelief, Von Stetten began the task of bringing German order into the Bakweri world. One German, delighted with the order he had brought to a village, observed that all that was now required was "the village postman going from door to door" (Ardener 1970:144). The German perceptions of the Bakweri had changed from a threat to be met and subdued by force to harmless inferior beings who needed the civilizing effect of German culture.

Perceptions of Indigenous Social and Political Systems

Often a colonial power's perception of the indigenous social and political structure is more important than its perception of the indigenous population, especially if it chooses to rule its colonies indirectly, using the native structure. In some cases, the situation was appraised correctly and rule proceeded smoothly. In other cases, an appraisal was made and a decision was made to alter the structure so that rule would be more efficient. Sometimes the colonial powers judged the indigenous structure wrongly and created situations that were never there before their coming. A particularly common error was to assume that the indigenous political system had a structure similar to that of the colonial power and functioned in the same ways. However accurate or inaccurate the initial appraisal, the result was almost always to freeze the situation as it was for all time, or at least until the coming of independence.

In his article "Indigenous Politics and Colonial Administration," J.A. Barnes sees colonial structures impinging differently on the indigenous political system depending on the latter's place in one of three categories: food-gatherers with small, politically autonomous units; primitive states with a centralized authority; and stateless agriculturalists with no central authority. Because of the progression of colonial expansion, empires had more early experience with the second category, that of the primitive state. It also came closer to colonial administrators' perceptions of the way societies ought to be organized politically. The result in many cases was the wholesale transfer to stateless areas of strategies for ruling based on a state organization. Barnes cites the example of Uganda, where the British were so impressed with the efficiency of the indigenous state system that they used Ganda models widely throughout the Protectorate (1960:223).

Since most of the areas of the world subjected to colonizing efforts were ethnically heterogeneous to begin with, accurate assessments were difficult to make. The consequences of policies based on misconceptions were often disastrous, contributing to the conflict inherent in multiethnic situations or creating conflict where earlier a precarious balance had averted strife. Frequently, the problem was compounded by the artificiality of the boundaries drawn around units to be administered. Only infrequently did the new political unit correspond to the cultural units involved. Both errors occurred, like textbook examples, in the Belgian administration of Rwanda-Burundi, where there were tragic consequences (see p. 80).

Perceptions Held by Indigenous Populations

Even when the colonial rule was one of benign neutrality based on more accurate perceptions than was the case in Rwanda-Burundi, for example, relations might be influenced by the perceptions and strategies of the indigenous population. As already mentioned, sometimes indigenous rulers took advantage of the colonial might to reinforce their own position. The strategy of the Australian aborigines was to reinforce the negative stereotypical view the white newcomers had of them so that they would be let alone and could maintain their integrity. The symbiotic, mutually respectful relationship of the Tungus and the Cossacks was strengthened by their joint perception of the Chinese invaders as a threat that could best be met by a united front.

The indigenous populations also perceive the characters of the foreign minority in ways shaped by their own cultural knowledge and access the advantages and disadvantages of different responses to the contact situation as they see it. The easiest, and therefore the most tempting, way to characterize the outsiders is good or bad, benevolent or wicked. Positive assessments frequently imply a desire to imitate, as in the following response by one of the participants in the last great Indian council of 1909. Chief White Horse, speaking of his train trip to the Council meeting said:

> It seems impossible how the trains go so fast, and this thought came to my mind: This is of the white people, who are so educated they can make the iron horse draw things across the country so fast. My wish is that the Indians will come to be like the white people, and be able to invent things, but the thought comes to me that this will be impossible. [Dixon 1913:211]

And the king of Duala (Cameroon), Bell Honesty, wrote to Queen Victoria in 1864 requesting permission to visit England for the purpose of being "enlightened" (Rudin 1938).

Negative assessments can be seen in the responses of the Chinese, who have always regarded any invaders as barbarians. Similarly, the Koreans caused the Japanese no end of anguish by their refusal to be grateful for the material improvements their masters had brought and by their persistence in referring to the Japanese as *wai nom*, or "evil little men." The Yaqui, on the other hand, watched the progress of their neighbors, the Mayo, under the tutelage of the Jesuits, and decided that they could take advantage of the Jesuit technology without much danger to their cultural integrity.

Changes in Perception

Just as the attitudes of colonial powers were subject to revision and change based on experience, so were the perceptions of the colonized. Out of their initial experience with British colonials, the Creoles of Sierra Leone forged and wholeheartedly accepted an identity as "Black English." Their sympathies were one with the English and the white man's burden in bringing civilization to Africa. In fact, they regarded themselves as excellent examples of British ideas and policies in Africa. As Leo Spitzer explains, however, their attitude gradually changed as they were confronted with more and more blatant examples of a change in the attitude of the British, from one that accepted the Creoles as Black English to one that viewed them as members of an inferior race:

> [T]he noble savage stereotype was replaced by the popular image of an ape-like black man in top hat and dark suit. As paternalism came to displace the ideal of equality through conversion too many Britons made Creoles feel like parodies rather than equals. [1971:104–105]

A change in attitudes of the indigenous populations toward the dominant power inevitably occurs as colonial subjects move toward independence. Benevolent paternalism is almost certainly resented as the subordinate people begin desiring and demanding equality as something due them. The mismatch between the perceptions of the colonizers and the colonized about relative status in pre-independence situations makes the whole colonial process seem to be characterized by conflict. The hierarchical relationship gives way to one of opposition, as each group perceives the other as an object of frustration.

Perception of the Contact Situation

The way the subordinate group perceives the contact situation is extremely important in influencing relationships. Members of the indigenous population try to assess the situation with an eye to the advantages to be gained from it. They may take the form of hitherto unavailable resources such as goods, education, employment, prestige, or political power that allows one group to strengthen its own position on the local scene. We have already seen how New World peoples tried to use the Spanish.

Indigenous groups that opt for goods and other tangible resources are affected in a variety of ways by their choice. The Yaqui were able to adopt Jesuit technology and the Christian church all the while maintaining a viable identity. The Creoles of Sierra Leone, on the other hand, absorbed more and more of British culture until they had only a derivative identity as "Black English."

The BaKongo on both sides of the Congo River between Stanley Pool and the Atlantic remained BaKongo in spite of their adoption of the Western technology provided by the Belgians. They retained their identity in large measure because of the way their perceptions of the West fitted into BaKongo thought. According to the BaKongo, Congolese science, particularly the areas of medicine and metal working, had been maliciously and systematically destroyed by the Europeans through the means of missionary teaching and state force. Europeans cleverly forbade the use of indigenous medicines so that people would have to come to the hospitals. There, foreign doctors would profit monetarily and would also choose some victims for the spiritual slave trade (turning some patients into zombies). These slaves then went to America, where they were put to work making the manufactured goods that the Congolese were forced to buy. Many BaKongo thought in 1959 that independence would mean that their indigenous medicine and manufacturing would be restored (MacGaffey 1972:58–59). It is not clear whether this kind of adjustment is common in the colonial experience but it was without doubt effective in the Congolese case. What is clear is that the perceptions brought to bear on colonial situations by all groups involved directly affect the responses to the situation and the strategies chosen by the various parties.

Purpose

The predominant motivations leading people to go forth and impose their will on others are the quest for sources of raw materials and markets for manufactured goods, the desire to spread one's moral philosophy or religion beyond the confines of one's own nation, the need for a place to put excess or undesirable populations, and the hunger for the kind of power gained by control over more land and more peoples.

Just as perceptions change over time, so do purposes. Many colonial ventures have their beginnings in isolated traders or frontiersmen. Germany's West African colonies and its colony of Western Samoa of necessity developed in this manner. Bismarck had prohibited all colonizing activity, but of course his restriction did not apply to merchants and traders. By the time he lifted the ban on German expansionism, all the foundations had been laid and colonies came into being literally as fast as agreements could be signed. Because of the actual ban, Germany is perhaps a special case, but we have, among others, Russian traders in Alaska and Portuguese merchants in the New World, where colonization followed initial contact made through trade.

Quest for Raw Materials and Markets

Many of the colonial powers whose ventures were sparked by the search for raw materials and markets had little if any desire to change the lives and habits of their new subjects. Change came about in the course of speeding up and organizing the production of desired commodities and creating or increasing the need for manufactured goods. Indeed, it was sometimes the very fact that new desires had been created that led to the realization by the colonial subjects that they were being denied access to more of what was now desired, and, in turn, led to movements for independence.

Change came about, even where there was little desire for change, by other routes as well. The arrival of the Spanish in Mexico, for example, set off a chain of epidemics of measles, smallpox, and the common cold that, in the space of ninety years, reduced the indigenous population by 90%. Whereas 500 Spaniards in 1521 would have had little impact on a population of 20 million, 200,000 Spaniards in 1605 did have an impact on a reduced Indian population of one million.

The mixture of races was not uniform throughout Mexico. There were little pockets of Indians in the less-accessible and less-desirable regions. Some, like the Yaqui in the northwest and the Maya in the south, fought successfully to retain an identity that they felt was distinctive from that of the Spanish or of the mixed populations. For the *mestizo*, independence came too late for a viable Indian identity. Most *mestizos* would not have been able to create an Indian image at that point even if they had felt it desirable to do so.

The British in Africa and India for the most part followed the Spanish model in their search for exotic products for home markets and for a place to sell their own manufactured goods. To insure this market they sometimes brought colonists to their colonies. Such was the case in British East Africa, where the Crown made numerous appeals to East Indians to settle there. Those who responded found themselves the richest settlers on the coast, with many Arab-Swahili in their debt. This action by the Crown was violently opposed by the British settlers, who saw their manifest destiny in the highlands of East Africa and wanted no competition from East Indians. They also saw their role in a somewhat different light from individuals in other Crown colonies. In 1906 John Ainsworth summarized these views: "White people can live here and *will* live here, not . . . as colonists performing manual labour, as in Canada or New Zealand, but as planters, etc., overseeing natives doing the work of development" (in Wolff 1974:54). They were able to do so because of two pieces of legislation: one prohibited Africans from growing coffee, thus forcing them to work for wages; the other, the 1902

Crown Lands Ordinance, gave British settlers jurisdiction over uncultivated land where the native ruler was incompetent to exercise that jurisdiction. Part of the impetus behind the rapid populating of new colonies was, of course, to prevent other colonial powers from taking them. In the case of British East Africa the competitor was Germany.

The British had a policy of indirect rule and did not attempt any sweeping changes in the native population except where necessary to smooth the way for business, which was the order of the day. Like the Spanish, the British precipitated change unwittingly. It occurred in the native social structure because the British assumed that all units had to have rulers comparable to those in the European tradition. When groups, such as the Nuer and the Dinka, did not have chiefs, the colonial officers simply appointed representatives who looked chieflike. Of the many problems inherent in this policy, Barnes mentions one that would figure large in the impact of any foreign minority on a native population, that is, the difference between the basis and kind of authority of traditional leaders as opposed to the kind of leadership demanded by the colonial administration.

> Under almost any scheme of colonial administration, the recognized chiefs, headmen, and councillors are intended to be mainly, if not wholly, administrators, like their superiors in the hierarchy. In the traditional society . . . , positions of leadership call for the exercise of political rather than administrative skills. [1960:229]

Furthermore, Barnes says that it is unlikely that traditional leaders whose positions derive from their esoteric knowledge of ritual or their ability to organize feasts will be either efficient or cooperative administrators.

More-obvious change occurred in the groups that chose to emulate British models, for example, the "Black English" of Sierra Leone. In many cases, however, the lid was kept on change for the sake of a peaceful atmosphere for commerce. The British legal system forbade native ways of resolving conflict, which, to British eyes, led to unnecessary bloodshed and violence. The infrequent but necessary feuds and warfare between groups over resources were also eliminated. The British system created societies in artificial states of equilibrium whose calm exterior hid terrible pressures building up just below the surface. These were to erupt in the many post-independence genocidal wars.

Missionizing

Change is often intentionally initiated by colonial powers motivated by missionary zeal. They believe that their own way is the true path and that it is their duty to herd as many wayward souls as possible onto that path. The Germans in the Cameroons and in Samoa are good examples of this mentality. Native homes were rearranged into neat rows of German-looking huts, and their daily lives were equally precisely organized.

The Inca of pre-Conquest Peru also believed it their divine mission to incorporate as many of the "heathen" natives as possible into the Inca empire and way of life. The empire imposed and regulated the style of clothing, language, legal system, marriage customs, and religion. In marked contrast were the Aztec of pre-Conquest Mexico, who made only those changes necessary to enable them to collect tribute and punish disobedience efficiently.

British colonial efforts in East Africa were justified both in English politics and for foreign consumption as a crusade against the evils of the slave trade.

One would have expected the Greeks, with their enormous self-pride, to have imposed their ways on the peoples they conquered, and indeed they did. Alexander, however, was able to appreciate some of the richness and wisdom of oriental ways and actively sought to graft some Persian traditions onto the Greek ideal. His efforts were equally actively opposed by many of his generals and by the rank and file.

The self-pride of the French is obvious in the administration of their colonies. They imposed the French system of justice, the French language, Catholicism—everything that was indicative of French identity. Promising youth of the indigenous culture were shepherded through the colonial schools and then sent to France for advanced education. When they returned they took up administrative posts and continued to promote French identity for everyone. Indeed, there was a time when societies having no relationship with France scrambled to keep up with the latest in French fashion. Among Americans at the time of the Revolutionary War, French dances, hair styles, dress, swordsmanship, and language were all the rage.

Removal of Undesirable Elements

Some colonies were opened as a result of an excess of undesirables in the home country. "Undesirable" was applied to a variety of people: individuals who adhered to a minority religious belief; those who had been found guilty of a crime, whether it was bankruptcy or murder; the unemployed; and, sometimes, groups that were just too numerous.

Australia is the best-known area to serve as a penal colony. For years England, followed by the rest of the Commonwealth, sent its prisoners halfway around the world to Australia. It was a harsh existence but no worse than life in a workhouse or prison. The individuals who settled Australia had not known pity or kindness in their own lives, and they did not show these qualities to the aborigines. The result for the aborigines was a mixture of extermination, miscegenation, and removal to the unwanted regions of Australia.

America too was a haven for the unwanted. Many settled in the colonies because they had been subjected to religious persecution in England. Some came because they were younger sons of large families and there was neither land nor position for them in England. Some chose life in the New World over debtor's prison in the Old, and others came to find their fortunes.

Competition

In all periods some colonial expansion resulted from competition, but it appeared more frequently during the periods of great colonial enterprise, the nineteenth century being one of the most noteworthy. During this period nations had no sooner become nations than they were seeking colonies, as if to validate their new nationhood. Italy had barely achieved unification in the 1860s when she began establishing colonial outposts in Ethiopia. The core of Eritrea, Assab, was acquired in 1882, and the colony of Eritrea, comprising all of Italy's Red Sea possessions, was established in 1890. Just one year earlier, Italy had purchased the entire Benadir coast from Kismayu to Cape Guardafui from the Sultan of Zanzibar. Britain encouraged Italy in her dreams of empire, for the lands a nonthreatening Italy explored and conquered would be unavailable to a threatening France.

Much of the nineteenth-century competitive colonialism was between the established colonial powers, Britain, France, and a rapidly expanding Germany. One of the more dramatic confrontations arose between Britain and France at Fashoda on the Nile in 1898. British expeditions had been trying to reach the Nile from Uganda in an effort to head off the French, who had plans for making the left bank of the river French territory. Although France reached the Nile first, under pressure at home and faced with ill-disguised threats of aggression from without, she finally relinquished all the Nile territory. One interpretation of the reconquest of Sudan by the British is that it was an attempt to keep France farther away from the British sphere of interest.[1]

Nineteenth-century explorations in the Pacific ended in competitive annexation until all the desirable lands had been claimed by one power or another. Britain had relatively little interest in acquiring Pacific territories but was finally forced into a policy of annexation because France and Germany were rapidly accounting for most of the lands in the Pacific. In 1898 the United States joined the colonial powers with the annexation of Hawaii, and she got the Philippines at the end of the Spanish-American War. The acquisition of the Philippines was an example of planned territorial expansion. After defeating Spain, the United States could hardly allow her to continue ruling her island possessions. At the same time, it was felt that it would be irresponsible to grant independence to the Filipinos when they were not yet ready to govern themselves.

The history of most of the lands acquired during bouts of competitive colonialism such as those described above would have been quite different if the colonial powers had not perceived the situations as competitive. As it was, once the colonies had been acquired, for whatever reasons, the different colonial situations developed along the lines of each national style.

---

1. The Sudan was important to the British for a variety of reasons. Sir Samuel Baker, who h   conquered the Sudan in 1822 while in the employ of Egypt, finished the conquest of the upper Nile in the 1870s and initiated the suppression of the slave trade. Ending slavery was often cited as a major reason for the British interest in the Sudan. In 1883, the prophet Mahdi set up an organized movement throughout the Sudan against Egyptian rule. In 1884 Britain obliged Egypt to give up the Sudan. General Gordon, who was sent to guide the evacuation, and all his troops were massacred by the Mahdi at Khartoum in 1885. The reconquest by Kitchener is sometimes interpreted as essential to restoring British prestige as well as avenging Gordon's death.

Summary of Forces of Colonialism

The first of three factors that shape the fates of ethnic groups made part of colonial empires is power, by which is meant both the varieties of power available and the use of it for specific ends. In many instances, power becomes the primary determinant of the course of colonial development. The second factor is perception, or the way in which the situation is perceived by both the foreign minority and the indigenous peoples; and the third comprises the many purposes behind colonialism. Two cases that illustrate the interplay of these factors and their consequences are the Yaqui of Mexico and the Hutu and Tutsi of Burundi.

Case Study: The Yaqui of Mexico[2]

Spanish colonial expansion into what is now Mexico was motivated largely by the desire for gold, other riches, and the exotic products of strange new lands. The Indians living in areas where those items existed in abundance very quickly came under the sway of the Spanish conquistadores. Those who did not expire from overwork, ill treatment, or epidemics found their lives radically changed. They were reorganized into centralized communities *(congregaciones)* whose focus was the Catholic church. This concentration facilitated absorption into Spanish ways. The Yaqui, in their mountain strongholds, were peripheral to major Spanish activities for most of the first century of the empire. The first contact with the Spanish was a skirmish between the Yaqui and Diego de Guzman in 1533. In an account that set the tone for all subsequent reports, Guzman lauded the great fighting ability of his Yaqui opponents. The next contact was somewhat friendlier. A Spaniard searching for silver, Francisco de Ibarra, found himself in Yaqui country in 1564. Because they treated him well, he helped the Yaqui in a battle with their traditional enemies, the Mayo.

Meanwhile the Spanish had set up headquarters 200 miles south of Yaqui territory, from which they subdued the Indians of the Fuerte River. By 1600, Jesuits were working among these groups, and the Spanish captain, Hurtaide, expanded his campaign northward. While pursuing a band of Ocoroni Indians, Hurtaide came to the Yaqui River,

2. For a more-complete account see Spicer 1962.

where he was confronted by Yaqui who told him that he was trespassing on their land. Hurtaide was not prepared for a full-scale battle and so he went back to put together a larger force. The first army he assembled, 2,000 Indians and 40 Spanish soldiers, was routed by the Yaqui. Persistent, Hurtaide then collected the largest army ever put into the field in that part of Mexico—4,000 Indians and 50 Spanish calvary. He was beaten even more resoundingly, wounded, and almost captured. The Spanish were unable to mount any military expeditions for almost a year.

The next move was made by the Yaqui, who, incredibly, sued for peace. Spicer (1962) explains this seemingly unaccountable move by citing the Yaqui's desire for a peaceful coexistence with the Spanish and other Indian groups and, more than that, for Jesuit missionaries to come and work among them. Whatever the actual terms of the treaty, the Yaqui remained free of the Spanish military presence. Moreover, they got their Jesuits. Between 1617 and 1619, 30,000 Yaqui were baptized. By 1623 the Yaqui were concentrated in eight towns along the Yaqui River, each with its own church. The next 120 years saw peaceful economic development for the Yaqui and the Jesuits living among them. By virtue of their military abilities, the Yaqui had been able to dictate the terms of their contact with the Spanish. They took advantage of new crops, livestock, and technology under Jesuit tutelage and built a harmonious social and religious life out of the new and the old cultures.

Threats to the Yaqui's peaceful life surfaced with the influx of Spaniards drawn by dreams of silver. In 1684 one of the richest silver mines of the New World was opened at Alamos, about 75 miles from the nearest Yaqui settlement. It was inevitable that as more and more Spaniards came into the area, they would encroach on hitherto inviolate Yaqui land. The situation was aggravated by an alliance between the governor of the Province of Sinaloa and various large landowners directed against the Jesuit program. After ten years of warning signals, the first Yaqui-Mayo revolt erupted in 1740. It began with the killing of a governor of one of the Mayo towns and continued with the battle cries of "Long live the King, Long live the Blessed Mary, Down with bad government" (Spicer 1962:52). A 6,000-man army, primarily of Yaqui, soon gained control of all the towns on the Yaqui and Mayo rivers. In continued fighting, however, it lost so many men (5,000 by Spanish accounts) that resistance was no longer possible.

The head of the Spanish forces was appointed governor of the province and immediately instituted restrictive policies. Indians could not leave their pueblos without permission, and they were subject to forced labor in the mines and on the haciendas. What had been Spanish practice since 1521 in other parts of Mexico finally came to the northwest. The Jesuits intensified their work among a declining Indian population until their expulsion from Mexico in 1768. The Franciscans, who replaced them, were never able to generate the same warmth or confidence, and the economic decline continued, intensified by floods and epidemics.

In 1772 the Crown instituted taxation and land allotment. These measures were designed to add to the Crown's income and make the Spanish settlers' lives more agreeable by giving them access to more Indian labor and more land. Local authorities were sufficiently fearful of Yaqui fighting abilities, however, to try persuasion rather than force in implementing the new orders. Persuasion had not the slightest effect. Yaqui belief in an autonomous Yaqui nation had much to do with the resistance. The Yaqui neither paid taxes nor gave up their landholdings.

During their last years of control in Mexico, the Spaniards fought among themselves and were ineffective as overseers of the empire. The Yaqui watched the Spanish struggles and correctly interpreted them as signs of weakness. In the Yaqui view the Spanish were no more to be feared than any of the neighboring tribes. The Yaqui were not forced to defend their tribal integrity again until Mexico had gained its independence and set about incorporating all Indians as full citizens of the new nation.

Summary of Yaqui Case

The case of the Yaqui under colonial Spanish rule illustrates how the factors of power, perception, and motivation work in concrete situations. Perhaps the key to their success in maintaining their independence was their military prowess. Quite simply, the Yaqui whipped the Spanish and the neighboring tribes often enough to make the others fearful and cautious. Perceptions, too, are crucial in explaining the Yaqui case. The Yaqui perceived themselves as an autonomous tribal unit with rights equal to those of any other group within their ken. That included the Spanish, whom they treated as they would any of the traditional Indian groups with whom they had contact. The Spanish had a healthy respect for the Yaqui warriors and considered them the equivalent of the Spanish fighting men. Motivation cannot be ignored either in this case. Spanish desire for immediate wealth led them to concentrate in those areas where fortunes could be made. That effectively kept them out of Yaqui territory until silver was discovered in 1684. Yaqui desire for the advantages that could be had from association with the Jesuits led them to make the advances that ushered in 120 years of peace and prosperity.

Case Study: The Hutu and the Tutsi of Burundi[3]

The operation of these same factors in Burundi, unfortunately, had tragic consequences, namely the genocidal warfare between the Hutu and the Tutsi.

On April 29, 1972 the attacks began, with some 10,000 Hutu and Mulelists attacking and killing Tutsi men, women, and children. On April 30 the counterattacks began, well organized and systematic, directed against the Hutu population and aimed indiscriminately at both those who had participated in the rebellion and those who had not. The slaughter of the Hutu focused on students, intellectuals, leaders, churchmen, and doctors. Three weeks after the first killings, between 80,000 and 100,000 people had been exterminated. This conservative estimate represented 3.5% of the total population of Burundi (Lemarchand 1975:50). These encounters were the culmination of a conflict between the numerically dominant Hutu and the politically dominant Tutsi the beginnings of which can be traced to the colonial administration of Belgium.

Burundi, contiguous with southern Rwanda in east central Africa, became part of the Rwanda-Burundi League of Nations mandate after World War I. It was administered by Belgium and continued under Belgian supervision as a trust territory after World War II. Although not much is known about early Burundi history, reconstructions of social composition have been proposed. The Burundi area was originally composed of Hutu and Twa peoples. In the thirteenth century, high-caste Tutsi (Tutsi Banyaruguru) moved into the area from the northeast, and in the seventeenth century, low-caste Tutsi Hima migrated in from the east. When the League of Nations mandate was established, Burundi was composed essentially of three groups: the Tutsi, the Hutu, and the Twa. Nilotic, cattle-herding Tutsi made up 14% of the population; Negroid-Nilotic Hutu agriculturalists 85%; and Pygmoid Twa hunters and gatherers and potters 1%.

---

3. This material is drawn from Lemarchand 1966, 1975; and Albert 1960.

Relationships within these groups and among them were extremely complex. The Tutsi, for example, can be subdivided into three categories—the Banyaruguru (north), the Hima (south), and the Basapfu (who are spread throughout the country and act as arbiters of both regional conflicts and conflicts between Banyaruguru and Hima). The Banyaruguru and the Hima are further subdivided into partilineages that are stratified as follows: very good families, good families, families that are neither good nor bad, and bad families. The Banyaruguru category alone has 43 patrilineages. The social distance between Tutsi strata was often more perceptible and significant in its social consequences than were ethnic differences between the Tutsi and the Hutu.

Traditionally, power was in the hands of the *ganwa* (princes of the blood), a small oligarchy who became identified as a separate ethnic group by the Tutsi and the Hutu. Lemarchand discusses the sense of solidarity that existed among those ruled by the *ganwa*:

> Their exclusion from the seats of power, together with their acceptance of the normative prescriptions underlying their traditional status, was enough to give them a sense of solidarity as an "outgroup" and this in spite of notable economic and social differences between and within each of these groups. [1966:405]

In addition to this feeling of a shared identity, the Hutu, Tutsi, and Twa were bound by patron-client ties based on their different subsistence economies.

No such sense of cohesiveness characterized the *ganwa*, who were always struggling among themselves for power. The king himself as a *primus inter pares* had little real authority, and so he, as well as the other *ganwa*, sought support from the Hutu and the Tutsi.

Three features held traditional Burundi society together in the face of a number of potential sources of conflict: the tendency of the *ganwa* to seek the support of both the Tutsi and the Hutu; the clientage that bound the Tutsi and the Hutu; and the unifying symbol of the king and the institution of kingship. In precolonial Burundi these ties cut across potentially devisive bonds of ethnicity such that antagonisms were not expressed as ethnic conflicts but rather as factionalism between unilineal descent groups.

Belgian administration changed all that. Charged with the care of two contiguous territories composed by and large of the same tribes,

Belgium made the decision to administer them in identical fashion. She perceived the situation in Rwanda to be one of a Tutsi aristocracy and a Hutu peasantry; accordingly she gave local rule to the Tutsi and ruled indirectly through them. Few Hutu were given access to either educational opportunities or political office. The same policy was instituted in Burundi. This situation, coupled with the psychological impact of the Hutu revolution in Rwanda in 1959, made the subsequent ethnocide in Burundi self-fulfilling and inevitable.

The inevitable ethnic conflict deriving from a situation in which one group is given access to power and prestige and the other, numerically superior, is denied that access came more quickly to Rwanda, where there already existed antagonisms between the Tutsi and the Hutu. In Burundi, conflicts along ethnic lines arose more slowly because of the complexity of existing ties and the importance of traditional loyalties based on region, clan, and clientage. Conflict was hastened, however, by the example of Rwanda, where the Hutu forced Belgium into allowing local elections in 1962. They gained 77% of the vote, and the Tutsi king and his followers went into exile. The Hutu in Burundi, sharing a similar underprivileged status, were encouraged by the success of their fellow Hutu in Rwanda and began agitating for access to material rewards and political influence. The Tutsi, for their part, were frightened by what had happened in Rwanda and were naturally suspicious of Hutu motives. Social equality and majority rule as far as the Tutsi were concerned meant the end of Tutsi supremacy and the beginning of Hutu rule.

Repressive measures in the post-independence years kept the Hutu in Burundi in a subordinate position, and the gap widened between their aspirations and their actual share of power and prestige. Frustrated in their efforts to change their status through socially acceptable channels, they turned to violence. Just as they had met previous efforts of the Hutu to bring about change so did the Tutsi meet the latest, violent demands — with even greater violence.

Summary of Burundi

Perception, or better misperception, is the factor that most influenced the fate of Burundi. The fact that Belgium incorrectly perceived Rwanda and Burundi as identical and ruled them accordingly led to the relevance of ethnic difference as a basis of conflict in Burundi, where it had not traditionally been a source of division. A bad situation was made worse by the perceptions of the Tutsi and the Hutu in Burundi of the situation in Rwanda and their subsequent acting on the basis of those perceptions.

Power is an important factor too. In traditional Burundi society, access to power was never accorded on the basis of ethnic differences between the Tutsi and the Hutu. Rather it was vested in the *ganwa,* who had to share it or at least share the things it bought with their Tutsi and Hutu subjects in order to continue to rule. Belgium took that power, as well as all that it could buy, and gave it to the Tutsi. Because they were supported by Belgian administrators, the Tutsi officials were under no obligation to share any of their power, and they did not.

Motivation plays a small but important role as well. Belgium acquired her mandate after World War I, but had no immediate interest in economic development. Initially she simply wanted to govern the territories indirectly in the most-efficient manner possible. Efficiency dictated that they be ruled as a unit, and the model was taken from Rwanda, which on the surface presented a much simpler situation. The Tutsi in Burundi, once they were given the power to rule for Belgium, were spurred by the motivation to continue that rule, which meant supporting Belgium.

It is dangerous to generalize about the colonial experience and its impact on ethnic groups. The variety of experiences discussed above should be ample warning. Some level of generalization can profitably be introduced, however, by looking at colonial situations in terms of certain factors that they all share, namely power, perception, and purpose.

Nations and
Nationalism

4

Nations and Ethnic Groups

NATIONS, BOTH LONG ESTABLISHED as well as emerging, become associated with ethnic groups at a number of points and in a variety of ways. Some writers maintain that nations and ethnic groups are incompatible and that, further, a country can only truly become a nation when ethnic loyalties disappear. It would greatly simplify our task if that statement were true, but it is not borne out in the majority of situations. In fact, there seems to be a resurgence of ethnic identity within nations and, in some cases, even a call for ethnic nationalism that goes beyond the bounds of the state. Both nations and ethnic groups can command the loyalty of their members without creating conflict or compromise as long as simultaneous expression of both loyalties is not demanded. In other words, a hierarchy of loyalties is unnecessary except when the two are called upon in the same situation.

Matters are further complicated by the fact that nations frequently borrow the imagery and rhetoric of ethnicity. That is not so difficult to do because nationalism and ethnicity do in fact share many features—a sense of peoplehood, common origin, at times a territory and a language. Moreover, when nations stand in a conflictive relationship with one another, the confrontation bears many of the earmarks of ethnic conflict.

It is not useful, however, nor does it correspond to reality, to speak of nations and ethnic groups as if they were the same entity or even as if they always behave in the same ways. The already complex relationship is further complicated by the fact that it changes from situation to situation. The complexity may be more easily dealt with in the following discussion if we examine the factors of power, perception, and purpose in the context of nationalism.

Nationalism as a Recent Phenomenon

Contemporary scholars maintain that nationalism is a relatively recent phenomenon. Hans Kohn, for example, regards the nations of today as fundamentally different from those earlier entities that we have also called "nations." He sees the primary difference as the national consciousness or "a living and active corporate will" (1944:15).[1] Benjamin Disraeli also regarded a national mind or will as an essential part of any definition of nation, but he went further to state that political institutions that are the outgrowth of the national mind are necessary machinery without which the nation will disappear. The nation, stripped of the machinery, becomes simply a people (in Deutsch 1966:21–22)

Disraeli is echoed by Weber in a remarkably succinct definition of nation:

> A community of sentiment which would adequately manifest itself in
> a state of its own; hence a nation is a community which normally
> tends to produce a state of its own. [1977:21]

Weber's definition includes what would seem to be two of the essential attributes of nations, the feeling of common cause or community and the machinery that implements it. We shall use this sense of nation as a working definition.

---

1. Three often-quoted definitions of nation illustrate Kohn's point. Pasquale Stanislao Mancini gave the following definition in an address at the University of Turin in 1851: "race, language, custom, and past history are nothing but inert matter into which only national consciousness [*conoscenza della nazionalità*] breathes life." In 1861, John Stuart Mill defined it as: "A portion of mankind may be said to constitute a Nationality, if they are united among themselves by common sympathies, which do not exist between them and many others—which make them cooperate with each other more willingly than with any other people, desire to be under the same government, and desire that it should be government by themselves, or portion of themselves exclusively" (in Snyder 1964:2). And Ernest Renan, in an address at the Sorbonne in 1882, declared: "Une nation est une grande solidarité constituée par le sentiment des sacrifices qu'on a fait et de ceux qu'on est disposé à faire encore. Elle suppose un passé, elle se résume pourtant dans le présent par un fait tangible: le consentement, le désir clairmant exprimé de continuer la vie commune. L'existence d'une nation est un plébiscite de tous les jours."

Modernization and Nations

Another argument for the relative newness of the nation as we know it has been made by Dankwert A. Rustow, who sees a relationship between modernization and nationalism. In this modernization process, which he characterizes as having equality of opportunity, a comprehensive division of labor, and science and industry, it is necessary to have a framework that will lend support. The ideal framework, for Rustow, is the nation-state of intermediate size. "Traditional feudal systems proved too cumbersome, dynastic and colonial empires too heterogeneous, and traditional tribes, principalities, towns and villages too small" (1968:2).

The social aspect of modernization, as Rustow sees Karl Deutsch's "social mobilization" (1953), is yet another factor in determining the shape of modern nationalism. "Mobilization" is the process of learning about a nationality that was made possible by the growth of networks of communication linking rural and urban areas. Before modernization those links were few.

Conditions of Modern Nationalism

Accepting at the very least that nationalism as we have known it since the nineteenth century is qualitatively different from earlier manifestations, we can begin to isolate the conditions giving rise to nineteenth-century nationalistic movements, and from there we can move to a discussion of the varieties of nationalism.

Four influences that brought about this kind of nationalistic sentiment were the French Revolution, the beginnings of anti-colonial feelings, the Romantic tradition, and the actions toward unification of feudal domains and consolidation of political boundaries inspired by the first three influences.[2] Nations arising from each of these movements differed from one another in fundamental ways.

---

2. This notion is similar to what E. K. Francis calls "risorgimento" nationalism. "The word *risorgimento* (derived from *risorgere*, which means 'to rise again') was adopted in Italy to describe the efforts made to awaken national sentiments among the Italians who were divided into several states" (1976:79). Francis goes on to state that, in its initial stages, risorgimento nationalism adopted ethnic arguments, while demotic arguments characterized the period of consolidation. I think that Francis's "demotic" is analogous to the kind of rational, bureaucratized, state-oriented nationalism I have posited for nations such as France, England, and the United States.

The French Revolution

"Before the Revolution there had been states and governments, after it there emerged nations and peoples" (Kohn 1944:573). The French Revolution wrought this change by effecting the rise of the third estate, which was less tradition-bound than the nobility and the clergy and eager to function not merely as a class with narrow interests but as representatives of all the people. Class privileges were abolished, the monarchy became a republic, and the administrative structure of France was rationalized. The patchwork of regions and feudal domains was replaced by the arbitrary but rational system of *départments*. "Nation was the slogan of champions of constitutionalism, secularism, equality, and centralization—of those who wished to modernize society and to rationalize its administrative structure" (Rustow 1968:8).

For Kohn, nationalism in countries such as Great Britain and the United States where the third estate was strong and active resulted in the rise of the nation-state and corresponding political and economic changes. In countries with a weak third estate, such as Germany, Italy, and Russia at the beginning of the nineteenth century, nationalism was primarily a cultural manifestation. "Among these peoples, at the beginning it was not so much the nation-state as the Volksgeist and its manifestations in literature and folklore, in the mother tongue, and in history, which became the center of attention of nationalism" (Kohn 1944:4).

Although the American Revolution ended the political domination of England, it did not rid the new nation of many Old World values. Noah Webster was one of the more outspoken critics of this retention of the customs and morals of former masters: "nothing can display a more despicable disposition in Americans, than to be the apes of Europeans" (cited in Kohn 1944:300–301).

Among the values retained was the preeminence of property as a basis for law and the vote. It had given rise to a class system in which the interests of property owners were favored at the expense of those without land. The situation was much the same as the one in France before the revolution, except that there the dominant classes were composed of nobility and clergy. The French Revolution, a revolt against narrow and self-serving class interests, provided the impetus for a second revolution in the United States in the 1790s, in which Jeffersonian Democracy triumphed over Federalism and its insistence on property.

Anti-Colonial Feelings

In chapter 3 we discussed the diverse definitions of society in colonial situations. Wallerstein suggested that we define a society not as a unit with a common culture but as a unit that at the minimum shares a common authority capable of maintaining itself. Within the "framework of such a common authority . . . the participants will begin to identify more and more with the nation-in-creation, first by the medium of the nationalist movement and even more, after independence, in many different ways" (1966:2). According to Wallerstein, it was the common-authority conception of society that nationalist leaders upheld. As the colonial period went on, the gap widened between the interests of empires and the interests of their colonies, and nationalist movements began to achieve their goals of independence.

Disruption of Indigenous Social Systems

Rupert Emerson offers a thoughtful discussion of the emergence of nations out of empires. His basic thesis is that "colonial nationalism is far less a response to oppression or neglect than to the widened horizons opened up by progressive colonial governments" (1960:45). He argues that two variables influence the rate and quality of the rejection of colonialism. The first is the degree to which the indigenous social system has been disrupted. The greater the disruption of the old system caused by the imposition of colonial rule, the quicker will be the assertion of nationalism. In most colonial situations, particularly those that were economically motivated, the indigenous systems have been replaced by modern Western modes of business and administration.

The second variable is the appearance of an elite whose Western education has given them the tools with which to implement their dreams of independent nationhood. These leaders can not only move their people by appeals to their desire to be quit of the empire but also can lobby for independence following Western rules. Emerson, in fact, sees Western education as providing access to seditious thinking (1960:52). A statement by Lord Lugard is perhaps the best commentary on Emerson's two variables:

> If there is unrest and a desire for independence, as in India and Egypt,
> it is because we taught the people the value of liberty and freedom,

which for centuries these people had not known. Their very discontent is a measure of their progress. [In Emerson 1960:77–78]

Styles of Colonialism

French Colonialism

Unlike England, France did not enunciate a mission to prepare her colonies for nationhood. She envisaged rather an enlarged French nation in which the citizens of her colonies would be citizens of France. France's message to her colonies clearly said that pursuit of national sovereignty was pointless, hazardous, and anachronistic in a world where interdependence characterized most relationships (see Emerson 1960). Among the Africans who supported this position was Felix Houphouet-Boigny, an Ivory Coast leader, who asked in 1957: "Is there a single country in the world which would offer to an African of my color, race, and stage of civilization, the liberty, equality, and fraternity we can find in the French community?" (ibid.:72). And in 1958, when de Gaulle authorized a plebiscite offering a choice of independence from or adherence to France, all the territories except Guinea voted for the latter.

Since the 1958 affirmation of ties with France, sympathies have shifted to nationalistic movements, fulfilling the goal articulated by Senagalese poet and leader Leopold Sedar Senghor: "The Community is for us only a gateway and a means . . . to prepare us for independence in the style of the British dependent territories. Beyond nominal independence—which is easy to obtain—it is real independence that we want to achieve" (ibid.:76). Emerson's thesis of the necessity of a Westernized elite is borne out in several former French colonies; Houphouet-Boigny and Senghor are only two of the many French-educated leaders.

Spanish Colonialism

Spain's colonies in the New World had a different purpose behind their struggles for independence. In fact, many of the Latin American nations came into being as the result of a conservative reaction. In Mexico the move for independence was led by members of the three classes that were entitled to *fueros* (privileges): the Church, the landed upper class, and the military. They were moved to this radical step because a new, liberal government had come into power in Spain and was threatening to do away with or at least drastically reduce the status these three groups enjoyed. After much agonizing it was clear to these advantaged groups in New Spain that the only way to retain their standing was to detach themselves from the Crown. They took this action in 1821. That it was a conservative movement is further attested to by the fact that the first ruler of the newly independent country was accorded the title of Emperor and ruled as a dictator.

The Colonial Legacy

Regardless of the particular circumstances surrounding the birth of nations out of colonies, there was always a family resemblance, the colonial legacy, if you will. Colson has made this point with reference to tribes:

> At least in Africa, tribes and tribalism as we know them today are recent creations reflecting the influences of the Colonial era when large-scale political and economic organization set the scene for the mobilization of ethnic groups based on linguistic and cultural similarities which formerly had been irrelevant in effecting alliances. [1968:201–202]

As in the case of tribes, many of the new nations were creations that reflected colonial institutions. As Rustow comments, the French divided West and Equatorial Africa into fourteen separate territories that then became reified in national boundaries at the time of independence. Belgium decided to rule Rwanda and Burundi separately but the Congo as a whole, thus setting the pattern for the post-independence nations. Britain overrode any significant cultural ties that may have obtained in her working out of a federation for the Nigerian nation-to-be. The abortive Biafran bid for independence was an attempt at reversing those decisions. African boundaries set at the time of independence and determined by colonial policies have by and large remained intact, with the exception of the formation of Tanzania. The importance of these boundaries will be discussed when we explore the nature of loyalties to ethnic group and nation-state.

The Romantic Tradition

The unification of Germany is the classic example of the influence of the Romantic tradition in the emergence of nations during the eighteenth and nineteenth centuries. Although Romanticism appeared in many guises, one of its basic tenets was a reaction to the Enlightenment emphasis on rationalism and universal rules of logic. In the arts this reaction was manifested in the attacks on Classicism. In literature, Classical themes were rejected; and fantasy, melancholy, and unrestrained passion dominated both poetry and prose. In philosophy, Cartesian rationalism was denigrated; and the irrational, mystic, and occult became topics of study (Borgese 1934). The term "Romantic" was also applied to the school of philosophy headed by Fichte and Schelling.

Individual Romantics had appeared in the visual arts, literature, and philosophy but the first collective manifestation was the German *Sturm und Drang* movement, a kind of cult of genius that first appeared in the early 1770s. Like many of the Romantic schools, it opposed rationalism and exalted intuitionism, mysticism, and what Borgese calls the new humanism of Herder, extolling originality and power (ibid.). Members of the *Sturm und Drang* also shared a hatred of the French (whom they referred to as the *Französchen*, or the "pygmy French"), in part, because France was recognized as the leader in cultural matters and was committed to a neo-Classic philosophy. Much of what constituted Germany's cult of Teutonism was also directed against the French. The few remaining vague anti-French feelings that persisted into the second half of the nineteenth century were given concrete support by the successes of the Franco-Prussian War; the Prussian state had only contempt for an enemy that had been defeated so easily and so overwhelmingly.

One of the prevalent notions of the *Sturm und Drang* group was the vision of Germany as the new Holy Roman Empire. Schelling was one of the advocates of the naturalness of a people who could be viewed as an organic whole. He was echoed in Novalis, who romanticized the state. As Kohn analyzed the situation:

> German nationalism substituted for the legal and rational concept of "citizenship" the infinitely vaguer concept of "folk," which, first discovered by the German humanists, was later fully developed by Herder and the German romanticists. It lent itself more easily to the embroideries of imagination and the excitations of emotion. Its roots seemed to reach into the dark soil of primitive times and to have grown through thousands of hidden channels of unconscious development, not in the bright light of rational political ends, but in the mysterious womb of the people, deemed to be so much nearer the forces of nature. [1944:331]

Romanticism and Political Philosophy

By the end of the nineteenth century, the artistic manifestations of Romanticism had begun to wane but it exerted an even stronger influence in the realms of politics and philosophy. The writings of Johann Gottlieb Fichte, in particular his addresses to the German nation delivered in the occupied city of Berlin beginning in December 1807, were used to support the reification of the German nation: "only the German—the original man, who has not become dead in an arbitrary organization—really has a people and is entitled to count on one, and . . . he alone is capable of real and rational love for his nation" (1968:111). Elsewhere he talks of the Germans within the Roman Empire:

> All those blessings which the Romans offered them meant slavery to them, because then they would have to become something that was not German, they would have to become half Roman. They assumed as a matter of course that every man would rather die than become half a Roman, and that a true German could only want to live in order to be, and to remain, just a German and to bring up his children as Germans. [Ibid.:123]

The notion of the innate superiority of the German and the German nation implicit in Fichte's addresses was also present in the *Sturm und Drang* cult of genius. It later served as the basis for Schopenhauer's Aryanism, Nietzsche's superman, and Wagner's glorification of "pure" German music. It appeared even more baldly in the writings of Heinrich von Treitschke, especially in his discussion of the Alsatian question.[3] Treitschke's flat statement of the right of the German Empire to prevent the permanent estrangement of her lost children is one of the best articulations of German manifest destiny, a destiny based on the idea of the superiority of the German people, an inexorable working out of the survival of the fittest, and the glorification of warfare in the name of the German nation. There, too, is the hatred of the French, which characterizes almost the entire coming-to-nationhood histories of the two countries.

---

3. "Who in the face of this duty to secure the peace of the world still dares to raise the objection that the people of Alsace and Lorraine have no wish to belong to Germany? Before the sacred obligation of these great days, the theory of the right to self-government of every branch of the German race—that seductive battle-cry of expatriated demagogues—will be ignominiously routed. These provinces are ours by the right of the

Slavic Nationalism

Slavic nationalism partook as well of the Romantic mode and developed along many of the same lines as had the German. The cosmopolitanism of Peter the Great shifted to a narrower nationalism, which began under the reign of Catherine II. Ironically, many of the Romantic ideas came into Russia via intellectuals whom Catherine had sent to western Europe to be educated. Their education included a hefty dose of Rousseau, and some returned to preach reform, including the emancipation of the serfs and the establishment of a constitutional regime. Catherine's response was to banish the reformers and return to the glorification of Russia in distinction to the West. The Empress, as well as historians, poets, and novelists, turned to Russia's magnficent past, especially the period before Peter, which was described by some as an Age of Innocence. Correspondingly, they depicted the Age of Enlightenment as a threat to the simple virtues and strength of the Russian soul.

Nikolai Mikhailovich Karamzin (1765–1826), an important figure in the Russian historical school during this period of rediscovery, wrote that the imperial greatness of Russia dwarfed even that of Rome. He believed that Russia did not need a new code of civil law based on the French model because she had all of her old decrees, and the will of the Czar was supreme anyway; and that Peter had been the cause of Russia's straying from the right path (see Kohn 1953).

Given this attitude about the force of the true Russian soul, it is not at all surprising to find the political philosophies of Fichte, Herder, and Lessing regarding the divine mission of the German nation reworked into the dogma of Russian nationalism or pan-Slavism. Germany and Russia also have similar policies with regard to peoples brought under their expanding nationalism: Teutonic indoctrination in the one case and Russification in the other. Because nationalism in these two countries springs from a belief in the destiny to reunite the Teutonic peoples and the Slavic peoples, they demand and expect conformity to the values and behavior of the master race. This requirement not only has impli-

---

sword; and we will rule them in view of the right of the German Empire of her lost children. We Germans, who know both Germany and France, know better what is good for the Alsatians than do those unhappy people themselves, who, in the perverse conditions of a French life, have been denied any true knowledge of modern Germany. We desire, even against their will, to restore them to themselves" (cited in Kohn 1944:582).

cations for the expansionism that characterizes both nations but also has import for the fate of ethnic groups that find themselves within the national borders. Divergence from the national character is tolerated only when it manifests itself in harmless areas, such as dress and food and perhaps music and dance. One reason for Russia's initial rejection of Polish overtures toward becoming part of the pan-Slavic movement was that the Poles were Catholic and showed no desire to convert to the Orthodox church (see Vysny 1977).

Writers on Romanticism have commented that some countries seemed to have resisted the extreme forms of the Romantic tradition. The United States and England are usually represented as being at one end of the Romantic continuum, with Germany and Russia at the other. Borgese explains the Anglo–Saxon immunity by citing the two countries' empirical and flexible nature, which rendered them less susceptible to the impact of "sentimentalism, medievalism, irrationalism, and nature worship" (1934). He contrasts writers such as Thoreau, Whitman, and Emerson to the Goethe of *The Sorrows of Young Werther*, Heine, and Novalis.

Open and Closed Nationalism

Kohn, in a similar contrast between the Anglo-Saxon nations and countries such as Germany and Russia, calls the former "open" societies and the latter "closed" societies. "Open" nationalism is generally territorially based and features a political society constituting a nation of fellow citizens irrespective of race or ethnic descent. "Closed" nationalism stresses the nation's autochthonous character—common origins of race or blood and roots in ancestral soil. In such an environment there is a conscious effort to preserve the purity of the nation and protect it from alien influences (1968:66). For Germany it was a small and logical step from this view of common origins to extolling race as the organizing principle of political entities. Hitler, in a letter to Rauschning, expresses this sentiment:

> The "nation" is a political expedient of democracy and Liberalism. We have to get rid of this false conception and set in its place the conception of race, which has not yet been politically used up. The new order cannot be conceived in terms of the national boundaries of the peoples with an historic past, but in terms of race that transcend those boundaries. [In Snyder 1964:168]

Unification: The Case of Italy

A few nations took their impetus from a combination of factors that led ultimately to the unification of feudal domains or principalities. Although Italy, as Louis Snyder suggests, enjoyed many of the features necessary for successful nationhood—natural boundaries, a common set of historical traditions, and a common language—they were not enough initially to overcome the separatist forces that divided the country. Those forces included the antagonism between North and South, the separate status of the papacy, and the pride of individual principalities—Rome, Milan, Venice, Florence, and Naples—that prevented them from relinquishing proud individual histories for a united Italy (1964:172). Also, Italy did not have a single strong state that could impose itself on the others, as Prussia did in Germany, where there had been similar problems of unification.

One of the most powerful incentives for unification in Italy was the desire to rid the country of foreign rulers, first the French and later the Austrians. The poetry of Vittorio Alfieri (1749–1803), especially the collection of anti-French diatribes, *Il Misogallo*, published in 1799 (see Snyder 1964:176), exhorted the people to rise up against the hated French. Throwing off the bonds of foreign tyranny was also the mission of the *Carbonari* ("charcoal-burners"), a nationalist secret society formed during the time of Napoleon and still operating during the post-1815 period of Austrian domination.

A somewhat more inclusive set of enemies was named in Giuseppe Garibaldi's appeal to the Sicilians dated May 5, 1860: "Left to themselves, the brave Sicilians will have to fight, not only the mercenaries of Bourbon, but also those of Austria and the Priest of Rome" (ibid.:188).

The fate of countries suffering under the rule of foreigners was perhaps best articulated by Pasquale Mancini in a speech given in 1851:

> The nationalities which do not possess a government issuing from their innermost life [*governo uscito dalle proprie viscere*], and which are subject to laws imposed upon them from the outside have become means for the purposes of others and, therefore, mere objects. [In Kohn 1968:65]

In 1861, the unification of most of Italy came to pass. Rome and Venezia were added within a decade (in his opening statement to the first Parliament in 1861, Victor Emmanuel described Italy as "Free, and nearly entirely united" [in Snyder 1964:192]). Although many ardent nationalists were happy with Italy's freedom from foreign rule, they felt that she was far from being a nation. In 1871 Giuseppe Mazzini called her "an inert organism . . . the ghost of Italy."[4] In fact, in many of his pronouncements, Mazzini saw the Italians as a chosen people, at one point even referring to their country as "l'Israeli dell'età moderna" (in Kohn 1946:183). He and others saw Italy's most important role as an imperial one, to bring civilization to her colonies. Implicit in Mazzini's urging of the Italian colonization of Tunis, Tripoli, and Cyrenaica was the belief that the Mediterranean belonged to modern Italy just as it had belonged to ancient Rome. Although the two leaders had quite distinct views of the relationship between the individual and the nation and different reasons for fulfilling Italy's imperial destiny, the philosophy of Mussolini is in many ways the logical outcome of ideas first expressed by Mazzini. Mussolini comments on the nation in his explanation of the political doctrine of Fascism:

> A nation, as expressed in the State, is a living, ethical entity only insofar as it is progressive. Inactivity means death. Therefore the State does not only stand for Authority which governs and confers legal form and spiritual value on individual wills, but it is also Power which makes its will felt and respected beyond its own boundaries, thus affording practical evidence. [In Snyder 1964:198]

Loyalties to Nation and to Ethnic Group

The impetus for nationalistic movements and the style of those movements themselves affected the relationships between ethnic groups and the new national entities. Regardless of the style of the relationship, however, the question of loyalties remains for each ethnically heterogeneous nation. The nature of one's attachment to an ethnic group, on the one hand, and to the nation of which one is a citizen, on the other, has been a topic debated by numerous writers on ethnicity and nationalism.

---

4. "Noi avremmo il contorno materiale, l'organismo inerte d'Italia; manca l'alito fecondatore di Dio, l'anima della nazione. I popoli che s'erano levati attonniti e presaghi di grandi cose a contemplare il risorgere dell'antica padrona del mondo, guardano delusi altrove, e dicono a se stesso: non è se non il fantasma d'Italia" (in Kohn 1946:190).

Ethnic and National Ties

Political philosophers do not agree on the values to be placed on ethnic group loyalties and national affiliations, but there is at least one question that most would agree is legitimate: What are the qualities of the ties that bind individuals to an ethnic group and to a nation? Further, how are these ties different, and what does that mean in terms of the relationship between the two groups?

Primordial versus Civil Ties

The qualitative differences between loyalties to an ethnic group and to a nation are usually likened to the differences between "primordial ties" and "civil ties." Edward Shils was one of the first to discuss the relationship between the two types of ties. In a passage that has become something of a classic he commented on its occurrence in modern societies:

> As I see it, modern society is no lonely crowd, no horde of refugees fleeing from freedom. It is no Gesellschaft, soulless, egotistical, love-less, faithless, utterly impersonal, and lacking any integrative forces other than interest or coercion. It is held together by an infinity of personal attachments, moral obligations in concrete contexts, professional and creative pride, individual ambition, primordial affinities, and a civil sense which is low in many, high in some and moderate in most persons. [1957:131]

Shils defines primordial attachments as intense and comprehensive, and most commonly arising from ties of blood and a sharing of common territory. Although Shils is not necessarily speaking of multi-ethnic nations, he offers a very useful way of approaching that kind of situation. Social scientists who have taken their direction from Shils view ethnic ties as positive building blocks of emerging nations.

Clifford Geertz (1963) discusses the problem of emerging nations, specifically the dilemma they face in forming an efficient bureaucratic unit. One solution is a legitimation of ethnicity and the primordial attachments that characterize it. In most emerging nations the only bases for delimiting political units are blood, language, race, locality—all components of primordial attachments—so that these of necessity are used to define political groups that are then raised to the level of national politics. In other words, these ties are not antithetical to the idea of the state but are the basis for power blocs, which then compete for state control. The integrative revolution is the sensible way to bring about a situation in which primordial and civil feelings are compatible. Integration occurs through the building up of larger and larger units on the basis of the original primordial ties. Ethnic blocs then become the functioning units of the nation, and eventually the consciousness of kind or primordial solidarity is extended into consciousness of the developing order (Geertz 1963).

Geertz also elaborates on Shil's concept of primordial ties. A primordial attachment, for Geertz, grows out of being born into a particular religious community, speaking a particular language, and following particular social patterns. The similarities of blood, speech, and custom at times have an ineffable and overpowering coerciveness (Geertz 1963). Like Shils, Geertz refuses the evolutionary view of society, which sees primordial ties as belonging to the past days of *Gemeinschaft* and not to be encountered in modern, urban society. That these ties do exist in modern society, indeed often emerge as a result of the forces of modern society, has certainly been adequately demonstrated, especially by the rise of ethnic-based interest groups in the 1970s.

Primary Group Ties and the Wehrmacht

"Cohesion and Disintegration in the Wehrmacht in World War II," by Shils and M. Janowitz, is a thoughtful study of primary-group affiliations and their relationship to a national affiliation. It is particularly interesting in light of the common image of the nationalistic German, ready to do all for the German nation. This stereotype was in fact reinforced by the stubbornness with which Germans fought right up to the end of the war. What Shils and Janowitz discovered, however, was that appeals to German nationalism had little impact on the fighting soldier. "For the ordinary German soldier the decisive fact was that he was a member of a squad or section which maintained its structural integrity and which coincided roughly with the *social* unit which satisfied some of his primary needs" (1948:284). Political, ideological and cultural symbols aided primary groups to resist disintegration only to the "extent that these secondary symbols became directly associated with primary gratifications" (ibid:281). In the cases of the men who did desert, the authors found support for the importance of the primary group. The army units with the highest rate of desertion were those made up of a heterogeneous ethnic population, usually with random mixtures of Austrians, Czechs, and Poles. Cohesive, primary attachments were rare in these units. In strong primary groups, many would-be deserters never deserted because they had been told by their superior officers that their comrades who stayed behind would be shot. Toward the end of the war still other units surrendered as groups after an open group discussion and with the approval of group leaders.

Germany realized that the more integrated a unit was the better fighting unit it would make, so the High Command took pains to create homogeneous units and to keep units together. This strategy helped keep the army functioning and in good spirits in the face of overwhelming odds until the close of the war, when it was no longer possible to maintain that policy. Then Germany was forced to put together hastily units made up of new recruits, transfers from the navy and the air force, older factory workers, concentration-camp inmates, and older married men who had been kept in reserve. When the 275th Fusilier Battalion was broken up, the 35 prisoners interrogated had only recently been scraped together from fifteen different army units.

Universal Significance of Primary-Group Ties

Martin Doornbos discusses both Shils and Geertz and concurs that primordial sentiments are universally significant. "Occurring more or less 'unspoiled' in *Gemeinschaft*, they may appear in modern societies in modified form" (1972:267). The distinction, it would seem to me, lies not so much in the difference between unspoiled and modified forms as in the fact that the more "modern" a society the more allegiances and attachments are possible. Choice then becomes a matter of strategy to be devised situationally. Doornbos's concept allows us to isolate a range of feelings, which characterize certain relationships, from other kinds of feelings. Moreover, if we are to understand the increasing reliance on ethnic identity as a reference group, we must investigate the quality of attachments to ethnic groups and see how it compares with the quality of other possible attachments.

Doornbos makes a distinction that is important for any heterogeneous situation where primordial ties are a possible area of recruitment. He distinguishes two dimensions of primordial bonds;

> namely the attachment to the particular focus as a *Ding an sich*, and also the solidarities evoked as a result of the cleavage with other

groups in the environment. . . . On the one hand, the primordial symbol receives increasingly intense attachments, while on the other hand it serves to reinforce group solidarity. [Ibid:269]

This distinction is particularly important because it allows us to separate members' perceptions of themselves from their perceptions of the group as it stands in relation to other groups in the society. In reality, this separation is often made, allowing primordial attachments to a group to remain intense but not to be used to intensify cleavages.

Some scholars maintain that primordial attachments such as ethnic ties are maladaptive and incompatible with the modern state because people invariably act upon them simply because they are there. In actuality, however, many of the disruptive issues in new states result not from conflict between the primordial ties of ethnic groups and the civil ties of the new state but from normal intergroup conflict that may have nothing to do with ethnicity. Some writers have questioned the wisdom of doing away with ethnic bonds as a way of promoting the state, and some, such as Doornbos, have gone so far as to question whether having *only* civil ties is a necessary condition for modernization. Doornbos argues that it has not yet been demonstrated that the creation of exclusively national identities (presuming the obliteration of subnational ethnic identities) would by itself lead to modernization without conflict (ibid.:278).

Arguments for Gradual Disappearance of Ethnic Ties

Social scientists who view ethnic ties as nonadaptive in modernizing situations and as incompatible with the modern nation also feel that with time and industrialization ethnic ties will disappear. In a book on nation building, Deutsch argued that "tribalism or any other social and political attachment to a small ethnic, cultural, or linguistic group" is a challenge to national integration and that, in contrast, the fully formed, fully integrated nation would be characterized by the sharing of a common language and culture (Deutsch and Flotz 1963:6). In his later writings, Deutsch seems to contradict these early contentions, but a great deal of social science theory was built on the 1963 book, and therefore it must be considered here. Deutsch could be said to have served the same purpose for those who see ethnic bonds as a detriment to nationhood as Shils did for those who take the opposite view.

Among those who argue that ethnic identity is transitional and will disappear with industrialization, some, like Seymour M. Lipset and

Stein Rokkan (1967), divide the progress toward complete industrialization into three phases. In the first, issues of cultural identity are
raised because directions coming from the national center cause resistance to develop. In phase two, these territorial resistances become
generalized into ethnic blocs, not unlike Geertz's ethnic building blocks
or the ethnism of Dov Ronen (dysfunctional for him). In the third
phase, individuals are redefined according to their function in the industrial process. This base of class interests will eventually cut across all
others.

The argument for the emergence of class interests at the expense of all
others with the advent of the industrial state is rather widespread. Some
interesting interpretations of it see certain kinds of industrialization and
effects of modernization as promoting ethnic differences that are inimi-
cal to subordinate groups. Mexico has been a test case for at least two
writers on this theme. Gonzalo Aguirre Beltrán speaks of "refuge regions," while Pablo Gonzales Casanova, more bluntly, uses the phrase
"internal colonization" (see Collier 1976). Certain regions or colonies
were originally established because the Spanish conquerors needed
cheap labor. The landowners' desires and those of the Church coincided
on this point. The task of the Church would be much easier if the
Indians were congregated in towns instead of being spread all over the
countryside.

In these refuge regions, the Indians have emphasized ethnicity and use
it to justify their exploitation of the economically marginal land that is
available. Concepts of territoriality, both individual and group, have
been developed and were buttressed by distinctive dress, language, customs, and political activity (ibid.:185). Today, in the San Cristobal region of highland Chiapas, the emphasis on these distinctive features is
greater the closer the Indian groups are to San Cristobal, the non-Indian
center. Moreover, one must adhere to group custom if one expects to
have the right to use the land. Forsaking one's Indian identity means
leaving one's livelihood in the region. In a sense, an Indian identity is
now used as a strategy, as a way of holding on to what one has.

Gonzales Casanova imputes a more-conscious exploitation to those in
power. He sees internal colonization as characteristic of nations. Prejudice, discrimination, colonial types of exploitation, and the separation
of a dominant population, with its own race and culture, are typical of
these situations. In San Cristobal and its environs, the non-Indian center
dictates the terms of commerce and credit, to the disadvantage of the

Indians who are forced to the center for market activities and for capital to invest in their land and in technological improvements. As colonies of San Cristobal, the Indian communities are exploited, dependent, and manipulated economically and politically, and they suffer from a lack of capitalization, facilities, and resources (Collier 1976).

Michael Hechter (1971) describes a similar situation in which industrialization has proceeded unevenly, so that the periphery is dominated by the core and, as a result, cultural or ethnic differences become heightened. These differences are played up by the core as a way of justifying its withholding industrialization from the periphery on the grounds that the latter is inferior and thus incapable of benefiting from technical advances. The differences are emphasized by the periphery, too, as a way of keeping what it has, on the one hand, and building a positive self-image, on the other. At later stages, the differences may also be used to negotiate economic or political claims. The Yaqui, as we have seen, are particularly effective in this type of negotiation, but they are not the only group to engage in this strategy.

Industrialization and its attendant changes, in the view of a number of writers, are positive forces. With true industrialization, class affiliation will override all other bonds, and internal colonies, refuge regions, and ethnic groups will be obliterated.

Increasing Significance of Ethnic Ties

Whether we have reached the stage of "true" industrialization is a difficult question to answer. What *is* true is that ethnic bonds have become increasingly significant worldwide. At one level, individual ethnic groups are asking for greater shares of the national goods. At another level, they are demanding total separation from the nations in which they find themselves, in an expression of "ethnic nationalism." The transformation of "ethnic discontents" into "ethnic nationalists" is part of the increasing (global) tendency to think in terms of membership in a particular ethnic group and to demand a separate political status for the group (Said and Simmons 1975). One example of this trend is the movement toward the formation of a Basque nation that would transcend the boundary between Spain and France and unite the Basques, who believe they have been artificially separated.

Abdul Said and Luiz R. Simmons see conflict as inevitable, because the state can be defined in terms of territory, population, and government, while the nation and/or ethnic nation is a conscious sense of shared peoplehood. Movements toward ethnic nationalism are given impetus by material increases in what Deutsch calls "social communication and mobilization." The technological revolution in communication increases the visibility of ethnic groups and conflicts and facilitates communication across national boundaries. Said and Simmons believe that improvements in communication contribute to conflict between ethnic groups and states. Of 164 violent disturbances that occurred between 1958 and 1966, 149 resulted from the conflict between ethnic loyalties and desires and the demands of the state, and only 15 were military conflicts involving two or more states (Said and Simmons 1975).

Better communication is only one reason for the upsurge in ethnic consciousness that has led to ethnic national movements. Walker Connor (1977) identifies three other contributing influences: modernization, self-determination, and a decline in annexation. Modernization is closely related to technological advances in communication. It is not new, but it had to reach a certain critical mass before it began to influence behavior. That occurred at the end of the nineteenth century in some nations and later in others. The term "self-determination of peoples" was used extensively by Woodrow Wilson and invoked in the Versailles negotiations at the end of World War I. But the doctrine was not proposed as a universal right until after World War II. It has been used increasingly since then, and, rhetorically at least, it has been a support for nationalist movements. The last factor Connor suggests is based on a change in the global political environment that has made it less likely that smaller powers would be annexed by their larger neighbors. Earlier it was quite common for a small nation or cultural group to ally itself with a larger power in order to avoid being annexed by yet a third power.[5] The climate today is more favorable, and the situation of small nations is correspondingly less precarious.

Which groups are likely to promote their ethnicity to the extent of a nationalistic movement? What are the motivating forces behind such movements? What are the requirements for success? There is no one answer to any of these questions, but we can begin by suggesting commonalities and probabilities.

---

5. In 1848 the Czech leader Havlicek opposed the creation of Bohemia as an independent nation because it would be too small to survive among all the great powers. Pan-Slavism was his answer to the question of Czech identity (Shibutani and Kwan 1965:452).

Separatist Movements

As Connor suggests, many separatist movements emanate from groups that are economically more advanced than the politically dominant group, for example, the Basques, Catalans, Croatians, and Slovenes. Emerson (1960) contends that these movements developed in the most-advanced colonies, where levels of expectation were the highest.

The four provinces of Spain that consider themselves Basque rather than Spanish, and are agitating for independence, are the most-industrialized, economically advanced region of Spain. The Basque nationalist organization, the ETA, is led by members of the middle class. The impetus for the separatist movement was the feeling that the industrialized Basque provinces were carrying the burden of the rest of Spain with no adequate compensation. Moreover, it was felt that any downturn in the Spanish economy would threaten the stability of the Basque provinces as well. These concerns were voiced primarily by the middle class, who control the major regional economic interests. The lower class—primarily unskilled workers—perceived no advantage in a Basque movement and aligned themselves with the Spanish socialist party, traditionally the workers' party. The concerns and economic interests of the upper class were national and international rather than regional. For this reason, they have been only passively involved in the ETA. The important point in this case is that the impetus for ethnic nationalism came from the sector whose privileges and power depended on the economic well-being of the Basque provinces. Basque nationalism was the obvious way to maintain their position.

Catalonia presents another example of a nationalist movement by a group that is economically more advanced than the politically dominant group. Catalonia is the northeast counterpart of the Basque provinces. It, too, is made up of four provinces: Barcelona, Gerona, Lerida, and Tarragona. Long desirous of separation from Spain, Catalonia presented a petition to the League of Nations after World War I asking for a separate national status. In that document the Catalans speak with pride of their long history and use that history as a weapon:

> We do not propose to speak of the little state which, separated from the empire of Charlemagne, became a great Mediterranean power,

imposing its language and its culture upon lands hitherto under Arab rule, and including in its domain the Acropolis of Athens . . . its parliament was the first in Europe and to it is due the first International Code of modern times: the "Consolat de Mar." [In Snyder 1964:240–41]

They go on to argue for a separate identity based on language and culture, which they say is recognized by the King and the governmnot of Spain.

It should not be surprising that Spain refuses to grant autonomy to Catalonia or the Basque provinces—they are the most-prosperous and self-sufficient regions of the nation. Conversely, it is easy to understand the motivations of the Basques and Catalonians. The fact that they have been independent in other periods of history lends weight to their demands and provides them with a powerful psychological incentive. Another strong argument is that the two regions are easily separable from Spain in geographic terms (see Spicer 1971).

Territorial Considerations

Territory is a crucial negative factor in such cases as Black nationalism and Native American nationalism. Even if it were possible for American Blacks and Indians to overcome internal divisions, they would still be confronted by a lack of a territory of their own. Demands for land to be set aside for each group have not been met, nor is there consensus among group members that separate territories are desirable. A territorial solution does not seem possible. As with every nationalistic movement, a strong ideology characterizes both the Black and the Native American movements. What is not clear is how long or how far such movements can go without a land base.

Role of the Intellectual

Perhaps as important as the question of a territorial base is the role of the intellectual or other elites in nationalistic movements. To some, a Westernized elite is indispensable to nationalism: "It is this elite—the new intelligentsia and the professional man—which translates to the local scene the nationalist experience and ideology of the West and serves as the crystallizing center for the inchoate disaffections of the mass" (Emerson 1960:44).

Weber also sees the relationship between the intellectual and the nation as a necessary and positive one, but in a different light. He stresses the unique properties of individual nations rather than some pan-Western nationalist strategy, saying that the significance of the "nation" is usually based on the assumption that cultural values are irreplaceable and can be preserved and developed only through the cultivation of the unique group. That, in large measure, is the task of the intellectual, just as the idea of the state is invoked by those who wield political power (in Stone 1977:21).

The role of intellectuals is fleshed out still further by Shibutani and Kwan. They argue that discontent is likely to appear first among the intellectuals, who have access to information about different ways of life, who can articulate the discontent and resentment of the people, and who can design utopias (1965:445–446). The intellectual is the one who articulates grievances, formulates nationalist demands, and eventually translates popular belief into a coherent ideology. Intellectuals also bolster national pride through their works, for example, the Mexican muralist Diego Rivera; the Polish composer Frederic Chopin and the Finnish Jean Sibelius; and the dean of Russian folk dance, Igor Moiseyev.

Emigré Intellectuals

Emigré intellectuals frequently develop nationalistic feelings before their counterparts at home do. Being an individual in another country makes one aware of the larger social hierarchy in which one's own country may rank very low. Frequently emigrés can initiate nationalistic movements without the fear of reprisal that they might feel at home. In the late nineteenth century emigré Armenians realized to their shame that their countrymen were perceived as backward and cowardly. This realization led them to efforts at reform. The most-frequent target of their attack was the Ottoman Empire, which symbolized backwardness and decay to them. Eventually a number of emigré intellectuals representing the Armenian Hunchaks and the Macedonian, Albanian, Cretan, and Greek revolutionaries banded together to form the Oriental Federation of Nationalist Groups in order to synchronize their efforts against the Ottoman Empire (Shibutani and Kwan 1965:451–452).

Ethnic minorities within Communist countries, specifically the Soviet Union and the People's Republic of China, theoretically have the right of self-determination. Official Communist ideology grants them the right to secede if they wish to. They do not, of course, and the result is a number of People's Republics within the Soviet Union and such autonomous regions as Inner Mongolia, the Sinkiang Autonomous Region (of the Uigur people), and the Kwansi Autonomous Region (of the Chuang people) within China. The effect of this strategy is similar to that of de Gaulle's plebiscite in French Africa, where all but one colony chose to remain part of France. It would be much more difficult for one of the Soviet or Chinese regions to declare its independence since these states are not geographically separate.

Conclusions

Nineteenth-century nationalism was brought about by the French Revolution, the Romantic movement, the reaction against colonialism, and, in some areas, the consolidation of petty princedoms to avoid incorporation into neighboring states. Anti-colonialism continues to be the driving force behind many emerging nations. Anti-colonial metaphors have come to characterize recent attempts at ethnic nationalism. In these cases the boundaries between ethnicity and nationalism become blurred, each borrowing strategies and metaphors from the other.

A large area of debate is concerned with the nature of loyalties exacted by ethnic groups, on the one hand, and nations, on the other, the contrast being drawn between primary ties and civil ties. But one does not have to give up allegiances based on primary ties such as ethnic group membership in order to function within a unit such as a nation, which operates on the basis of civil ties. Rather, the two kinds of attachments exist side by side, and determinations about which is appropriate are made according to the situation. Conflict erupts when subordinate groups perceive an advantage in claiming rights based on some form of primordial loyalty and set themselves up in opposition to the dominant society. In a different situation primary ties are supportive of national efforts. The Wehrmacht in World War II, as described by Shils and Janowitz, is a case of this sort. Ultimately, what we must conclude is that the relationship between ethnic group and nation, ethnicity and nationalism, is a complex one and depends on the environment out of which nationalism arose and the environment in which contemporary nations and ethnic groups find themselves.

"Strangers in the Land"

5

IF IT IS TRUE THAT CONTACT with groups and individuals who are perceived as different from oneself is necessary in order to make one's ethnic identity relevant, then the context and process of immigration is a prime contributor to ethnicity. The migration of human populations is certainly not a new phenomenon, witness the passage from Ezekiel 27:7 that provides the title of this chapter. However, as with colonialism and nationalism, we shall limit our discussion to events of the past two or three hundred years; and the three factors of power, perception, and purpose will guide our discussion of immigration.

Nineteenth-Century Immigration

Nineteenth-century immigration was qualitatively different from what had gone before, just as nineteenth-century colonialism and nationalism were different, and for the same reason—the communications explosion. It was not simply the slow, steady increase in linkages between individuals, groups, and nations but a monumental change due to the rapidity with which technology advanced. Important for immigration was the internationalization that this progress prompted.

Marcus Lee Hansen stresses the international quality of the nineteenth century in his discussion of the great waves of immigration. He cites four features characteristic of the last century that are relevant to immigration: the international competition to capture the trade of the seas;

the internationalization of banking and finance that accompanied commercial expansion; the importance of foreign markets and the steady market among emigrants for products from the home country; and the growth of imperialism; that is, the concept of a commonwealth of nations was simply a recognition of the fact that nations existed that had been created by groups of settlers (1948:6–9).

A futher point made by Hansen is that the term "immigrant" came into usage only in 1817. The process of immigration had gone on in the seventeenth and eighteenth centuries, but the individuals involved were called "emigrants." They migrated *out of* something. By 1817, they were migrating *into* something—nations. Both the quality and the sheer quantity of the immigration were impressive. Some 50 million people left their homes in Europe between 1815 and 1914. According to Hansen, it was a period of free trade in people, or rather people's labor. The underlying reason for the tremendous market in human immigrant labor was the old idea that every land should devote itself to developing the resources with which Nature had endowed it. The stumbling block in the rapid development of resources seemed to be a lack of labor; hence, the excess labor of Europe was sent to facilitate this great worldwide exploitation of materials.

In order to speak with precision about the relationship of immigration to ethnicity and ethnic identification, we must talk first about the impetus for immigration. As we saw in the contexts of colonialism and nationalism, the purpose underlying choices of behavior is crucial in shaping the experience. Individuals may have specific motivations, but certain general categories of motivations appear over and over again. We must then consider the nature of the population, both the groups that are emigrating and the groups receiving them. A third area to be investigated is the immigration process itself, which is usually characterized by a number of stages. At each point strategies, responses, and initiatives are important. Ethnic succession is a phenomenon of the utmost significance to all those involved in the immigration process. Yet another factor that has to be considered is the role of the culture broker in immigrant adjustment. It is clear from recent articles that this role is much more complex and vital than we have hitherto thought. We have to be aware of ties to the old country as well as people's knowledge of events in the old country. Both ties and knowledge affect the immigrants' behavior and values. Finally, there is the phenomenon of internal migration, which is somewhat akin to internal colonization. We must ask what are the similarities and differences between immigration from one country to another and internal movements within a single nation. We must distinguish between migration from rural to urban areas and vice versa and migration associated with the expansion of frontiers.

There are negative and positive reasons for immigration. Among the former are persecution in the country of origin, population pressure, and slavery. Among the latter are perceived opportunities in the new country or region, both short- and long-term. Another positive impetus is more difficult to label, but it is something we might call a sense of patriotism. The best example of it is the settling of Israel; many of the Jews who immigrated had been well-off and comfortable in their native land.

Negative Motivations

Persecution

In the Country of Origin

Persecution in the country of origin commonly takes the forms of religious persecution and political oppression. Antagonism based on perceived inferior social status appears less often. Two groups that were victims of nineteenth-century religious persecution are the Molokan, who fled from Russia, and Christians from the area of what is now the nation of Lebanon. The Molokan held a belief different from that of the dominant Russian Orthodox faith. They were first removed to the Caucasus region, and when it became clear that they were not going to be allowed to live and worship peacefully, many immigrated to Canada. Although the religious atmosphere there was favorable, the climate and soil were too different from what the Molokan were used to, and they moved again, this time south into the United States and northern Mexico. For most of the twentieth century the Molokan in northern Mexico lived in harmony with their neighbors, but recent government colonization projects in the area of the Russian settlement have created antagonism between the Molokan and the Mexicans. The Mexican colonists regard themselves as the rightful owners of the land by virtue of nationality and view the Molokan as foreigners with no rights at all. Once again the Molokan are on the move.

The Christian Lebanese[1] immigration to the United States and Mexico began for many of the same reasons. The Maronite and Melkite rites were regarded as potential threats to the numerically dominant Lebanese Moslems, and so after years of persecution, the Christians left their homes rather than give up their faith. Quite a number of them went to Mexico, where many occupy positions of great social status today. Why have the Lebanese Christians succeeded while the Molokan have not? First, both the Maronite and Melkite rites were close enough to Roman Catholicism that the Lebanese happily became Catholics, but there was no such religious compatibility for the Molokan either in Canada or in Mexico. Second, the Lebanese soon occupied strategic positions as middlemen, while the Molokan continued their isolated existence as large-scale wheat farmers. Third, the Lebanese intermarried with Mexican nationals, especially after the second generation. This practice was very rare among the Molokan, who often chose to remain unmarried rather than marry out of their group. Yet many Lebanese actively maintain their Lebanese identity in spite of their successful accommodation to the Mexican nation. The price of this kind of integrity for the Molokan has been a never-ending series of migrations.

Now, as in the past, people also leave their homes because they harbor unpopular political ideas. In the complicated case of the Maltese now living in England, Australia, the United States, and Canada, political conformity in Malta had become synonymous with membership in the Nationalist party, which is dominated by the Church. Most of the emigrants belonged to the Malta Labour party, which is secular and also anti-Church. The Church has been all-powerful in Malta since Britain removed the island from the jursidiction of Sicily in 1802, and returned it to the Order of the Knights of Malta, thus establishing a direct link to Rome. The Church fulfils many of the functions of a political party and, in fact, is coterminous with the Nationalist party. Parallel and interdependent military and ecclesiastical bureaucracies have steadily increased their domination of Maltese society during this century. Many Maltese have responded to the growing oppressiveness of their government by leaving (see Dench 1975).

A more straightforward case is that of the Highland Scots, who fled Scotland after the failure of their uprising in 1715 brought about repris-

---

1. Lebanon did not become a nation until 1941. "Lebanese" is a convenient way of referring to the people from that area.

als. They had been loyal to the House of Stuart and refused to accept George I of Hanover.

Attitudes in the Receiving Nation

The response of the receiving nation toward immigration that occurs for reasons of religious or political persecution is usually a generous one. To take the United States as a prime example, immigration laws have always made exceptions for victims of these kinds of persecution. Even in the anti-immigrant period, from the 1880s to the 1920s, there were loopholes in the laws. Of course the loopholes were fewer and smaller for members of "undesirable" groups, such as southern and eastern Europeans, but the kindred-spirit feeling was still there for those who had suffered religious or political oppression. Persecuted groups allow the receiving society to bask in perceptions of itself as generous, benevolent, and tolerant.

Socially Inferior Groups

Groups that emigrated because they were regarded as socially inferior were generally viewed similarly by the receiving country. The Irish, driven by hunger and persecution in Britain, came to the United States in great numbers in the mid-nineteenth century. Many occupied the same niche of unsavory and illegal activities that the Italians were to fill later. The undesirable social image of the southern Italians crossed the ocean with them and remained for several generations in the urban areas that they tended to populate. The fact that these groups were viewed as socially inferior left them little option in their choice of ways to survive.

The eastern Europeans who came in large numbers to the United States and Canada at the end of the nineteenth and beginning of the twentieth century had been unskilled laborers and farmers in the Old World. They continued to provide strong backs and arms in their new homes. Many led shortened and weary lives in the coal fields, where the mines and breakers devoured men and boys with an appetite that diminished only when the coal gave out or became uneconomical to mine. They were good workers, often hired in preference to poor whites from the American South. Poor whites deprived of jobs voiced bitter resentment against "those damn hunkies" who took the bread out of the mouths of the "100% Americans" (see Lantz 1958).

Today, refugees from Pakistan, particularly those from Bangladesh, are perceived as inferior on both social and cultural grounds. They were persecuted in their native country and have been treated almost as badly in England. Following a recent decision, England has been actively re-patriating Pakistanis who entered the country illegally.

Population Pressure: The Irish Potato Famines

The nineteenth century was a time of increased population pressure in Europe, which was aggravated by a number of famines and depressions. One of the most dramatic interactions of overpopulation, famine, and emigration occurred in Ireland in 1846 and 1847. Conditions had been unstable, largely because of the proportion of the population that lived on the land. In 1840 only 8% of the people lived in towns. Most of the Irish depended on the farms for their existence, specifically on one staple crop, the potato. Absentee landlords owned the land, and most of them were indifferent to the conditions under which their tenants lived. The landlords were alien conquerors working in a "system produced by centuries of successive conquests, rebellions, confiscations and punitive legislation" (Woodham-Smith 1962:20). The landlords regarded Ireland as a resource from which one extracted as much income as possible. The Irish hated them, and, according to the Earl of Clare, brooded over their discontent in sullen indignation (ibid.:21). The hostility of the tenants made it unpleasant if not danger-ous for the landlords to live on their property, even if they were so inclined. Most of them managed their lands and tenants through mid-dlemen, whose pay was based on the amount of money they could bring their employers. A common way of increasing income was to split the farms into smaller and smaller parcels in order to collect more rents.

Between 1779 and 1841 the Irish population underwent an incredible growth — 172% (ibid.:29) — such that by the time of the potato famine it was over 9 million. The lack of industry meant that the Irish laboring class had to have land or it would starve. Many families lived on half-acre plots. Their survival and, more, that they increased their numbers under these conditions, were due solely to the potato. No other crop could have supported so many people on such small landholdings, and no other crop could have been grown so easily and inexpensively. Un-fortunately, as Cecil Woodham-Smith points out, no other crop was as dangerous. Potatoes, unlike grain, do not keep and cannot be stored from season to season. In the best of years, many Irish came close to starvation in the summer months when the old crop had been used up and the new one was not yet ready. Moreover, a population adapted to the potato, the cheapest of all food sources, was in no position to replace it with crops that would surely be more costly. Even if that had been possible, a shift from potato cultivation to some other staple would have required several years and demanded a drastic reduction in the population.

The situation in Ireland in 1845 was precarious at best. In August the potato blight was reported in England. By September it had reached Ireland, and the potato crop was destroyed. While the British government made some efforts to prevent wholesale starvation, many absentee landlords responded to the plight of their tenants by evicting them for non-payment of rent. In some cases, tenants who were not in arrears were evicted, thus adding to the general misery of people who could have been self-sufficient. In the most famous of these evictions, 300 tenants in the village of Ballinglass were turned out on March 13, 1846 in order to turn the property into grazing land.

> The scene was frightful, women running wailing with pieces of their property and clinging to door-posts from which they had to be forcibly torn; men cursing, children screaming with fright. That night the people slept in the ruins; next day they were driven out, the foundations of the houses torn up and razed, and no neighbor was allowed to take them in. [Ibid.:71–72]

In 1846, when the potato crop failed again, the Irish, having starved the preceding year, were in no condition to resist disease and another year of privation. The British government had concluded that it was dangerous to encourage dependence on the government by continuing to send relief to the Irish. Moreover, if such relief were to be forthcoming, the government maintained that it should properly come from the landlords. To make matters worse, much of the Continent was suffering from famine and disease. Some landlords did reduce their rents or eliminate them altogether, but these acts of humanity were by no means universal. On September 20, 1846, Simon Dunane, from County Limerick, wrote to his landlord that the only way he could pay his rent would be by selling his oats. But since his potato crop was gone, that would mean starvation for himself, his wife, and his six children.

"Nevertheless, since fear of eviction was in the very blood of the Irish peasant, grain was sold, rents were paid, and Simon Dunane, with his fellows, flocked, starving, to the depots" (ibid.:123).

One of the ironies of the famine years was that grains and other foods continued to be exported. By the end of the 1846 harvest, 60,000 tons of oats alone left the country. The British government was against any scheme for limiting exports, claiming that the Irish merchants could import low-priced foods. What the British did not consider was the total lack of commerical enterprise in Ireland, which made this argument ludicrous.

The alternative to starvation or death from typhus and relapsing fever was emigration. During the famine years 1,250,000 Irish left their homeland for North America. Even more went to Liverpool, Glasgow, and the ports of South Wales. In the beginning, the emigrants were relatively healthy and self-supporting. They were able to pay for passage on decent ships and thus managed to arrive at their destinations in good condition, ready to work. As the famine years went on, however, the state of the individual emigrant deteriorated until half-starving, fever-ridden men, women, and children were being crammed into the holds of "coffin ships." Their passage was paid in one of two ways: their emigration was assisted by the landlords and the government or was prepaid by relatives already in North America.

In 1846 the landlords were given an incentive for shipping their tenants to North America. The Poor Law transferred complete responsibility for the Irish peasantry to the landlord class. The cost of emigration was about half the cost of maintaining a pauper in the workhouse for a year; and it was a cost paid only once, since it was difficult if not impossible for an emigrant to return to Ireland. Because the old and the sick were the heaviest drain on the landlord's purse, they were the first to be packed aboard the ships. Their destination was almost always Canada, since passage to that country was cheaper than to the United States, and immigration was not subject to the same restrictions. In 1846 over 100,000 Irish left for Canada; 17,000 died on the voyage and 20,000 died in Canada. Thousands of the survivors poured across the border into the United States.

Although Americans had sent an unprecedented amount of relief to Ireland during the famine years, there was no welcome for the emaciated, indigent immigrants who seemed to be reaching their cities in hordes. In the best of times, when the Irish immigrant was a sturdy laborer unafraid of hard, dangerous physical activity, he still felt the brunt of anti-Catholic, anti-Irish sentiment. By 1847 that feeling had deepened to an active dislike.

> By a curious piece of reasoning, the Irish starving in Ireland were regarded as unfortunate victims, to be generously helped, while the same Irish, having crossed the Atlantic to starve in Boston, were described as the scourings of Europe and resented as an intolerable burden to the taxpayer. [Ibid.:248]

The immigrants were regarded as stupid, dirty, superstitious, untrustworthy, diseased, and in despair (Hansen 1948:161). The Irish brought no technical skills with them, and most of them were not fit for manual labor. As a result they found work in unskilled, irregular jobs that paid poorly: they unloaded ships and cleaned yards and stables; some were weavers, some servants. All were resented by the American public.

The rural, potato-farming Irish peasant became a city dweller in the United States. Many immigrants had no other choice, since they had no money to take them farther than the port at which they debarked, but in reality, the Irish peasantry were more suited to an urban environment. They were totally unused to any kind of agriculture except potato cultivation, unlike the Germans and Swedes, who were farmers of long experience; and they placed great value on sociability and interaction with other human beings, especially with other Irish. Commentary from the few Irish who did move west to farm and did so successfully clearly shows their feelings of loneliness and loss. So the majority of the Irish remained in the cities, living in slums and eking out a livelihood doing menial labor. They were scorned by the respectable and exploited by the less respectable (Woodham-Smith 1962:269). In the eastern cities it took a long time for the Irish to be accepted, but those who ventured further west had quite a different experience. Many of the Irish who came to San Francisco before the end of the nineteenth century reached positions of high status and political power, as opposed to the Irish laborers and domestics in the East. There were two reasons for their success: the Irish who were able to travel to San Francisco began with more resources than the ones who remained in the East; and San Francisco was a new city, without an "establishment" already occupying all the prestigious positions (see Walsh n.d.).

Slavery

Slavery has had a long history, possibly as long as that of human beings living in social groups, but it is not until the great periods of colonial expansion that we see slavery on such a scale that its effects are still with us. It has been responsible for the transportation of hundreds of thousands of people from their homelands to countries where their labor was needed as well as for the enslavement of indigenous populations, as in many colonial ventures in Africa and in the Dutch East Indies.

Spain in the New World

Initially, enslavement of the indigenous peoples characterized Spanish colonization of the New World. After the initial scramble for easy loot in the form of gold, silver, and precious stones exhausted the supply of such items, the Spaniards turned to other ways of making a profit. Two of these were mining and plantation cash-cropping, both labor-intensive enterprises. Over the protests of the ecclesiastics, the conquistadores put large numbers of Indians to work in the mines and on the plantations. The results were disappointing, for the Indians died in large numbers. They were unused to such steady, punishing physical labor. In the mines they could not accommodate to being underground most of the time; and on the plantations, they were unable to adjust to the hot, humid tropical climate, which was excellent for sugar cane and tobacco but devastating for people used to a temperate dry environment. As the Indians died the Spanish found themselves without workers. The solution was to import slaves from Africa, and that they did on a grand scale. The Africans proved to be much better suited than the Indians to the climate and the work, and, also important, they were more resistant to disease.

Blacks in the United States

Africans were transported to America for much the same reason—to provide labor, primarily for the plantation economies of the South. Slavery there differed greatly from slavery in Spanish Latin America, and as a result the contemporary situation also differs. From their beginnings, the Southeastern colonies sanctioned slavery. Initially the number of Blacks brought over was small because the already enslaved local Indian populations were sufficient for the colonists' needs. But in time the plantations became established and began to expand, producing good crops of rice and indigo, and the manufacture of pitch and tar steadily increased. By the beginning of the eighteenth century, larger importations of slaves became necessary. The Indians had rebelled, and the colonists had decided that they were too dangerous and untrustworthy to use as laborers. This image was reinforced by the Yamassee War of 1715–1717, which thoroughly frightened the colonists, especially those in South Carolina (see Willis 1971:100). Blacks were the obvious solution as a source of labor that could be controlled. By the beginning of the eighteenth century, Blacks already outnumbered whites; by the end of the century the ratio was two or three to one (ibid.:100).

Viewing the Indians as enemies and fearing the masses of Black slaves who were actively engaged in subversion, the planters of the Southeast found themselves in an unenviable situation, albeit one of their own making. To make matters worse, the Southeast was an area of bitter struggle between empires. The French, the English, the Spanish, and the Americans all sought control where their interests diverged from the English. One of the planters' great fears was that the Indians and the Blacks would join forces against them, and in such a case there could be only one outcome. Their response was to play off one Indian village against another and the Indians against the Blacks.

The harshness of the slave code, the deliberate separation of Indians and Blacks, and proscriptions against marriage with Indians and Blacks all led to the perpetuation of distinct groups of people in North America. The whites maintained control and forced all other groups into subordinate positions. In Spanish Latin America the situation developed differently. Although the Indians initially outnumbered the Spanish by approximately 20 million to 500 (in 1519), the effects of disease and warfare drastically reduced their numbers, and by 1605 only a little over a million Indians survived. At the same time the Spanish population kept increasing. Many men came to New Spain unmarried, and others left wives in the Old World. Far from having laws against marriage with nonwhites, the Spanish gave more land and privileges to those who married than to those who remained single. The result was predictable—Spaniards married both Indians and Blacks. The population of Mexico today is an example of 500 years of this process—over 80% are classified as *mestizo* (literally "mixed").

Forced Immigration

Although events in the new homeland may evolve differently, certain characteristics are shared by all situations of importation of slaves. The most important is that the slaves have no power. In Stanley Lieberson's (1961) terms, they are subordinate migrants, but of a special sort. The Irish certainly occupied a subordinate position in the United States, but most of them came voluntarily, as free men and women, and were entitled to the protection of the laws of the land. Slaves were regarded as property and therefore came under the laws pertaining to the buying, selling, and maintaining of property. They were in a psychologically less-favorable position than other kinds of subordinate migrants, whose situations might be equally harsh or even harsher. But the latter could at least claim to be human beings.

Positive Motivations

Perceived Opportunities

Rural Migrants

Many people undoubtedly leave home and country because they believe their opportunities will be greater elsewhere. In the great period of immigration in the nineteenth century, much of the exodus was by rural peoples seeking land and opportunity. They came from Germany, England, Ireland, Scandinavia, and eastern and southern Europe. Almost all of Europe had undergone rapid population growth, and pressures on the land had begun to be felt. Families had to divide hereditary plots into smaller and smaller units, until the farms became so tiny that they were unable to support those who worked them.

The Germans and the Scandinavians, in particular, sought the comforting solidity of large tracts of land that they and their descendants could farm productively. They were attracted by the vastness of the American Middle West and the Canadian plains, where there was room to expand. Land away from the eastern seaboard was not expensive, and all that was required to be successful was the willingness to work and a knowledge of farming. Many prosperous European farmers who left Europe during the depression that followed the Napoleonic wars had the knowledge and will as well as the capital to make a good start.

The reactions of Americans and Canadians to these prosperous, hard-working, and for the most part Protestant immigrants were clearly favorable. All these qualities were familiar to and valued by American and Canadian society. These attributes acquired even greater significance as the settlers they characterized began to be compared to the dreadfully poor, ill, and frequently Catholic immigrants forced to seek asylum abroad. Many settlers favored the United States, which had made good land readily accessible to the right sort of immigrant and had a good road system. By the 1820s, Canada began to compete for immigrants. After the Canada Company started offering such inducements as cheap land and credit, many settlers went there, especially the English, who, all other things being equal, seemed to prefer being under a British flag (see Hansen 1948).

In Latin America the rate of immigration gathered speed after the various independence movements succeeded in throwing off the yokes of Spain and Portugal. Many individuals seeking to improve their lot headed for Latin America in the belief that the best opportunities in the United States were already taken. Others were lured by the tropics. Hansen remarks that in seasons that saw 200 to 300 Germans going to the United States, 2,000 to 3,000 were going to South America. Some of the enthusiasm for the tropics disappeared under the strain of coping with unstable governments. Immigration continued, however, although at a slower pace.

Another area that proved attractive to Englishmen whose desire to live off the land had been frustrated by lack of opportunity at home was the British colony of Kenya. Lower-class Englishmen quickly saw the advantages of the cool highlands and settled down to growing coffee. They did so well that their antagonism toward British attempts to parcel out land to Africans and to induce East Indians to settle in Kenya is not surprising.

Not all immigrants seeking opportunities were farmers or had emigrated in order to farm. The newcomers also included owners of small businesses, commercial entrepreneurs, skilled laborers, and traders. Many of them filled unoccupied economic niches in their adopted countries, but the process of finding the appropriate niches often involved painful trial and error.

Chinese immigrants to the west coast of the United States went through just such a process. Their immigration began in 1848 with the Gold Rush in California. They were employed at first as manual laborers, and then went on to help build the railroads. They were so disliked that in 1882 the Chinese Exclusion Act was passed. Even with the subsequent decline in immigration, dislike and harassment of the Chinese continued. The factories would not hire them, and whenever the Chinese went into manufacturing for themselves they were pressured to withdraw from competition with white-owned firms. The economic niches left to them after the whites had selected their empires were in the categories of wage laborers and the self-employed. Some were employed as domestic servants, cooks, and gardeners, while others operated laundries, restaurants, import outlets, and groceries. As described by Ivan Light in a book on ethnic enterprise in the United States, "the classic small businesses of prewar Chinese were, in this sense, monuments to the discrimination that had created them" (1972:8).

In other countries, Chinese entrepreneurial immigrants fared better. In Thailand, they stepped quite early into the world of business and trade, unhampered by any kind of restrictive measures. This tolerance can be explained partly by the fact that the Thai enjoyed what has been described as ethnic confidence. "The Thai not only developed a great civilization but were fortunate enough to maintain their faith in it unbroken" (Skinner 1963:13).

Lebanese immigrants to the Isthmus of Tehuantepec in southern Mexico were particularly successful in carving out a lucrative economic niche for themselves. The first Lebanese families came into that area toward the end of the nineteenth century. They were drawn by the potential of the transisthmian railroad (then being built) for bringing wealth to those who had the initiative and the capital to invest in the towns along its route. One of these towns was Juchitán, and one of the first Lebanese to reside there opened a hardware/general drygoods store. Commercial establishments were practically nonexistent, since the town was principally the center of a large agricultural district. Until the coming of the railroad there was no need for any more than the minimum number of stores in addition, of course, to the daily market.

The traditional economic activities for the Zapotec men of Juchitán were farming and fishing. The women processed and sold what the men raised or caught. When the opportunity presented itself, it was the women who went into commerce, opening stores and trading, while the men continued in their time-honored labors. Lebanese and Zapotec women competed amiably. The Lebanese businesses tended to require larger initial investments of capital. The Zapotec therefore did not regard them as direct competitors, and, in any case, the market was large enough to accommodate everyone.

By the first decade of the twentieth century, the Lebanese controlled two of the three major cottage industries—hammock making and weaving of artifacts out of palm fiber. The Lebanese function as middlemen between Juchitán and the outside market in these two crafts. The Zapotec feel that they are treated fairly and are willing to let the Lebanese continue in their role. The third, developed somewhat later, was the gold-washed jewelry industry, which has always been under Zapotec control. Significantly, it does not employ the large number of workers that the other two industries do.

Returning to the Homeland

Unlike numerous other nonfarming immigrant groups, the Lebanese in southern Mexico did not have an ideology based on making a profit quickly and then returning to their native land. Whether or not this ideology is realized, it is an important feature of immigrant groups as diverse as southern Slavs in United States coal-mining towns and Pakistanis in London. Having such an ideology implies certain values and behaviors and colors perceptions. From the beginning the commitment of such immigrants is to their homeland, and they leave behind them the items that they value—property, kin, and spouses. They send most of their earnings back home because that is where their future lies and because they are not competing for status in their temporary home. They make few changes in life style or attitudes except those necessary to accommodate local norms. They live in self-circumscribed communities made up of people from the same country or region. Except in rare cases where cheap labor is needed and there is no local source, these attitudes and behaviors generate considerable antagonism.

The Slavs in coal-mining areas were bitterly resented by the poor whites who had to compete with them for jobs. The resentment surfaced in comments about their tendency to cling to foreign ways— eating strange foods, speaking a strange language, and worshipping in the wrong fashion; about their willingness to give up their rights, and their corresponding sympathy for socialism; about their suspected contempt for the "real" Americans who were loyal citizens, Protestants, and Democrats. Such antagonisms polarize natives and immigrants still further and lead each group to reinforce its boundaries.

Individuals will immigrate in order to feel at home. One may object that "at home" is a difficult concept to define, and, further, that it is difficult to separate patriotic motivations from economic considerations. True, but some instances of immigration will not fit into any of the more-easily bounded categories of motivation. They involve three reasons for "going home": a return to the old country by second-generation immigrants, a crisis in the homeland, and mass immigration to a newly created or liberated homeland.

Children of immigrants or generations even further removed from the immigration experience sometimes return to the land of their ancestors. Often the return is sparked by a curiosity arising from years of hearing about the "Old Country" and participating in traditions more or less attenuated by translation to a new environment. These returns have occurred during all periods of immigration history. They are almost always individual decisions; only rarely is there an organized return at the level of the group. One such instance is the back-to-Africa movement promoted by Marcus Garvey and his Universal Negro Improvement Association. Although it has been described as the single important large-scale nationalistic effort, it never actually resulted in mass emigration of blacks (Lieberson 1961).

Since the civil rights movement in the sixties and the subsequent rise of ethnic consciousness on the part of Third World peoples as well as "white ethnics," returns to the ancestral homeland have increased. Many are simply visits, but others are permanent moves.

The beginning of World War II witnessed the patriotic return to Germany of thousands of people who were living settled, peaceful lives in various parts of the world. Not all immigrants feel such nationalistic fervor, but in times of real crisis many may be unable to resist the magnet of the homeland. The emotion is similar to what one feels when one is away from home and hears others maligning that home. One's immediate impulse is to leap to its defense even though in ordinary circumstances one may critize "home" equally vehemently.

Immigration to a newly created or liberated homeland is almost without exception a mass phenomenon. In the last century there was a move to populate Liberia with freed American slaves. The first of the newly liberated colonists arrived in 1820, and the colony was founded two years later. Although having nothing in common with the native population save color of skin, the American Blacks made a success out of the venture, and Liberia became an independent republic in 1847. As is the case in Israel today, the immigrants brought with them much of their previous lives. The Liberian constitution is modeled on that of the United States; the official language is English; and the currency is the U.S. dollar.

Between the founding of Israel in 1948 and the census of 1961, some 1,198,000 people had immigrated to Israel, making up 63% of the population (Klaff 1977:104). Although Jewish identity and a sense of a long-delayed return to an ancient homeland were the motivating factors in this rapid populating of the country, this unity of motivation did not produce a unity of population. Gradually, the social distinctions between the Ashkenazim and the Sephardim, between European and Oriental, created a social hierarchy.

Nature of Immigrant and Native Populations

In the previous discussion of reasons behind individual and group decisions to emigrate, we saw some examples of acceptance or rejection of immigrants because of perceptions of their characteristics and condition. Perhaps the most forceful of these examples was that of the immigrant Irish before and during the potato famine. When they were strong, healthy, and unafraid of hard work, they were accepted even though their being Catholic made them different and therefore suspect. Once the famine had caught hold, the sick, poverty-striken, frightened immigrants were no longer welcome and were met with scorn and violence.

We also saw how the composition of the groups *into* which the immigrants moved could affect the nature of the relationship. The Irish in the eastern seaboard cities were superfluous and, worse, competitors for the unskilled laborer jobs. They were passionately resented by those who already occupied that niche. Easterners were also secure in their interpretation of the social hierarchy, which placed the Irish at the bottom. In San Francisco, however, the Irish were judged as individuals who were better or worse businessmen, entrepreneurs, and capitalists. Society in the West was as yet unformed and therefore freer of prejudices. People were still judged on the basis of their abilities and not yet on their family name.

An individual's age and relationship to a larger social unit often shape the immigration experience in crucial ways. They influence strongly the ultimate fate of the individual or group whether it be assimilation, integration, or separation.

The Maltese in London

Maltese immigrants now in London illustrate a case of assimilation accelerated by the personal characteristics of the immigrants. Their immigration derives from dissatisfaction with the political state of Malta, in contrast to the immigration of the nineteenth century, which was primarily responsive to economic cycles and in which there was no desire to remain abroad permanently. Maltese society in the twentieth century, however, is perceived as more oppressive, and immigration is a way of escaping from the stifling hand of Church and State. It is not surprising then that twentieth-century immigration has been a movement of individuals, 72% of whom are male. Sixty-five percent of these men immigrate between the ages of 15 and 25, 79% are bachelors on arrival, and 47% have no close relatives at their destination. It is precisely these kinds of persons who would chafe the most under the restrictions of post–World War II Malta. Having left Malta to assert their independence, these young men are reluctant to establish relationships with other Maltese. In fact, the evidence seems to indicate a tradition of discouraging any kind of Maltese identity or community. In a study of the Maltese in London, 35% defined themselves as English (37% regarded themselves as Maltese, and the rest were uncertain as to their status); only one-third felt that the Maltese in London were a cohesive group, while one-half of those interviewed stated flatly that no such community existed; and 55% said that one should not encourage closer association between Maltese immigrants (Dench 1975).

In addition, there are both positive and negative aspects of the way in which the Maltese fit into London and of the social interaction among themselves, all of which reinforce their rapid assimilation. Unlike many immigrants, the Maltese do not need the services of culture brokers. Most of them speak English, and they are not defined by the British as "coloured." It is not difficult for them to find employment above the level of unskilled manual labor. In fact 25% have jobs classified as nonmanual, primarily as restaurant and hotel employees, in contrast to the less than 5% of Jamaicans in London who have risen above the manual-labor category. Finally, both by necessity and by preference, there is a high degree of intermarriage between Maltese men and English women, who are supposed to be less stuffy than Maltese women. Insofar as the English women are not Catholics raised in the anything-but-liberal spirit of the Maltese Catholic Church, that assessment is probably accurate.

What of the interaction among the Maltese? There is a kind of café society typical of Maltese immigrants that under other conditions might be a source of communal feeling. Geoff Dench argues that it does not function that way for the London Maltese because their ethos is founded on the rejection of a religiously grounded community life. Moreover, it does not offer any viable alternatives. The Church, which is the major focus of social and political life in Malta, has no power in London. Only 36% of the Maltese immigrants continued to observe its minimum requirements. There is only apathy toward the Maltese Catholic Centre in London. Worse still, there is active antagonism between the Maltese who accept and those who oppose the traditional church-based social order. In short, Maltese immigrant society in London is split by factions, and the result is the absorption of the Maltese into the larger London community.

Pakistanis in Industrial Cities of England

The Pakistanis make an interesting comparison with the Maltese, since on the surface their personal characteristics are very similar. Their ultimate relationship to England, however, is very different. There is little integration and almost no assimilation of Pakistanis in the larger community. The difference has to do with the British perceptions of the Pakistanis and with the latter's goals.

Because of the tradition of primogeniture in Pakistan, many people were left without the security of a land base. Some of them emigrated in order to earn money with which to purchase land in Pakistan. For them the "significant others" were kinsmen and fellow villagers back in Pakistan (Dahya 1974:98). Significantly, the emigrating Pakistani could immediately find a congenial community of fellow countrymen in any number of industrial cities in England. In fact, one could even find a community of one's own language/dialect, religion/sect, or village. For the most part, single male Pakistanis emigrate, seeking employment for several years until they can purchase a piece of land at home, at which time they return, settle down, and raise a family. While in English cities, they rely heavily on the services of Pakistani brokers, men who have been there long enough to know the language and the ropes. More likely than not, the new immigrant will live in the central area of one of the textile manufacturing cities in a rooming house owned by other Pakistanis. Until he gets a job he will pay no rent, and his other expenses will be taken care of by his countrymen. He will probably get his job through the services of an ethnic entrepreneur. It is a close, comfortable, communal life, in which all the needs of the immigrant can be satisfied within a few blocks of his home. He lives among people of his own kind; he can buy sundries and foods from Pakistan in neighborhood stores run by Pakistanis; and if he wishes to return home for a visit, he can buy his ticket through a Pakistani travel agent. In short, his is an encapsulated community—it is institutionally complete.

The objections raised by the British to the Pakistanis' seemingly low standard of living are based on British notions of minimal requirements. The Pakistani point of view is quite different. The Pakistanis are used to high-density living conditions, much denser, in fact, than conditions in the industrial townhouses. Because most of them had no bathrooms, water, or electricity in Pakistan, the old homes in the British cities that have these facilities seem luxurious. And what hardships and deprivations the Pakistanis do suffer are regarded as only temporary, since they will soon be returning home and to an enriched style of life as a result of their stay in England.

Why have the Pakistanis developed so differently from the Maltese? Much of the difference stems from the goals of the immigrants themselves—the Pakistanis were willing to suffer privations in England for the sake of a better life in Pakistan. The Maltese by and large had no illusions about returning to a Malta made better by increased economic stability. Another part of the explanation lies in the attitudes of the English toward the two groups. Unlike the Maltese, the Pakistanis are regarded as "coloured," and that has limited their flexibility in the labor market. Most of them are employed as unskilled labor, mainly in the textile mills. Very few of them speak English, and so they are forced to rely on brokers and the insulated Pakistani community. Because of their menial jobs, their language difficulties, and their tendency to congregate in what outsiders regard as slums, the English place them toward the bottom of the social hierarchy.

The Chinese Abroad

In comparing the adaptation of two different immigrant groups to the same environment, we saw how differences of motivation and goals as well as related attitudes on the part of the host country affected the immigration experience. Let us now examine the experience of the same people in two different settings in order to see the influence of purpose, perception, and power on the group concerned. The Chinese in Thailand have built a solid economic niche for themselves. They are accepted by the Thai, and many of them have become Thai. The Chinese in Malaysia also have a strong economic position but are a separate and feared segment of the population, ostracized even when they convert to Islam. Chinese immigrants to both these areas began arriving in great numbers during the nineteenth century. They emigrated for the same reason—to make their fortunes. In both situations, the Chinese who left their homes were almost without exception single males. If the times, the motivations, and the personal statuses were identical, what then accounts for the difference in the way the two groups fit into their adopted homelands? Let us first look at the homelands themselves.

Chinese in Thailand

Thailand is one of those happy countries that has never known foreign domination. The two monarchs who guided her fortunes from 1851 to 1910, Mongkut and Chulalongkorn, so impressed the colonial powers with their plans for modernization that they signed trade treaties with Thailand instead of annexing her. One effect of indigenous rule is that the elite in Thailand are Thai and always have been. Any group with social and political ambitions does well to imitate them, and that is precisely what many Chinese have done. The Thai make this process relatively simple: Thai citizenship is automatically conferred on anyone born in Thailand; and anyone who uses a Thai name, speaks the language, and behaves as a Thai is accepted as one regardless of his or her ancestry. Also important in explaining what G. William Skinner (1963) calls a high rate of Chinese assimilation is the fact that there have never been any sort of travel restrictions on the Chinese in Thailand. They have been allowed to live and travel where they please, and thus ghetto situations have been avoided. Between one-third and one-half of

Thailand's Chinese live in Bangkok and its environs. Since Bangkok is the main port of entry, this community is continually being reinforced by new arrivals. However, it has not developed a separate, cohesive identity because the Chinese are not a homogenous group. They are split by dialect differences and by an incipient class structure based on occupational and economic considerations. If, in the past, there had been antagonism and restrictive legislation on the part of the Thai government, the Chinese might have been welded into a cohesive unit by a sense of opposition. Should Thai policy change in the future, it is not clear whether there are enough non-Thai Chinese to form an effective community. To summarize, Chinese in Thailand were rewarded by becoming Thai and many did precisely that.

Chinese in Malaysia

The experience of Chinese immigrants in Malaysia differed from the beginning. Formerly a British colony, Malaysia underwent a period of intensive immigration in the nineteenth and twentieth centuries, when cheap labor was needed for the rubber plantations and the tin mines. The two largest immigrant groups were the Chinese and the Indians/Pakistanis. The Chinese were and are predominant in the city of George Town, Penang (today constituting 71.5% of the population). In the form of indirect rule that Britain applied in Penang, each of the ethnic communities was administered through intermediaries essentially as a separate unit. Later the British lumped all the Muslims together in a single administrative category, but by then the ethnic separation had already become a fact. The Chinese, administered through a *Kapitans China,* very quickly organized into a closed, tightly integrated community with such traditional corporate groups as *kongsi* and secret societies (Nagata 1974:38).

Since independence, the Malays have been in control politically, although they are barely a numerical majority in the country. Because of an earlier policy of Malay self-sufficiency, much of the present Malay population is rural, in contrast to the Chinese, who are predominately urban and who control most businesses. In fact, the common stereotype of the Chinese is as the urban controller of the Malaysian economy. Because there are almost as many Chinese as Malays, the latter feel threatened. For this reason the special privileges accorded to Malays by the Second Malaysia Plan and similar government projects are carefully guarded, and any switching of identity from Chinese to Malay is discouraged (ibid.:35).

The real separation of the Chinese is made apparent by the treatment of Chinese converts to Islam. A common traditional saying held that any convert to Islam was said to *masok Melayu* ("become a Malay") (Freedman, cited ibid.:39). As Judith Nagata suggests, there are degrees of "becoming Malay," but Chinese converts are rarely described by this phrase, no matter what the degree. The Chinese Muslims, for their part, maintain their own association, separate from the other Muslim organizations. Although they are practicing Muslims, most of the Chinese converts prefer to think of themselves as Chinese. They still practice many traditional Chinese customs and have no illusions about the Malays' regarding them as anything but Chinese.

In fact, hostilities between Malays and Chinese are very real. In August 1965, Singapore was separated from Malaysia in an attempt to resolve the tensions between the ethnic Chinese, who were the dominant group in Singapore, and the Malays, who controlled the Malaysian government. An indication of continuing difficulties are the riots that broke out in May 1969, when 180 persons died in conflicts between Chinese and Malays in the capital city of Kuala Lumpur.

These two examples clearly demonstrate the influence of the receiving population and situation on the immigrant group. In Thailand, the Chinese entered a stable situation in which a self-confident, indigenous population governed itself efficiently and progressively. Because the nation was modernizing, there were opportunities for the immigrant that did not have to be wrested from others. Malaysia, in contrast, was initially under a kind of laissez-faire rule that facilitated the growth of separate institutional structures for each ethnic group. Further separation and suspicion were generated by the fact that Chinese immigrants gravitated toward the urban areas, where they outnumbered the Malays.

Stages in the Immigration Process

Since the nineteenth century, when immigration began on a great scale, people have been talking about it, its effects on the immigrants, its effects on the receiving societies, and, more recently, its implications for action based on ethnicity. All the talk and most of the scholarship made certain assumptions about immigration. It was thought to be an event that had a beginning and an end, usually marked by departure from one port and arrival at another. It could be classified as illustrating one of several monolithic models. Finally, it was either positive or negative for the immigrants or the hosts, depending on which of the monolithic models it followed. Let us consider some of the frequently cited models.

Race and Ethnic Relations: A Societal Theory

Lieberson has proposed a societal theory of race and ethnic relations to account for differences in the outcome of contact situations in which each group tries to maintain a social order compatible with, if not identical to, its precontact way of life. He considers social, political, and economic institutions in terms of two major types of contract situations: those involving the subordination of an indigenous group by an immigrant group, and those involving the subordination of an immigrant group by the indigenous population (1961:77). The kind of contact situation will determine whether conflict or assimilation will occur.

Lieberson's theory derives from Western observations of and assumptions about immigration and contact situations. One major assumption was that immigrant groups either fought or were assimilated. They did not do both or neither, or begin with one and go on to the other. There was no sense of the influence of the particular situation. Another missing ingredient was the consideration of motivations other than institutional, specifically the power of a sense of opposition to generate identity retention.

Theories about Assimilation

Like Lieberson, Milton Gordon based his theories on the American experience. In *Assimilation in American Life* (1964), he discusses three philosophies that have been and are popular in the United States: Anglo-conformity, melting pot-ism, and cultural pluralism. The first assumes the desirability of maintaining English institutions (as modified by the American Revolution), the English language, and the dominance of English-oriented cultural patterns in American life. This philosophy, according to Gordon, has probably been the main ideology throughout

American history. It has seen periods of great popularity and times when it seemed to be held by only a few. It has prompted a variety of responses, ranging from murder and rioting to anti-immigration legislation to pseudo-evolutionary theories of race. Throughout its history, the guiding principle of Anglo-conformity has been that immigrants must not harbor competing ideologies and traditions.

Since at least the eighteenth century, a second philosophy has had supporters. They saw America as a melting pot that would, out of the diverse raw materials of its citizens, create a totally new blend, culturally and biologically. America would not be simply a modified England. The derivative nature of American culture, implicitly supported by followers of Anglo-conformity, was first attacked by Frederick Turner in 1893. He argued that the dominant shaping force in American life was the moving and varied western frontier, which was the crucible in which immigrants were Americanized and the composite nationality that is the hallmark of America was created. The crucible image was transferred to urban America and immortalized in 1909 in the play *The Melting Pot* by Israel Zangwill.[2]

The third philosophy, cultural pluralism, dates from the beginning of the twentieth century and stems, Gordon suggests, from idealistic members of the middle class who went off to the slums to do good deeds. There, two realizations struck them: One was that immigration/assimilation policies had terrible effects on immigrant families. Forced assimilation led to the splitting of generations, with children being ashamed of older family members who could not or would not change as fast as they. The second was that forced assimilation led to ethnic self-hatred. Jane Addams was one of the first to articulate the value of other cultural traditions, as she dealt with peasant women at Hull House in Chicago. These women were gradually given back their pride in Old World traditions as they taught weaving. Out of this initial sympathy for other cultures and the traditions of which they were being

---

2. "There she lies, the great Melting Pot—listen! Can't you hear the roaring and the bubbling? There gapes her mouth—the harbour where a thousand mammoth feeders come from the ends of the world to pour in their human fright. Ah, what a stirring and a seething! Celt and Latin, Slav and Teuton, Greek and Syrian—black and yellow—. . . . Yes, East and West, and North and South, the palm and the pine, the pole and the equator, the crescent and the cross—how the great Alchemist melts and fuses them with his purging flame! Here shall they all unite to build the Republic of Man and the Kingdom of God. Ah, Vera, what is the glory of Rome and Jerusalem where all nations and races come to worship and look back, compared with the glory of America, where all races and nations come to labour and look forward!" (Zangwill 1909:184–185).

deprived grew the idea that the United States ought not only to tolerate cultural pluralism but to nurture it. That meant the preservation of the communal life and significant portions of the culture of immigrant groups within the context of American citizenship, including political and economic intergration into American life.

Ethnic Myths and Realities

Since the 1960s we have seen scores of ethnic revitalization movements as well as larger-scale, more-militant movements of ethnic nationalism. It is hard to reconcile them with philosophies of Anglo-conformity or melting pot-ism. Worse, does this ethnic resurgence mean that the immigrants never gave up their identities at all, but have been hiding them until the time was ripe? I would argue that our perception of the situation in the past has been rather a misperception. We saw uniform assimilation, or tried to impose it, where the reality was much more complicated. We posited one melting pot where in fact there were many. That meant that within certain narrow boundaries homogenization occurred but that beyond those boundaries separation was the rule. Cultural pluralism has been attacked by every possible constituency. On the one hand, groups agitating for ethnic nationalism are already far beyond the notion of cultural pluralism and are arguing instead for their own nation. On the other, liberal intellectuals who support ethnic pluralism on the grounds that diversity and variety are good things to have in our society are attacked by people who argue that ethnicity and the "spurious social philosophy of pluralism that ra-tionalizes it" are the worst threats to individuality and personal au-tonomy (see Patterson 1975). Their attack is based on the premise that ethnic identity is a *group* identity and that where it reigns individual identity must suffer. Meanwhile people have responded to the govern-ment reification of ethnic differences, which has led to a system of re-wards for emphasizing one's ethnic heritage.

Ethnic Revitalization and Assimilation: Recent Explanations

Seeing the immigrant as an actor in an ongoing process of adjustment to his or her surroundings sorts out much of the jumble we had made of the immigrant response by thinking of it in institutional, either-or terms. Marilyn Trueblood suggests, in an article on Portuguese immigrants to New England, that there are different stages in an immigrant's accommodation to a new life and that these stages call forth different adaptations. She isolates two concepts and applies them to directions of change—Americanization and ethnicity. But she makes the important point that, although on the surface these concepts seem to point to oppositions, they are in fact parallel and represent a similar orientation: "identification with a group having a culture and history that is a source of pride and that allows one to augment his opportunities" (1977:158).

A newly arrived immigrant realizes that, in order to be accepted by his adopted homeland, he has to overcome certain disadvantages that are more class-related than ethnic-specific. For example, in comparison with the average American, he probably has less education, does not speak English with ease, and, as a result of these two factors, holds a poorly paying, low-prestige job. To change his status, he will learn English and will send his children to school. Other features of American life begin to enter his life—watching television or driving a car—and will make his change of status easier.

Trueblood points out that the immigrant can appear to be an American, but unless he identifies himself as an American the Americanization process is not complete. At the point where assimilation has almost become a fact, the immigrant has a choice of behaviors. He has mastered the behavior appropriate to his adopted home but he can still refer to pre-American values and behaviors. It is here that Trueblood argues for flexibility and frequently ethnic revitalization. With the self-confidence generated by success in the American system of just managing to survive for a number of years, immigrants can emerge from the protective coloration of being anonymous Americans. "The energy that went into consolidating their positions as Americans can now be turned toward diversifying their roles. One of the facets of their identity that they begin to cultivate is the ethnic self" (ibid.).

Since the 1960s, having an ethnic self is often strategically wise, and the number of individuals who engage in this kind of revitalization has increased. Trueblood comments that the upsurge in ethnic identification for the Portuguese-Americans in the New England town in which she worked has come about during the 1970s. The most active participants are those who also feel most secure in their American status (ibid.:163). Part of this renewed interest in an ethnic identity has resulted from competition with other ethnic groups in the area, and part is the result of the efforts of a local Portuguese-American intellectual who is interested in glorifying the contribution of the Portuguese to history.

Although instances of ethnic revitalization have certainly increased in the 1960s and 70s, Trueblood has touched upon a much broader phenomenon here. At bottom, human beings adapt to their environment not simply to survive but to thrive. When circumstances change, so do their adaptive strategies.

Cultural Brokers

An indication that immigration is a continuous process is the presence of individuals who span both the world of the immigrants and the home they have chosen. In the literature on developing countries and peasant societies these individuals have been given various names— cultural brokers, middlemen, mediators, go-betweens. They almost always have some personal qualities that allow them to move between two worlds or two classes or two groups of people, and they use these qualities to help others bridge the gaps. As Trueblood persuasively argues, it is not that these middlemen are the only connection between the two worlds—frequently there are institutions like schools, unions, or churches—but that they can take a personal interest in the individual who is trying to make the connections and tailor their strategies to his peculiar needs. Both brokers working toward a goal of Americanization and those working toward ethnicity are most in evidence when people are undergoing a change in status and need leadership. Both rely on intellectual and social advantage, particularly the second kind of broker.

The broker working toward Americanization must know the institutional structures of both the immigrant and the host society. The one promoting ethnicity as a way of life has to know the special qualities of the immigrants' past that are likely to contrast with American society and therefore appeal to a nostalgic immigrant population. It is not merely a question of convincing immigrants to act upon their cultural knowledge; in most cases it means imparting that cultural knowledge. Louis Wirth describes the process as one whereby the immigrant intellectual influences his fellow immigrants' self-image by "recovering, disseminating, and inspiring pride in the group's history and civilization and pleading its case before world public opinion" (1944:361). He speaks both for and to his people.

Sometimes the sense of a tight, ethnic community is promoted by cultural brokers not as a means of instilling pride in the ways of the Old Country but in order to retain control over a dependent population. For example, it is to the advantage of Pakistani brokers in the industrial cities of England to keep their clients removed as much as possible from English life and custom. In their dependence the clients provide a living for the brokers that would disappear if all the Pakistanis were to become English. In some cases, brokers are flexible enough to make the shift from promoting assimilation to promoting ethnicity. Similarly, those who wish to maintain their positions by keeping their clients ignorant may eventually see the handwriting on the wall and make the transition. Caroline Brettell, in an article on the Portuguese in Toronto, documents the first kind of shift, from dealing with new immigrants to imparting a sense of Portugueseness. "The political arena, in which at present the Portuguese remain unrepresented, is a focus for the patron-broker; his skills can be turned toward mobilizing ethnicity" (1977:178).

With some immigrant groups, for example, the Chinese, the brokerage role is taken by members of the kin group. The kin group provides other services as well, often acting as a credit institution. This style of immigration is very different and requires a relatively stable community over time and the eventual immigration of whole families.

Our recognition that there are different kinds of brokers who serve different functions is an advance in our understanding of the immigration process. It reminds us that immigrants are, after all, individuals who are responsive to their surroundings and who make choices based on their perceptions of those surroundings. Let us also recognize the fact that contact between the immigrant and his home country does not normally cease when he arrives in the country of his choice.

Immigrants and Their Country of Origin

Certainly the bulk of the literature on immigration has focused on people and their adopted homelands. That is understandable, since researchers' primary interest was in the immigrants' ability to assimilate or their tendency to remain separate. There has also been some interest in the effect of immigrants who return to their country of origin. Using interview material primarily, Theodore Saloutos (1956) produced one of the pioneering works in this area. He worked with repatriated Greek-Americans and was concerned with their reasons for returning, their attitudes toward both America and Greece, and their efforts at readjustment.

Studies of returned immigrants are outside our area of concern, since members of dominant national groups cease to be ethnics once they return to their own country. But it is essential to consider the flow of information from the old country to the new. Studies that assumed that communication ceased with the sailing of the ship had somewhat more reason on their side in previous times, when communications were very poor. However, even when letters took three months to reach their destination, there was still an exchange of ideas and information. Another source of news from the old country was the constant stream of new immigrants. Very few studies of the immigrant experience take this constant exchange of information into account. Significantly, those that do concern Puerto Ricans and Mexican-Americans. For both groups there is a pattern of continual visiting between the United States and the original home. Mary Sengstock, in an article on Middle East immigrants to the United States, argues that the easing of immigration restrictions, with the elimination of the 1920 quotas, and improved transportation and communication have made it possible for still other groups to visit back and forth. Increased communication between the old country and the new, in terms of both individuals and information, means that radical changes in the old country may have an impact on the self-perceptions of immigrants new and old. Furthermore, studies of Old World countries of origin that are undergoing upheaval and change and their extra-national population can sharpen our understanding of immigration and immigrations by answering the following questions: "Does contact with the country of origin increase identification with one's national origin? Does it slow the acculturation and assimilation process? What effect is produced on the culture and social patterns of the migrant community?" (Sengstock 1977:57).

Immigrants from Iraq in Detroit

The earliest immigrants from the Middle East came to Detroit in 1910. They had left an area where one's primary identification was with one's village, tribe, kin group, and religion. With few exceptions, they came from one village in what was to become northern Iraq and were bound by many cross-cutting ties. Moreover, they were separated from other villages by differences in dialect, religious subdivisions, and kin affiliations. Until 1932, when Iraq became a nation, there were no national ties to override these divisions, so the early immigrants identified themselves as Chaldean Christians from the village of Telkaif, stressing their church and their village (ibid.:59).

The homeland from which recent immigrants have come is a very different one. It is now a nation, and one that is actively trying to purge itself of the traditional loyalties and divisions and replace them with a unity based on Arab nationalism. The recent immigrants reflect these changes. They are likely to have come from an urban rather than a rural background; as a group they are more educated than the earlier immigrants; they practice either the more-dominant Latin rite of the Catholic church or a more-modernized version of the Chaldean rite; their economic base tends to be derived more from modern business practices than from self-employment; and they identify themselves as Iraqis or Arabs rather than as natives of a particular village, town, or city.

Recent immigrants thus form a less-insulated group within the city of Detroit because they come from a more-urban, less-traditional setting within the old country, but at the same time they are nationalistic. Contact between the old immigrants and the new has brought about slow but significant changes. Although most older immigrants still prefer to identify themselves by village and religion, they have supported the recently established Arabic language class and have shown an interest in the package tours to Iraq sponsored by the Iraqi government.

The newer immigrants, with their very different allegiances, have employed different strategies and behaviors. If the Detroit community is not to be fragmented by different values, there will have to be a merging of the two systems. Sengstock indicates that the process is already under way.

Internal Migration

Individuals and groups who cross national boundaries change from being nationals to being ethnics. Equally important in forming, reinforcing, or destroying ethnic ties is the process of internal migration. It may take the form of chain migration (immigrants moving in stages as they establish outposts along the way), rural peoples moving into urban areas, or rural peoples filling frontier areas as opportunities arise.

A great deal has been written about rural-to-urban migration patterns. Mitchell, for example, discusses the impact of innumerable African tribes coming together in the Copperbelt region of Africa. Previously separated by as much as a nation, they were now interacting with each other in an urban mining situation. They reinforced their ethnic boundaries in order to cope with their new urban environment. Social interaction was no longer European-African but African-African, a situation that encouraged the drawing of boundaries and the demarcation of territories.

A similar situation obtained in the United States when Blacks from the southern states and Slavs from the Northeast moved into coal-mining towns in Pennsylvania, West Virginia, and Kentucky. An additional difficulty in this area that was not present in the Copperbelt was the core of resident population, who resented both groups. Still, the result was the same—the reinforcement of ethnic boundaries.

A somewhat different experience characterized American chain migration. Many immigrants went first to an urban setting and, from there, moved into available rural areas. Turner has argued that this expansion created a frontier melting pot in which differences were forgotten in the common sharing of hardships and the general democracy of the frontier. In some instances, when the Irish moved westward, for example, boundaries were maintained as groups found it more profitable to mark themselves off from other groups and lay claim to certain properties.

S.R. Charsley (1974), in an article on the formation of ethnic groups, describes a situation in Kigumba, a subcountry of northeast Bunyoro in western Uganda. For a long time the population of this area was much smaller than the actual carrying capacity of the land. As population pressures in surrounding areas increased and the political situation in Uganda created hordes of refugees, the Kigumba region began to attract immigrants. Although the indigenous ethnic organization there was very weak, the newcomers formed definite ethnic communities even though there was no crowding or competition for resources. Charsley makes a forceful anti-melting pot case for Kigumba and further demonstrates that groups adapt their customs to new situations. He describes the categories or subsystems that arose out of the migration as not simply the prolongation of pre-migration patterns but as the result of interaction between these customs and the requirements of the receiving society. The resulting subsystems come to be patterned in new ways but, because all the groups migrating to the area meet with the same requirements, they are patterned in ways that have parallels throughout all the ethnic groups present (1974:355).

Few studies such as Charsley's exist. Part of the explanation for their absence is that scholars have reified the rural–urban contrast to the point where if urban is characterized by heterogeneity then rural must be homogeneous. Unless Kigumba is a unique occurrence, this contrast is neither valid nor useful. If population growth continues in developing nations at its present rate there will be more and more internal migration as excess population flows into previously sparsely settled areas. At that point, reinforced ethnic identity as a result of migration becomes a real and relevant issue.

Immigration and internal migration are two processes whereby previously separated groups are brought into contact, thus creating a situation in which ethnic identity may be manifested. Whether or not an ethnic identity becomes salient and the nature of that identity depend on certain features of the immigration process. While each case undoubtedly has unique characteristics, it is still subject to the effect of these general features: the motivation for immigrating; the stages in the process; the presence of brokers—either of nationalism or ethnicity; perceptions of the receiving society; and the characteristics of the new situation. The examples discussed in this chapter demonstrate that, while it is useful to be able to make general predictive statements, it is the singular coming together of features in the process that determines when and how a particular ethnic identity will appear.

Conclusions

The last three chapters have discussed the most important larger contexts that shape the development and maintenance of ethnic identity. The three contexts of colonial empires, nations, and immigration have affected the salience and nature of ethnic identity during the past two centuries in ways qualitatively different from previous manifestations. The great nineteenth-century race for empires reflected a desire for new markets, new lands to explore, and new subjects to conquer. All would add to the power and comparative prestige of the colonizer. Differences between colonizer and colonized in terms of power, perception, and purpose led to the demarcation of boundaries—in many cases, ethnic ones, between groups.

Similar processes were at work in the rise of the various nationalisms in the nineteenth and twentieth centuries. The fate of ethnic groups within new or emerging nations was influenced by the purpose behind nationalism, whether it resulted from anticolonial feelings, the French Revolution, Romanticism, or the consolidation of feudal domains.

Finally, the immigration of individuals from old nations to new ones or the migration of peoples within nations prompted by a desire for new opportunities created situations conducive to the rise of ethnic consciousness.

Those are the contexts. In the next chapters we shall explore the how and why of ethnic identity. We shall see, given these larger contexts, under which conditions ethnic affiliation is displayed rather than any of the other affiliations available to people, and, once chosen, the way an ethnic identity is negotiated and manifested.

Strategies — Possibilities
and Constraints

PART THREE

Symbols, Stereotypes, and Styles

6

SYMBOLS AND STEREOTYPES, and the product of those two, styles, are ingredients in human interaction in general. Without them we would be confronted with a hopeless proliferation of unique objects, and we would be unable to predict the behavior of others. George Herbert Mead goes even further to require that individuals not only be symbolizers but be "significant symbolizers" in order to create and sustain predictability and eliminate discrepancy and misinformation. The importance of this demand is underlined by the fact that every society has ways of defining, regulating, rehabilitating, or isolating unreliable symbolizers (Mead 1934).

For interactions in which ethnic identity is a factor, symbols, stereotypes, and styles assume even greater significance. Interactions between different ethnic groups or between ethnic groups and national cultures are based on incomplete knowledge of each other's culture. The cultural knowledge shared by members of the same group is much greater than that shared by members of different groups. Interaction between different groups tends to take place in terms of mutually recognizable symbols and stereotypes. For example, American Indians who want to attract Anglo audiences advertise their benefit performances with flyers depicting Plains style Indians in feathered headdresses and bustles and the performances themselves will feature Plains War dancing. These symbols signify "Indian" to most non-Indians, and the Indians know it. Similarly, posters for Mexican national holidays feature copper-skinned women with braids wearing china poblana (the full skirts and ruffled blouses worn in the Mexican Hat Dance) and men with sideburns and charro pants and jackets. Although few Mexicans conform to this particular stereotype, it has a high recognition factor.

Definitions

Symbol

In the above examples, the china poblana and charro outfits and the feathered headdresses are each a symbol in the sense of the word as Webster defines it: "something that stands for or suggests something else by reason of relationship, association, convention, or accidental resemblance; esp: a visible sign of something invisible." The invisible somethings are Mexican identity and American Indian identity. Webster further describes a symbol as "an act, sound, or object having cultural significance and the capacity to excite or objectify a response." We respond to these symbols in a manner appropriate to Mexicans or American Indians. Knowing what they are, we know the proper behavior toward them. In the discussion of symbols by Cohen, we find the same basic features. He defines symbols as "objects, acts, concepts, or linguistic formations that stand *ambiguously* for a multiplicity of disparate meanings, evoke sentiments and emotions, and impel men to action" (1974:ix) and states that they are objective and collective and therefore observable (ibid.:x). In other words, symbols are multi-meaninged visible signs that promote action.

Stereotype

Stereotypes are often but not necessarily built on symbols. Stereotypes generally pick out some conspicuous attribute or attributes and let it or them stand for the whole. For example, ballet companies traditionally divided their female dancers into tall women and short when height was the salient attribute. Once categorized in this fashion, they were then matched with roles. Short dancers could be Nubian slaves in *Aïda* and the cygnets in *Swan Lake*; tall ones were the priestesses and the two tall swans. What distinguishes a stereotype from other kinds of categorization is its relative permanence or inflexibility. In other words, stereotypes are less responsive to conflicting evidence than other types of categories.

Style

Style as exhibited by an ethnic group, is composed of symbols, forms, and underlying value orientations (Royce 1977:140). Or as defined again by Webster, style is a "manner or method of acting or performing, esp. as sanctioned by some standard." Style implies an element of choice. "Tradition" is the term most frequently used to describe the factor that bound and characterized ethnic groups. Style, however, more accurately corresponds to the reality of ethnic identity and interaction. Tradition implies conservatism and a body of values and symbols that have been passed down for generations in the same form. That is clearly not the case for much of ethnic style. Ethnic groups are not conservative in their self-presentation. Rather, the symbols they display change in response to changing situations. In the days when most Zapotec women went barefoot, they used to dance *sones* barefoot. Today they dance them in the latest style shoes because to be barefoot implies either old age or poverty. In their minds, "tradition" is served just as well shod as unshod.

Style also involves flexibility. The word "tradition" conjures up images of individuals born into the world with the burden of values, lore, and institutions from the distant past. What calamities would transpire if an individual were to refuse that burden? To display a style, in contrast, means that there has been a conscious selection of a particular manner and, implicitly, the rejection of other possible styles. That does not mean that there are no constraints that limit choice. It does mean that where there is no choice there is no style. For example, when Zapotec of the middle or upper class speak Zapotec, they have selected that language rather than Spanish or, for some, English. When lower-class Zapotec speak Zapotec, it is frequently because that is the only language they know. They are not displaying an ethnic style although they may well be viewed as and define themselves as traditional Zapotec. The essence of ethnicity is room to maneuver, flexibility of strategies, and tactics of choice. Viewed in this way, "style," rather than "tradition," is the appropriate term.

Symbols of Ethnic Identity

Selection of Symbols

For a symbol to be effective, it must have meaning for both the people who display it and the people to whom it is displayed. The most powerful symbols are those that have some strong universal implication or those that have been forged in the interaction, however minimal, between groups. In the former category would go most of what Stanford Lyman and William Douglass (1973) define as ethnic cues; that is, aspects of appearance and behavior that have ethnic significance but that are beyond the control of the actor. Harold Isaacs (1975) speaks of the same phenomenon when he says that more than anything else, the body (physical characteristics such as skin color, body shape, or hair) is a badge of identity that instantly establishes who are the "we" and who are the "they." Physical features are so important, he argues, that we have many ways of creating differences if they are not already there or of accentuating those that do exist. Attitudes toward these universally recognized features change over time, and interpretations vary from group to group. What makes them powerful is that they are there, immediately visible and available for use as symbols.

The other category of symbols arises from the contact between different groups. The process of symbol selection is a complex one involving incomplete knowledge, perceptions distorted by strained situations, and more-or-less accurate imputation of motives.

All human groups can be identified by certain attributes, just as all human groups are conscious of the greater importance of some features. Groups in isolation certainly have symbols by which they identify themselves. With contact, those symbols may remain the same and do double duty by representing the group to the outside; they may be used only within the group and not in interaction because they are not salient to the other groups and therefore not effective as symbols of identity; or they may be replaced by new symbols built out of the interaction itself. In all cases, a process of mutual education characterizes the development and maintenance of effective identity symbols.

Symbolic Continuity

Language is frequently the focus of identification. It is readily apparent when two groups do not have a common language; language difference is usually one of the first markers of different identities. As the contact period continues, however, it becomes more and more difficult to use language as the primary or only means of identifying either self or other. Then other symbols often take on greater significance, sometimes those that had been there from the beginning but had been accorded less attention because they were less apparent than the language difference. Among the Mayo Indians of Sonora, the *tebatpo kurus*, or house cross, one of a number of items in the Mayo ceremonial repertoire, is the primary symbol of identification. Many Mayo still speak the Mayo language, yet the presence of the house cross is sufficient to indicate Mayo-ness, and the absence of it labels one a non-Mayo no matter what other attributes of Mayo identity one might have (Crumrine 1964).

Culture heroes are other symbols that have long lives and the ability to survive contact situations. In order to remain useful as identity markers, however, heroes often must develop a repertoire based on contact; that is, a culture hero deals with the trauma of contact and provides solutions, just as he did with pre-contact catastrophes; or a culture hero continues his leadership, teaching his people how to manage post-contact developments and technologies.

Intergroup Symbols

Among the Lubovitch Hassidim (Levy 1975), the relevant symbols within the group are not all the ones by which outsiders identify the group. Orthodoxy is the primary identification feature within the Hassidic community, which perceives itself as consisting of four groups ranging from the most orthodox to the least so. Each group can be identified by certain symbols or behaviors that stand as symbols, but the subtlety of this differentiation is lost on the outside world, for which it is irrelevant. For outsiders, only a few symbols out of the whole repertoire are significant—beards, ear locks, wide-brimmed black hats, and long black coats.

Symbolic Development

Symbolic development is probably the commonest response to interaction because the flexibility and responsiveness that it indicates are qualities necessary for survival. Groups that are too rigid to engage in this kind of interchange are poor risks for surviving as anything other than marginal members of larger societies.

Symbolic development may result from a blending of new elements with old or from the adoption of altogether new symbols. The Zapotec have shown remarkable success in blending symbols. The women's festive dress, which is famous all over Mexico, consists of successive overlays of Spanish, French, English, and Chinese elements on an Indian foundation. Today's dress would scarcely be recognizable to Zapotec on the eve of the Spanish Conquest, yet it stands quite effectively as a symbol of Zapotec identity. Zapotec dance is another example of syncretism. In the Zapotec *son*, the woman's dance style is a combination of a waltz and an Andalusian fandango. There is nothing to connect it with the dances of other Indian women. The man's style, however, is pure Indian, with its bent-forward posture, relaxed knees, and zapateados (footwork characterized by heel and toe taps).

In the adoption of new elements, the group's interpretations of these features may differ from those of the donor group. The Mesquakie Indians, for example, have incorporated the United States flag into their ceremonial system but with a distinctively Mesquakie interpretation. In their view, the flag was first planted on the dance ground by United States soldiers. That act symbolized the beginning of a long and friendly relationship. It showed that the Anglos needed the Mesquakie to dance and maintain the religious component of life, while the Mesquakie needed to remain at peace with the Anglos (Crumrine 1964:49).

In a discussion of symbol formation, Cohen (1974) speaks of the gradual separation of legitimating symbolic formations from the groups that created them, thereby leading to a kind of autonomous existence for the symbols. The way is then paved for the adoption of the same symbolic cult by different interest groups, among which it acquires quite different functions and interpretations (ibid.:6). As Cohen argues,

> It is indeed in the very essence of the symbolic process to perform a multiplicity of functions with economy of symbolic formation. The

more meanings a symbol signifies, the more ambitious and flexible it becomes, the more intense the feelings that it invokes, the greater its potency, and the more functions it achieves. [Ibid.:32]

This is exactly the case with a certain category of very powerful symbols, those that had negative connotations for the labeling group. In the process of adoption, the negative aspects are reversed and become positive virtues. One of the best-known reversals is that of "Yankee Doodle," the earliest version of which was a cavalier poet's rhyme ridiculing Cromwell—"Nankee Doodle Came to Town." It first appeared in the colonies in 1775, courtesy of a British army surgeon who changed "Nankee" to "Yankee." His purpose in altering the bit of doggerel was to poke fun at the appearance of the American troops. There was nothing one might call a uniform for the Continental army, and outfits ranged from ragged assortments of what was handy to the showy uniforms of a Maryland company of militia. The latter were the butt of the line "stuck a feather in his cap and called it macaroni." "Macaroni" was the term then current in England to refer to a group of fops who had introduced a particularly flamboyant style of dress in 1772—wide coat skirts, many ruffles and ribbons, and hair piled high with an excess of feathers. They were called "macaronis" because the style was associated with Italy (whether rightly or wrongly, we do not know). Taken as a whole, the verse was meant to imply that Americans were rough and ill-mannered, lacked good breeding, and in general showed no appreciation for the finer things in life.

The Americans, on their part, viewed the British as arrogant, posturing swaggerers, in contrast to the image of themselves that they found satisfying to project: Americans, unlike those decadent British, were open, forthright, honest, and possessed of all the good, homespun virtues. "Yankee Doodle" suited their purposes admirably, and they took it over as *their* symbol. To add insult to injury, they played it at the surrender of Cornwallis at Yorktown in 1781. Because the verse was so well known and had such a satisfying rhythm, it was constantly appearing in new guises. The Americans continued to be able to laugh at themselves and in the process turn what others regarded as failings into virtues. The following parody appeared during the Revolutionary War and remained popular throughout Washington's presidency:

And there came Gen'l. Washington
Upon a snow-white charger
He looked as big as all outdoors
And thought that he was larger.

[Leach 1949, vol. 2:1187]

Physical Features

Physical features frequently appear as markers of ethnic identity because they are immediately visible and also because they are difficult to change, thereby lessening the chance of deception or an attempt to "pass." A less-explored but nonetheless useful explanation is that they can generate an immediate affective response. In other words, they fall into a category of symbols that is difficult to ignore. Isaacs (1975) gives several classes of primary affective symbols. Perhaps most significant is the human body and its different figure types, skin colors, and hair. Not only is it possible to classify all human beings on the basis of these fundamental features but it would run directly against human nature not to do so. As noted above, however, that by no means implies consistency of interpretation.

Body

Height and body shape can be used to identify individuals from relatively long distances, and when combined with movement patterns, provide almost infallible means by which persons can identify each other. These features invariably are culturally loaded; we value certain combinations of height, body shape, and movement and do not value others. In some systems, the combination of slenderness, delicacy of facial features and bone structure, and above-normal height spells breeding or aristocratic blood. Persons who have these attributes acquire power and respect in their own societies and are accorded the same by outsiders who have a similar view of the world. The opposite traits—a thick or heavy body, large and undefined facial features, and squatness—then become associated with a lack of power. Individuals of this type are not accorded respect and are, in fact, ridiculed and made scapegoats.

In situations of conflict, values such as these can have tragic, indeed morbid, consequences. In the genocidal war between the Tutsi and the Hutu in Burundi, the Tutsi had been given positions of power in the colonial government. Being Nilotes, they were tall, slender, fine-boned people. The group that of necessity became subordinate were the Hutu, a Bantu people, who are short and heavy and have broad noses. The stereotype acquired additional cultural loading by the division into Tutsi pastoralist and Hutu farmers. For whatever reason, pastoralists, particularly nomadic ones, have been romanticized both within their own societies and by Western observers.[1] Having suffered under these stereotypes for years, ever since Burundi became a colony and the romantic aura of the Tutsi was given concreteness by positions of authority, the Hutu had their revenge in the fighting that erupted in 1972. Observers reported seeing piles of Tutsi hands and feet. In their anger and frustration, the Hutu had lashed out at the most-visible, most-hated symbol of their subordination—the superior height of the Tutsi—and had literally cut them down to size.

A similar attitude pervaded the American South in antebellum years. In an 1860 sketch of Southern society, Daniel Hundley described the real Southern gentleman as invariably a man of aristocratic lineage, tall, slender, and usually characterized by "faultless physical development" (in Taylor 1969:152). A similar description of the aristocratic Edward Clayton in the novel *Dred* (1856) is given by that most perceptive of Southern critics, Harriet Beecher Stowe:

> tall, slender, with a sort of loose-jointedness and carelessness of dress, which might have produced an impression of clownishness, had it not been relieved by a refined and intellectual expression on the head and face. The upper part of the face gave the impression of thoughtfulness and strength, with a shadowing of melancholy earnestness; and there was about the eye . . . that occasional gleam of troubled wildness which betrays the hypochondriac temperament. [Ibid.:161]

In Stowe's description, we find all the traits so commonly associated with refinement, including a romantic temperament that leans toward melancholy and wildness. Her description is interesting as well for its allusion to the fine line between refined Southern gentlemen and poor whites. The latter also are tall and slender but they are described with terms such as "lank" and "raw-boned," and their features are "ill-formed" or "formless" as opposed to "finely chiseled"; their skin is

---

1. An exception to the generally favorably viewed nomadic peoples are the gypsies. They have certainly been romanticized and envied for their freedom, but at the same time they are held in bad repute and regarded with suspicion.

"sallow" or "pinky" rather than "of a pale hue." There is a rather nice description of them in Thompson's *Hell's Angels*: "sharp faces and long-boned bodies that never look quite natural unless they are leaning on something" (1967:202).

For every culture that associates slenderness and delicacy of body type with good breeding, there is undoubtedly one that values robustness. The Zapotec, for example, cast critical eyes on thin or small women and make such comments as "it is only her skin that keeps her bones from falling apart" or hint at the sickly nature of thin women, "she is like the *siempreviva*[2]—one moment she is dying and the next she is restored." Zapotec women will tighten the armholes of their *huipil* (traditional blouse) so that their upper arms will bulge out and make them look sleek, well fed, and prosperous. Women not blessed with bulk will wear two, three, or even more petticoats to give the proper illusion. And, finally, when Zapotec women converse or even pass each other in the market, they stroke each other's upper arms and comment favorably on their plumpness or, in the case of not so plump arms, question the other woman's health.

Color

Perhaps even more than body shape, color unquestionably marks identity. Within certain limits, one can alter one's body shape but not one's skin.[3] As with body shape, preferences and dislikes for certain colors shift so that no one color is favored or disliked everywhere or for all time. There are shifts in the values assigned to color as groups try to escape negative images, bolster positive ones, or force other groups to change their attitudes.

One general attitude that derived from the colonial experience was the association of light skin color with high status and dark skin with low (Isaacs 1975). The dominance of whiteness was supported by racial mythologies perpetrated by Europeans to justify their subjugation of darker-skinned peoples. In the Philippines the Spanish preference for light skin was incorporated into local values (ibid.). It was later rein-

---

2. The flower known as the "everlasting." In this case, it makes an appropriate metaphor for sickly persons who manage to survive.

3. The difficulty of changing one's skin color has never prevented people from attempting it, and there are myriads of folk theories about ways to lighten skin. The reverse process, that of darkening the skin, was made famous by more than one writer who wanted to experience the life and problems of Blacks firsthand.

forced under the American occupation, when, in striving to look American, the lighter-skinned Filipinos had the advantage. As the image of an independent Philippine nation came into favor, brown skin was associated with independence and white became the color of colonialism. As is frequently the case, attitudes were bolstered by a myth: When God made human beings, whites were produced when he took his creations out of the oven too soon, blacks were those left in too long, and Filipinos were those left in just the right length of time.

For the Creoles in Sierra Leone, the term "Black English" was initially favorable, both in their own perceptions and in the view of the British, who thought it admirable and charming that these people should try to imitate their betters. After evolutionary theory became popular, however, British attitudes reversed themselves and the term "Black English" then conjured up ludicrous images of apes trying to imitate Europeans. Black as a color was no longer a benign characteristic.

Not all preferences for lightness of skin derived from colonialism. Isaacs describes an indigenous version of Indian prehistory in which the light-skinned conquerors, "Aryas," come in and dominate the dark-skinned "Dasyas." Classical Hindu texts associate colors with caste groups in a hierarchy from light to dark: white with Brahmin at the top, bronze or yellow with the middle groups of Kshatriya and Vaisya, and black with the Sudras at the bottom. Preferences for light skin strongly influence marriage decisions within castes. In those instances where color does not correspond with caste as it is supposed to, there is a handy folk explanation: "Beware of a black-colored Brahmin and the white-colored Chamar [untouchable leatherworker]; they can only be handled with shoe in hand." Isaacs explains that the reversed skin colors could only come about through illegitimacy, and illegitimate children are always crooked and in need of punishment (1975:59).

Whiteness or light skin is not valued everywhere. The Zapotec associate light skin in women with sickliness, while the Filipinos associate it with undercooked dough. The Chinese have described white foreigners as being as cold and dull as the dead ashes of frogs. And pity the poor individual who has to go through the winter without a "Florida tan."

The slogan "Black is Beautiful" is the most-recent and most-striking reversal of traditional color symbolism. By its use, the Black Power movement has attempted to force white society to accept a new definition of the situation that is favorable to Blacks. This aggressive strategy is designed to put the dominating group on the defensive. Blacks are emphasizing the centuries of white oppression and using color symbolism as a medium through which claims and adjustments can be negotiated (see Lyman and Douglass 1973). The alternative to this kind of offense is the more-passive engaging in collective impression management, which implicitly plays by the rules laid down by the dominant group. It is a negative rather than a positive strategy and, except in unusual circumstances, does not lead to a positive "community-forming" venture (see Weber 1947).

So important are the physical symbols of identity that we create them when they do not exist. Among the many ways of creating markers are scarification; tattooing; filing or blackening of teeth (or inlaying them with precious stones); head deformation; piercing of ears, nose, lips, and tongue; shaving hair in patterns, shaving it off completely, or not cutting it at all; painting caste marks on the skin; and circumcision. In areas where ethnic groups have been in contact for relatively long periods of time and physical differences are very slight or nonexistent, rulers or dominant groups sometimes find it necessary to make distinctions using artificial symbols. Jews have had a long history of being singled out by artificial markers. In 1215 Pope Innocent III ordered them and Moslems to wear identification badges. Christians and Jews living under the caliphs after the spread of Islam were required to dress distinctively so they could be identified. In parts of Spain, Jews had to dress in yellow and were forbidden to wear turbans; and the Nazis required that they wear the Star of David.

Language

In addition to the physical reality of language difference that distinguishes groups from one another, language has an emotional aspect for both the user and the hearer. The impact of a language stems from its particular sound as well as from its familiarity. The widespread idea that language shapes behavior took scholarly form in the writings of Edward Sapir and Benjamin Whorf. Sapir declared in 1939 that the "real world" was to a large extent unconsciously built on the language habits of a group. And Whorf followed the same line in 1958:

> Language is not merely a reproducing instrument for voicing ideas but rather is itself the shaper of ideas, the program and guide for the individual's mental activity, for his analysis of impressions, for his synthesis of his mental stock in trade. . . . We dissect nature along lines laid down by our native language . . . we cut nature up, organize it into concepts, and ascribe significances as we do largely because we are parties to an agreement that holds throughout our speech community and is codified in the patterns of our language. [In Isaacs 1975:96–97]

Even though there are equally strong scholarly arguments on the other side, many people continue to believe Sapir and Whorf. We are inclined to argue along the lines of "language equals culture" whenever we have to deal with a group that speaks a different language, particularly if that group is in competition with us. It is then that we have recourse to emotional stereotypes that link language with character traits—French is the language of love, for example.

Languages often become the symbolic focus of conflict. When India became a nation, each of the many different language groups naturally wanted the distinction of providing the official tongue. When the decision was finally made, India had fourteen official languages, including Sanskrit, which some 300 people claim as their first language even though it is not spoken.

Forbidding a language is a strategy employed by many new nations and by old nations plagued by troublesome ethnic groups. Spain tried this tactic with both the Catalans and the Basques. The edict was rescinded when it became obvious that it had had little or no effect other than making the two groups more determined than ever to survive as distinct peoples. The English tried a similar strategy in Ireland, forbidding the use of Gaelic. Like the Basques and the Catalans, the Irish simply went underground.

Similarly, reviving a language is frequently one of the first strategies of groups that are in the process of strengthening or re-creating their identity. In developing nations with large numbers of people who are illiterate in their own language and have only a minimal knowledge of the national language, ambitious programs are necessary to make those individuals literate first in their own language. In Mexico these programs have been strongly promoted in recent years following changes in government policies toward Indian groups. The official platform of the Instituto Nacional Indigenista (INI), the government organization that handles Indian affairs, includes an emphasis on cultural diversity. The success of the literacy programs has been due to the foundation established by the personnel of the Summer Institute of Linguistics, which, for years, has been promoting literacy in indigenous languages. As a result of SIL work, government programs had available to them grammars, dictionaries, texts, and a corps of literate Indians who could help train others. One of the benefits of such a focus has been the increased status and self-pride generated in and for indigenous peoples.

Stereotypes and Stereotyping

Stereotypes concentrate on only one or a few attributes and let them stand for the whole. Stereotypes must have some base in reality but they rarely reflect all its complexity. They involve "either/or" judgments and are not evaluative. That in part explains their persistence in the face of conflicting evidence.

There is no doubt about the stubbornness and pervasiveness of ethnic stereotypes. Once a stereotype becomes conventional, it is not arbitrary in its criteria (although it may be selective in its application) even though it may be inaccurate. Stereotypes result from observations made during interactions between groups or individuals. We learn stereotypes the same way that we learn our own culture, because they are part of it. We are socialized into the meanings of stereotypes, and our attitudes are reinforced by interaction. In a persuasive argument Shibutani and Kwan suggest one reason for the persistence of stereotypes: Since an actor's intention cannot always be determined by one act alone, many different interpretations are possible of any single act. So stereotypes can and do persist in the face of what could be contradictory behavior. We are selective in our perceptions, seeing only what is relevant to our interests and seeing only cues that confirm what we expect to see. Therefore, once stereotypes are learned, people are perceived in terms of them. "The more firmly established the expectations, the more easily they are confirmed." Contradictory evidence usually does not alter the concept because contradictory evidence is not even noticed (1965:91).

Stereotypes persist also because they are not merely labels for categories but implications for programs of action. Knowing who a person is means knowing one's own appropriate behavior. That behavior derives from the motives one imputes to other individuals on the basis of stereotypic knowledge. In the case of groups that interact over long periods ot time, motives, expectations, and corresponding patterns of behavior fall into a routine from which it is hard or unpleasant to escape. In this way, the behaviors that are maintained would seem, on the surface, dysfunctional for at least one of the groups.

Isthmus Zapotec women interact with Huave women in the market. The Zapotec have a reputation for being shrewd businesswomen not above cheating anyone who lets herself be cheated. The Huave, in contrast, have never been known as traders or merchants. They sell surplus produce or fish in their own villages to Zapotec businesswomen, who then sell it in Zapotec towns at a profit. The Huave expect never to get the better of the Zapotec in business dealings, not even on their own turf. Over the years, a strategy has evolved in which the Huave women calculate how much they need to raise the asking price in order to break even or, under optimum conditions, to make a small profit. The Zapotec women know that they cannot cheat outrageously very often or they will find themselves without a source of marketable produce. But it is also true that they would lose credibility and eventually business if they did not cheat. Role expectations dictate that the Zapotec and the Huave continue in their respective behaviors.

When confronted directly with evidence contrary to one's stereotyped view, one can override it by using another category—for example, "he is not a Black; he is a friend." As a last resort, one can fall back on "the exception that proves the rule."

Because stereotypes are developed and perpetuated in groups, it is difficult for an individual to escape them even if that is desirable. A person's inner impulses and overt actions may be restricted because the consensus of the group may not support them (Shibutani and Kwan 1965:93). This situation becomes particularly problematic in a period of rapid social change. Then consensus breaks down and so do prescriptions for action.

In the American South during the Civil War and the Reconstruction period patterns of behavior that had developed over centuries began to be challenged. If the abolitionists were correct, Blacks could no longer be regarded as childlike, happy-go-lucky, and requiring supervision. They were now to be treated as human beings, as adults capable of taking care of themselves. What place was there in a world in which the slaves were freed for the patriarchal Southern family based on the premise that Blacks were less-advanced members of the family who needed care and attention?

The violation of venerable codes of social interaction generated hostilities on both sides and only reinforced the old stereotypes. Every time a freed Black got into trouble or was incapable of taking care of himself, the response from whites was, "We told you they were like children; without our supervision they are incapable of advancement." In many cases, the reaction was like that of parents whose child had betrayed them. Now the child had to be taught a lesson. This attitude was intolerable to many of the emancipated slaves, as it undoubtedly had been during the years of bondage, and they reacted with hostility. Sometimes it took the form of acts of violence; sometimes it involved buying up land of former masters who could no longer pay their taxes. Other freedmen were bewildered by the rapidity of the change and the lack of preparation for it. There was no longer a stable, predictable pattern for any of the actors in the scene now being played out in the South.

Matters were made infinitely worse by the breakdown in the role of the Southern white male. The men returned from the war to find that their wives and female relatives had gained a certain independence from having had the management of plantations and businesses thrust upon them. They had clearly shown that they could manage on their own. Along with the loss of the slaves, many lost their plantations as well. Without all the elaborate patriarchal structure, they had no reason for being, at least none that they could have understood from their past experience. The rise of the Ku Klux Klan and the steady increase in the number of lynchings can be seen as a response to the breakdown of a world where everyone shared knowledge of the categories, stereotypes, and social rules — a world where each individual knew his or her place and did not challenge its appropriateness. In Klan activities men were, in fact, acting out the pre-war role for the Southern male; they were riding off to battle the forces of evil, and they were doing it for Southern womanhood. Southern women, they felt, had always needed protection from the sexual appetites of Black men, and the danger was even greater now that those men were free.

Just how unreal were these attempts to recreate antebellum Southern culture was memorably demonstrated by the women's response to the actions of their men. In 1930 the Association of Southern Women for the Prevention of Lynching was formed in Atlanta. Its members declared:

> Lynching is an indefensible crime. Women dare no longer allow themselves to be the cloak behind which those bent upon personal revenge and savagery commit acts of violence and lawlessness in the name of women. We repudiate this disgraceful claim for all time. [In Hall 1977:53]

If that statement were not clear enough, the Association went on record in 1934 with an indictment of white supremacy:

> The crime of lynching is a logical result in every community that pursues the policy of humiliation and degradation of a part of its citizenship because of accident of birth; that exploits and intimidates the weaker element . . . for economic gain; that refuses equal educational opportunity to one portion of its children; that segregates arbitrarily a whole race . . . and finally that denies a voice in the control of government to any fit and proper citizen because of race. [Ibid.:54]

Hall's analysis concludes that much of the rage of the white Southern male toward the Black man derived from the "Southern rape complex," which was based in turn on the stereotype of the Black man as a sexual agressor. In the antebellum South, the sexual threat was kept in check by the precarious balance of the patriarchal system and the consensus that characterized it. Since the Civil War there has been a slow and painful process of reworking categories and adjusting to new rules. Stereotypes have a remarkable tenacity, however. Some counties in Mississippi have responded to the sexual threat to white schoolgirls posed by mandatory desegregation by segregating their schools along sex lines. White girls are still kept separate from Black boys.

Freedom of Action and Stereotypes

All societies allow individuals more freedom of choice in some areas than in others. Western society usually allows great latitude in an individual's choice of friends, spouse, and occupation. Being able to act out of choice and natural inclination rather than in response to some external dictation implies that one's actions correspond rather closely to one's feelings. Normally one does not have friends whom one does not like or marry someone incompatible. Areas that are more closely restricted by conventions of the society, where one may not follow one's own inclinations, are sometimes areas of conflict for the individual. In these instances it is necessary to look at the way in which individuals comply, at the "style" of the action rather than at whether or not it is carried out at all (Shibutani and Kwan 1965:94). Desegregation, for example, may have forced interaction between Blacks and whites, but much of it is tense, ungraceful, and reluctant.

In Isthmus Zapotec society, marriage traditionally was arranged by families rather than by individuals. Preferred marriages were between families of the same social status that had other close ties as well. Marriages that linked Zapotec families without these similarities and connections were allowed, but no one was pleased by them. Worst of all were marriages between Zapotec and non-Zapotec. Not only was there no benefit to be gained by them but they were threatening to the integrity of Zapotec society—either the outsider spouse had to be admitted to the secrets of Zapotec society or the Zapotec spouse would be lost to that society. Whenever such a marriage loomed, all kinds of arguments, pleas, and threats were marshalled. The godparents of the erring Zapotec bride- or groom-to-be would be enlisted to talk sensibly to their charge. Unhappy parents would threaten to disinherit their child. If the couple remained stubborn in the face of all this, the marriage would be allowed but the celebration would be quite different from that of an intragroup wedding. The point was to demonstrate, in this threatening, antagonistic, and unhappy situation, the superiority of Zapotec custom to any and all outsiders present.

In 1972, a Zapotec man from Juchitán married a non-Zapotec woman from Oaxaca city. All the usual pre-wedding routines were fulfilled— negotiating between the families, sending out the invitational bread, and so forth—but the Zapotec also went through the old custom of having a speechmaker lecture to the bridal couple and others involved in the wedding about their respective obligations. That was done, as is required, in formal, flowery Zapotec. Few modern weddings within the Zapotec community still go through this ritual. The bride wore a Western-style wedding gown for the church ceremony, as do Zapotec brides, and then changed into the Zapotec festive costume for the celebration that followed. The women guests were requested to wear

Zapotec dress, and they all did, although such clothing is rarely worn to Zapotec weddings. The women frequently wear modern pants suits or cocktail dresses.

Music for the wedding was supplied by three different groups: The most traditional music was played by a flutist and a drummer (this music is not for dancing and is hardly ever heard at weddings now); the music for Zapotec dances (*sones*) was played by a small Zapotec band; and, finally, music for popular social dances was performed by a nineteen-piece orchestra then popular in the Isthmus region. Ordinary Zapotec weddings have only the small band, and it plays both *sones* and popular dance music. On this occasion, however, it was important to impress the outsiders with the antiquity of Zapotec tradition (flute and drum music) and with the affluence and modernity of the Zapotec themselves (the orchestra). Although the bride did not know the Zapotec dances, she was required to dance the *mediu xhiga*, which is done by the bridal couple at one point in the celebration. She was guided through the motions by several older Zapotec matrons.

Like the music, the food and drink provided at the party represented both the old Zapotec tradition and the well-to-do modern family— turtle eggs, *gueta bingui* (chopped shrimp coated in cornmeal), deep-fried hot peppers, and whole small crabs washed down with cold beer, on the one hand; and chicken and ham sandwiches, peanuts, and vegetable salad, accompanied by brandy and highballs, on the other.

Categories of Stereotypes

There are regularities in the way ethnic categories are evaluated even though each ethnic stereotype may be unique (Shibutani and Kwan 1965:95). These regularities depend on the relative position of the stereotyped groups in a system of stratification. A limited number of relationships exist: groups may be stratified; they may be in opposition; or they may be cooperative.

Perhaps the commonest kind of relationship is that characterized by stratification, where one group is perceived as dominant and the other subordinate. As long as the latter does not pose a threat, it is characterized by such adjectives as "childlike," "happy-go-lucky," "irrational," and "emotional"—words that describe benign inferiors who need to be guided through life. Groups in subordinate positions are often given favorable attributes, including friendliness, physical strength and endurance, courage, and virility. These traits are also associated with animals that human beings value. People perceived as inferiors who are structurally subordinate frequently are assumed to be closer to animals than to human beings. Therefore they have all the animal-like qualities but lack those that characterize the higher orders, such as rationality, abstract reasoning, and logic.

What happens in dominant-subordinate relationships when the participants begin to interact in other than stereotypic ways is well illustrated in *Prospero and Caliban*, a classic study of the psychology of colonialism (Mannoni 1956). The author argues that the colonial is perfectly happy as long as he is able to project his fantasies on the world around him. When he is forced to realize that the subordinates he has imagined as creatures of his subconscious are real beings with claims to freedom and human dignity, he is outraged and indignant.

> What is resented in Caliban is not really his physical appearance, his bestiality, his "evil" instincts—for after all it is a matter of pride to keep half-tamed apes or other wild animals in one's household—but that he should claim to be a person in his own right and from time to time show that he has a will of his own. [1956:117]

Women and Blacks in the antebellum South occupied the same functional category and were described with just such adjectives as appear above—"emotional," "childlike," "irrational." Countless novels contain a scene in which the master of the plantation is about to leave on a long trip or has to sell his slaves because of some misfortune. At one moment, the slaves are weeping at being separated from their beloved master, and at the next are laughing and singing because somebody has begun to play the banjo. Just like children! Women were denied access to many subjects in school because it was thought that they could not think abstractly or rationally, and to attempt to teach them would simply destroy all their lovely qualities of sentimentality, emotionalism, and moral purity.

These attitudes apply only to inferiors who are regarded as harmless. When they are perceived as dangerous the adjectives are very different. Now those same people are "cunning," "treacherous," and "deceitful." Diaries and letters written by Southern women in the days of slavery reveal the relationship that all too frequently existed between white and

Black women. For the white man, the Black woman was a source of sexual gratification—she was "warm," "childishly affectionate," and "sexually exciting." For the white woman, the Black woman was a threat: she came between the mistress and her husband; the Black woman's children were a constant reminder of an illicit union and made a mockery of marriage and family; and the mistress's own children were wooed away by the Black woman in her role as Mammy. So in the white woman's words, the Black woman was a "slave to her sexual appetites," "deceitful," and "treacherous."[4]

Similar characterizations occur in the stratified situation among some Australian aborigines (Tonkinson 1974). The Jigalong Mob aborigines live on a mission station where they must interact with Christian missionaries. The latter apply such descriptions as "childlike," "being in the childhood of humanity," "lost in darkness," "happy-go-lucky," and "lazy" to their charges. When the aborigines refuse to be converted, they are said to be "too ignorant to understand the message of God" or "incapable of reasoning like human beings."

The relationship with the missionaries is interesting when viewed from perspective of the aborigines. The first whites with whom they came into contact were the cattle station owners. The aborigines evidently thought of the white cattlemen as regular guys, who were honest, hard-drinking, hard-working men with healthy sexual appetites. Whatever their faults, hypocrisy was not among them. They were called "white fellas" by the aborigines and were perceived as intelligent, benevolent, and tolerant. Then came the Christian missionaries. At first, the aborigines tried to interact according to the rules generated from their stereotypes of the white fella. When they failed spectacularly, they were understandably puzzled. These white men, after all, were just like the others. What contradicted their stereotypes was the fact that these new white fellas, soon known as "white fella Christian," said that drinking was bad, sex that was not sanctified by marriage was bad, and there was only one God, who would see that you went straight to Hell if you did not believe in him. Because the cattle station owners had established a live-and-let-live relationship with the aborigines, a

---

4. Some relationships between white and Black women were warm and loving, and many endured until death. But the structure of the social situation itself militated against affection and trust.

traumatic conflict of cultures had been avoided, but that was no longer the case. The aborigines, whose income depended on the existence of the mission, soon learned to accommodate to the new regime even though they did not like it. A major cause of their unhappiness was that the white fella Christians preached morality, good behavior, and Christian charity but did not practice it. They were hypocritical, and the aborigines remained unconvinced and unconverted.

As Shibutani and Kwan note, in stratified situations in which the dominant group is perceived as having basically good intentions, it is characterized as benevolent, tolerant, intelligent, honest, and self-controlled. That is how the aborigines viewed the cattlemen. When the dominant group seems to be out only for its own good, these characteristics do not apply. Such was the case with the aboriginal perception of the white fella Christians, who were asking the aborigines to adopt values and behavior that they themselves belied.

The second kind of relationship may occur when groups are perceived as being in opposition. While usually there is an uneven distribution of power, the underdog is somehow able to mount an opposition, even if it is only a moral one. These situations are frustrating for both sides, as the two groups compete for the same resources (Shibutani and Kwan 1975:100). Objects or individuals that are regarded as frustrating are described as "hypocritical," "unjust," "ruthless," "selfish," "cold," "cruel," "arrogant," "exploiting," "deceitful" (ibid.:101). Subordinate groups that are upwardly mobile usually characterize the dominant group in terms such as these. It is one way of rationalizing the way of the world; after all, it is only by being hypocritical, selfish,and ruthless that the top group manages to keep all the resources for itself. If the sense of frustration heightens to the point where either group is regarded as dangerous—that is, if the dominant group sees the subordinate group resorting to force to gain a share of the resources, or the subordinate group sees the top group about to take away some of its meager resources or use force to prevent it from acquiring what rightly belongs to it—the adjectives will change so as to allow the groups to justify their own violent or ungenerous impulses. The enemy becomes "aggressive," "cunning," "treacherous," "brutal," "clannish," and "corrupt." Any action is justified if you are dealing with such people, and mere passive resistance will not work in the face of aggressive cunning.

The third type of relationship is one of cooperation, with groups coexisting peacefully and sharing resources sometimes in a symbiotic manner. Because of the mutual advantage of cooperation, the parties involved wish to promote this kind of relationship. They believe in the worthiness of their partners, viewing them as "trustworthy," "hard-working," "benevolent," "friendly," "strong," and "intelligent." One tries to ignore one's partners' faults and seek out their virtues. The symbiotic relationship between the Tungus and the Cossacks in north-west Manchuria engenders precisely this kind of behavior. The Tungus criticize the Cossacks for the theft that occurs among them, thievery being unknown among the Tungus. The Cossacks recognize the difference and praise the honesty of the Tungus. On the other hand, the Cossacks, whose violence tends to be premeditated, criticize the Tungus for their random violence when drunk. The Tungus agree and say that this weakness on their part is deplorable (ibid.:88).

If the evaluation of ethnic groups depends on or is affected by their relative positions in a stratified system, one would predict that as their positions change so would the adjectives applied to them. For example, have American Blacks progressed from being childlike and happy-go-lucky to being dangerous, aggressive, and clannish? Or what kind of metamorphosis did the Japanese-Americans of the Pacific coast undergo during World War II, when they became potential enemies? And what about the transformation afterward?

In situations of competition or conflict, stereotypes are frequently employed to make the task of dealing with one's competitors somewhat easier. They allow people to live with their consciences.

Pervasiveness of Ethnic Stereotypes

In order for interaction to occur at all in multi-ethnic settings, there must be shared understandings and common conventions. This necessity gives rise to ethnic stereotypes, which are generalizations about the different groups they describe and which indicate appropriate attitudes and actions toward those groups. We "see" situations and individuals in terms of our predetermined and often inflexible definitions of them. Anything not contained in our definition we generally do not "see."

It is important in ethnically heterogeneous societies that members of each ethnic group realize that they are perceived in terms of certain stereotypes; that they view themselves in terms of stereotypes; that they perceive other groups along stereotypic lines; and that they understand the content of these different sets of stereotypes. The task is not as monumental as it might appear. We grow up learning the contents of stereotypes and how to fit others and ourselves into stereotyped categories. We initially put new groups appearing on the scene into the best-fitting category with which we are familiar. Gradually we learn to make finer distinctions, and a separate category may evolve. It is more difficult to appreciate the pervasiveness of stereotypes. Most individuals realize that they are perceived in terms of stereotypes and that they use stereotypes to aid them in categorizing others. Less obvious is the fact that we all have stereotypes of ourselves that affect our interactions. That we tend to view others from our own cultural vantage point means that the better we understand that perspective the better foundation we will have for understanding our perceptions or misperceptions of others.

Style

Cohen offers a cogent foundation for the development of style in his book on the strategies of Hausa traders in Yoruba towns. Retribalization

> is a process by which a group from one ethnic category, whose members are involved in a struggle for power and privilege with the members of a group from another ethnic category, within the framework of a formal political system, manipulate some customs, values, myths, symbols, and ceremonies from their cultural tradition in order to articulate an *informal* political organization which is used as a weapon in that struggle. [1969:2]

Cohen makes three important points. (1) He sees the process of retribalization as the result of increasing interaction between groups, a point of view that has gradually replaced older theories of isolation as a necessary factor in the retention of tradition. (2) Retribalization is a dynamic process not a retreat to conservatism. The fact that styles constantly change precludes thinking of them as conservative. (3) Groups are well aware of the value of traditional styles as weapons in the struggle for control over political and other resources.

The Zapotec of Juchitán

Cohen's three points are amply illustrated in Juchitán, where Zapotec style is a dynamic, constantly changing complex that does not preclude the use of other styles in some circumstances and that is consciously used as a way of obtaining and maintaining power and prestige.

Juchitán, with a population of 37,686, is the second-largest municipality in the state of Oaxaca. The sprawling city is connected to the rest of the nation by two major highways, the Carretera Panamericana and the Carretera Transistmica, and one railroad, the Ferrocarril Panamericano. It was founded in the fifteenth century as a colony of Tehuantepec, the capital of the pre-Conquest Zapotec kingdom in the Isthmus of Tehuantepec. Juchitán began as a Zapotec village and remains consciously Zapotec to this day. Eighty percent of the city's populace are Zapotec; the other 20% —the "others"—include Mexicans, Italians, Japanese, Lebanese, Spaniards, North Americans, and a few representatives of other Isthmus Indian groups. What the 20% have in common is a sense of allegiance to the Mexican nation rather than to the city of Juchitán. The lack of commitment to Juchitán is one of the primary features that sets them apart from the Zapotec.

Juchitán is not alone in its Indian-Mexican, local-national dichotomies. These oppositions exist in a number of other smaller and similar-sized cities in Mexico, but what makes Juchitán unique is its celebration of an Indian identity and its ability to impose that definition on the rest of the inhabitants. Zapotec control of Juchitán is not just a moral triumph; the Zapotec control the city socially, economically, and politically. Three factors have enabled the Zapotec to maintain their position of dominance: rivalry or a sense of opposition; local autonomy; and early prosperity.

Rivalry or Opposition

The Zapotec of Juchitán were never isolated from other groups. Before the Spanish Conquest, the Zapotec and the Mixtec fought each other on some occasions and allied to fight the powerful Aztec on others. They also had contact with other Indian groups such as the Mixe, Zoque, Chontal, and Huave in the southern Isthmus area. After Conquest, the Zapotec continued their traditional rivalries. The earliest recorded instance of Zapotec nationalism dates from 1533. In that year a criminal complaint was lodged by three Mexican Indians who charged that the Zapotec governor had had them flogged because they were Mexican and not Zapotec (Códices Indígenas del Estado de Oaxaca, cited in Covarrubias 1946:204).

As the colonial period progressed, rivalry began to develop between the Zapotec of Juchitán and the Zapotec of Tehuantepec. Rivalries between Latin American cities are frequent, especially when they are close neighbors and compete for the same resources. In the case of Juchitán and Tehuantepec, which are only 17 kilometers apart, fuel was added to the rivalry by the perceptions each city held of the other. As far as Juchitán was concerned, Tehuantepec had no local pride, allying itself with whatever group happened to be in power. It had sold its Zapotec heritage for political favors. Tehuantepec, for its part, viewed Juchitán as an ignorant country backwater whose inhabitants clung to their old ways and were hostile to progress.

After independence from Spain and during the time that the Isthmus had the status of a territory, a subprefecture was established in Juchitán. It prompted a population growth that provoked the jealousy of Tehuantepec. Since Juchitán was part of the district of Tehuantepec, the latter city could and did exercise its authority in such a way as to maintain its own prominent position and so roused the ire of Juchitán. The constant quarreling between the two cities often erupted into armed conflict. From the 1830s to the 1850s, Melendez, the political boss of Juchitán, made periodic raids against Tehuantepec. At one point he succeeded in holding the entire city captive for a year, during which time he extorted many "loans." Tehuantepec had its chieftains, too, and hostilities were reciprocated. The constant state of turmoil in the Isthmus wasted the time and energy of the state government, whose armies would come back to Oaxaca City after resolving a quarrel only to have to turn around and return to the two bickering cities. In May 1857, under Governor Benito Juarez, the state issued a decree designed to end the fighting. Juchitán was elevated to the status of *villa* (a political division that enjoys independent government at the local level) and was thus removed from the political control of its rival.

However, the uneasy peace was broken again, less than ten years later. A regiment of soldiers from Tehuantepec betrayed their fellow Istmeños and their country by joining forces with the French army in the Isthmus during the short reign of Maximilian and Carlotta. On September 4, 1866 they attacked Juchitán, which had been actively anti-French, and routed its inhabitants. But they had judged the Juchitecos poorly, for, on the following day, a coalition of Juchitecos and Blaseños (residents of San Blas Atempa) defeated the entire French army, regiment of traitors included, and rid themselves of both the foreign and the local oppressors at once.

Although the French left Mexico shortly thereafter, Tehuantepec remained a source of antagonism. When Porfirio Diaz was a young rebel trying to battle the forces of corruption at the national level, he had the strong support of Juchitán, while Tehuantepec worked actively against him. But when Diaz was well into his thirty-year dictatorship, Tehuantepec would give lavish celebrations in his honor when he visited that city. The festivities catered to the foreign, particularly French, tastes of the dictator. As soon as Diaz stopped fighting corruption and became corrupt himself, Juchitán turned against him.

Such differences in political attitudes between the two cities generated physical violence well into the twentieth century. Efrain Gomez Pineda continued the tradition established by Melendez when he attacked the city of Tehuantepec early in the century with a force of 200 men; and many purely local rivalries were carried out in the confusion of the years of the Revolution.

There are no longer pitched battles between the two cities but the rivalry continues in political and economic spheres. Tehuantepec, associated with centralism and authoritarianism, is more often rewarded with political appointments, hospitals, and schools in return for its cooperation with state and national governments and with PRI (Partido Revolucionario Institucional), the political party in an essentially one-party system. Juchitán is a thorn in the side of state and national politicians and an embarrassment to PRI. The Juchitecos have consistently ignored higher authorities when they felt that their interests were being subverted, and in the municipal elections of 1968, 1971, and 1980, they refused to support the PRI candidate.

An episode that occurred in June 1974 illustrates the view of the two cities held by those in power. Tehuantepec invited Señora Echeverria, the wife of the president of Mexico, to be the sponsor of the annual Vela Sandunga. She accepted, but she also accepted an invitation from Juchitán to visit that city. She arrived in the Isthmus wearing the Tehuantepec version of the festive dress and spent 15 minutes in Juchitán, where she declined an invitation to visit the restoration of the church, refused the food that had been prepared for her visit, and turned down the plans for a children's park proposed by a local engineer. Leaving Juchitán smarting under the insult of her whirlwind visit, she went by motorcade to Tehuantepec, where she spent three days and became an honorary Tehuana.

Local autonomy

Local autonomy, the second factor in the development and persistence of Zapotec style in Juchitán, is the only one of the three not shared with Tehuantepec. Were it not for the fact that Tehuantepec does not enjoy local autonomy, Juchitán's freedom could be explained by the tenuous political control higher authorities exercise over the Isthmus in general. As it is, one must consider the early political development in the southern Isthmus and the manner in which it affected the two largest cities in that area.

Tehuantepec has always been the "big city" of the Isthmus. It was the residence of the Zapotec king before Conquest and had the only sizeable population in the Isthmus. At the end of the fifteenth century, Juchitán was only a small Zapotec settlement to the northeast of Tehuantepec. It had been granted the status of colony by the Zapotec king. During the colonial period, Tehuantepec remained the political seat of the Isthmus because the Spanish had a policy of disturbing local organization as little as possible. Juchitán continued to be an unimportant hamlet and consequently enjoyed considerable local freedom. It had no Spanish officials or troops and few visitors. Order at the local level was maintained by a series of strong men and political leaders (*caciques*).

Tehuantepec not only had the full panoply of Spanish secular authorities but also the burden of supporting the Church after the city became the seat of the Bishop of Tehuantepec. Even after Juchitán had outstripped Tehuantepec in population, Tehuantepec remained psychologically the "big city." Its status was confirmed when the transisthmian railroad made a detour around Juchitán but ran right in front of the homes of Tehuantepec's most-prominent citizens.

Being the hub of political and ecclesiastical authority for the Isthmus has brought many benefits to Tehuantepec, but it has also made it impossible for the city to maintain or develop any sense of local identity that is not a reflection of state and national identities. Juchitán has had to wait longer and fight harder for benefits and improvements, but its aggressive nationalism has thrived under conditions of relative local autonomy.

Early prosperity

Early prosperity means wealth that is available before a local culture is absorbed by the dominant or national culture. It is wealth that is sufficient to fashion a style that can compete successfully with that of other groups. This kind of prosperity characterized the Isthmus Zapotec. Their wealth stemmed from land and the capital built up from land ownership.

Since the Zapotec came into the Isthmus from the Valley of Oaxaca, they have made their living from the land and the nearby lagoons. The majority of the Zapotec men have always been farmers and to a lesser extent fishermen. The environment is one in which it is possible to produce a surplus, whether it be of maize from the two harvests a year, from the catch of fish and shrimp, or from the planting and harvesting of tropical fruits so desirable to people in the colder, highland regions. The Zapotec women, traditionally and as an extension of their domestic duties, have processed and sold the surpluses. The cash from the sales was quickly converted to gold, which could be used as capital in other ventures.

The Zapotec had good reason to accumulate a cushion of capital. The climate on the southern coastal plains is capricious. Although it is suitable for growing two crops per year and cultivating lush orchards of tropical fruit, too often there are years of drought followed by years of floods. Thus it is imperative to have enough savings to survive the bad times.

Good years generally outnumbered bad, and individual Zapotec families gradually increased their capital to the point where they felt secure enough to begin investing it. Land and livestock were early purchases. Income property and businesses came later, after the building of the transisthmian railroad in the mid-nineteenth century. The building of the railroad had brought in hundreds of laborers, engineers, and speculators and with them new opportunities for money making. The influx meant that the hitherto mostly farming towns now had to provide hardware stores, hotels, grocery stores, restaurants, and banks. Although the migrant speculators were sharp competitors, the Zapotec women boldly seized opportunities to open businesses or to buy up valuable property. For them to do so was only natural — selling, acquisition of capital, and investment were all part of the woman's role in the domestic economic unit. There was never any thought that the man should abandon his fields and lagoons for a life of business. Land was the stable force, both mystically and practically. Owning and working land made one respectable. When businesses failed, when two trains a day instead of 20 rolled across the Isthmus, the land was still there.

Capital allowed the Zapotec to compete successfully with outsiders in the new business opportunities that suddenly became available in the mid-nineteenth century. Local Zapotec households could compete with the wealthiest of the outsiders who came to the city then, just as they are able to do now. Further, Zapotec women have never been conservative economically although they certainly demonstrate a shrewd business sense. They have always been willing to consider new ventures, and the Zapotec economy has benefited from their enterprising nature. In contrast, one might point to the numerous Indian groups in Mexico who, lacking capital or an active marketing tradition, remained subsistence farmers while outsiders took over control of businesses and income property. The final degradation for these groups often came when they were deprived of their miserable plots of land and forced to work as wage laborers for outsiders on that same land. As it stood, the coming of the railroad to the Isthmus found the Juchitán Zapotec ready. The railroad brought money and opportunity; it made the fortunes of some families and it solidified the fortunes of other, already established families.

Although Juchitán had been a Zapotec city from its founding in 1486, the elaboration of Zapotec style as we know it today began in the last half of the nineteenth century. It was only at this point that there was sufficient surplus and cash to develop the truly awe-inspiring array of symbols of Zapotec identity. Barth's (1969) contention that people will only continue an identity that can compete with other identities is appropriate to the Zapotec case. Put very simply, it costs as much to be an upper-class Zapotec as it does to be an upper-class Mexican, and the symbols, while different, are equally impressive. A Zapotec matron on her way to a fiesta presents a magnificent sight. Her costume of heavy velvet will be covered with myriads of embroidered flowers and trimmed with yards of Swiss lace, and her arms, fingers, ears, and neck will be adorned with thousands of dollars worth of gold jewelry.

Elaboration of Zapotec Style

The elaboration of the Zapotec style complex seems to have begun toward the latter half of the nineteenth century, and it reached a peak of development during the Porfirian period (1876–1910). At this point, all three factors essential for the elaboration and persistence of Zapotec cultural identity were operating in Juchitán. The rivalry with Tehuantepec, although present since the Conquest, had intensified because of Tehuantepec's support of the French and Juchitán's rapidly growing population, which made Tehuantepec uneasy. Juchitán's local autonomy was greater than ever because of the severing of the ties that had bound it to Tehuantepec. At the same time, Juchitán avoided coming under the control of the state or the nation. Finally, the Juchitecos, for the first time, had the means with which to create a Zapotec style that could not be overlooked or easily equaled.

The following account, although of a *vela* in Tehuantepec, illustrates both the opulence of the Zapotec style and the foreign elements that went into its creation:

> To entertain Porfirio [Diaz] on his visits to his beloved Tehuantepec in the manner to which he was accustomed, she [Dona Juana C. Romero] built a "chalet," the only European, two-storied dwelling in town to this day. Great balls were given in his honor, and Diaz seldom missed the yearly *vela bini* [vela of the people] given by Dona Juana in a specially built "ballroom," an enclosure of white and gold wooden columns, roofed by a great canvas canopy and hung with crystal chandeliers. It was compulsory to dress for the *vela bini* —the women in the ceremonial Tehuantepec costume of lace, spangles and fringe of gold which Porfirio preferred; the men in black serge suits and stiff collars despite the unbearable heat. . . . Dona Juana gave out little carnets with pencils attached for the guests to write beforehand the partners with whom they would dance lancers, polkas and waltzes. A great supper was served, with rows of roast turkeys, platters of cold cuts and rivers of imported wine. [Covarrubias 1946:233–34]

We have no comparable description for *velas* in Juchitán at this period. Statements of older informants indicate, however, that in many cases Juchitán *velas* emphasized Zapotec elements rather than the foreign fashion so popular in Mexico during the Porfirian period. In Juchitán, hostesses served Zapotec foods such as turtle eggs, seafood delicacies, and sweets rather than turkey and cold cuts; and Zapotec *sones* alternated with waltzes and mazurkas.

Zapotec style in Juchitán has changed since the Porfirian period, with new elements added and old ones abandoned. At the same time, it has maintained an internal consistency and a correspondence to basic Zapotec values. *Velas* are still held under enormous canvas tents, but the chandeliers have been replaced by hundreds of electric light bulbs hung on wires. The miles of metallic paper cut into lacy designs that run around the perimeter of the enclosed area and wind around the columns are reflected in huge pier glasses set at intervals around the floor. The women still wear Zapotec dress, although the floral patterns seem to have become larger and more brightly colored; and, although stiff collars have disappeared, many men are still pressured into wearing suits and ties. The lancers, mazurkas, and waltzes have been replaced by their modern equivalents, but traditional *sones*, which have changed little, still open the *vela* early in the evening, mark the change of *mayordomos* (ritual sponsors), and bring the *vela* to a close early the following morning.

Juchitecos have steadfastly refused to charge admission to their *velas*—all may come, and do, but only invited guests are assured of a chair. The sponsoring cooperative society absorbs the costs. In Tehuantepec, the *velas*, now very few in number, sell tickets to defray expenses. *Velas* are perhaps the most-concentrated expression of Zapotec style, and, in Juchitán, unlike all other Isthmus cities, the number of *velas* remains constant—new *velas* are continually being created as some of the old ones die.

Elements of Zapotec Style

Two styles exist side by side in Juchitán—Zapotec and Mexican. These contrasting ways of life are not simply collections of symbols and values chosen at random, nor does Zapotec style represent a conservative traditionalism. Both styles are coherent complexes of symbols and values that have developed over a long period of time. Neither are the two styles mutually exclusive. The Zapotec experience no feelings of cultural inconsistency when they adopt elements of Mexican national culture.[5] More or less "pure" displays of style are ordered and manipu-

---

5. The reverse is not relevant since followers of Mexican national style never display any elements of Zapotec style.

lated in terms of sets of different kinds of social relations and situations. This is probably true of most active local styles confronted by the national style.

Some overt features of Zapotec style, such as the man's narrow-brimmed, high-peaked felt hat, decorated with heavy silver braid, and the white cotton pants and shirt, are almost never seen in Juchitán now, while others, like the *zuquii* (oven made from a large pottery jar in a matrix of mud) and the hammock, are a part of daily life. Most features are not purely Zapotec, but, rather, demonstrate some degree of syncretism—Zapotec has many Spanish loan words; the women's festive dress imitates French ball gowns of the nineteenth century; the *sones* closely resemble the waltzes of the last century; the fiesta system utilizes elements from many sources—but, as a complex buttressed by values, they effectively mark off what is Zapotec from what is not (Royce 1975).[6]

The symbols of what is considered to be Zapotec are constantly being revised as Juchitecos move with the times. Dishes and bowls are still thrown to one's friends during the parades associated with *velas*, but now they are made of plastic instead of the pottery of ten years ago. The white flounce on the regional costume is rarely made of Swiss lace, which is almost unavailable now; one sees instead permanent-pleated Dacron ruffles. The content of Zapotec style has changed gradually over the years, but the purpose to which it is put remains constant. It is manipulated by members of the Zapotec middle and upper classes and, in certain instances, by the Zapotec lower class in order to retain economic and political power within Juchitán in the face of opposition from outsiders.

The greatest contrast between Mexican and Zapotec styles is in the area of basic values. Both the Zapotec and the Mexicans value money and work hard to acquire it, but the similarity ends there. For the Mexicans, money means increased educational opportunities, which, in turn, mean higher status and a larger income. It also makes possible a

---

6. Other overt features of Zapotec style are the long, full skirt and *huipil* (blouse), for everyday and festive wear; the *bidaani quichi'* (starched white lace headdress); gold coin jewelry; facility in and the ability to compose poetry and songs in the Zapotec language; woven and dyed palm artifacts; *xiga gueta* (painted and lacquered gourds); the observance of local holidays; the *velas*; the use of frangipani and jasmine blossoms in ritual observances; and such special foods as iguana, armadillo, turtle eggs, seafood delicacies, and *bupu* (a festive drink consisting of a thin corn gruel flavored with chocolate and topped by a foam of beaten chocolate and frangipani blossoms).

higher standard of living; the acquisition of expensive consumer goods such as modern appliances, television sets, stereos, and cars; travel; and expanded opportunities for one's children.

In contrast, very few of the local Zapotec spend money on expensive consumer items; even fewer build modern homes or buy cars. Most travel is done out of necessity rather than for pleasure. Expensive elaboration of certain elements, particularly dress, *velas*, and intellectual activities, and selective incorporation of elements from non-Indian traditions give the Zapotec middle and upper classes full rein to express their personal wealth and success. Simply put, the Isthmus Zapotec style can be manifested in just as extravagant and costly a fashion as the Mexican national style.

Maintaining Zapotec style does not imply that one must sacrifice the desirable aspects of Mexican style. Zapotec middle- and upper-class children are educated in the finest universities in Mexico, and their national-level education enables them to write poetry in Zapotec and theses on the history of the Zapotec race. The Mexican custom of celebrating a girl's fifteenth birthday in a grand manner to introduce her to society has become a legitimate way for the Zapotec to increase their social prestige. The Mexican institution of the Christmas *posada* (re-enactment of asking for lodging), transformed in many ways, is now incorporated into the Zapotec cycle of fiestas.

Among the Zapotec, money is used primarily for entertaining one's friends and kin, for expanding one's network of friends and fictive kin, and for maintaining one's social obligations. Charity is extended willingly to friends and kin who are in need but not to strangers. The saddest figure in the Zapotec world is the person who has no living relatives and who has lost all his friends because he has failed to maintain his social obligations. Money is not a crucial factor in fulfilling obligations to friends, however, as the following story illustrates.

Don Silahyn was an old man who had no living relatives in Juchitán. His daughter-in-law, who lived across the Isthmus, sent him small amounts of money at irregular intervals but, by and large, he was taken care of by friends. He fulfilled his obligations to them by daily visits and sometimes by giving them little gifts he fashioned out of scraps of colored paper and other odds and ends. He also managed to contribute small sums of money to the *velas* of his closest friends. In return, he was sent gifts of food, was invited to the *velas*, and was looked in on from time to time to be sure that he was not ill.

Don Silahyn died in the summer of 1974 after many days of battling a respiratory infection. Throughout his illness there was always someone to sit with him no matter what hour of day or night. Friends or neighbors bought food and medicine for him and paid the doctor. The same people made the funeral arrangements and notified his daughter-in-law. His funeral was modest but respectable. Don Silahyn was dressed in clean, new clothes and laid in a coffin that sat in the big room of his house. The coffin was surrounded by candles and white flowers, and a constant stream of women dressed in mourning came to sit with the body.

As the hour for the burial approached, more women arrived to sit in the room with the coffin, and men now began arriving too. Instead of sitting in the inner courtyard, as is customary, the men carried chairs out to the sidewalk and sat in the street in front of the house. That was a way of showing Juchitán that Don Silahyn did not die friendless. About 40 people accompanied the hearse on its slow procession through the dusty streets to the cemetery and waited there while the coffin was lowered, the men taking turns lifting shovelfuls of dirt onto the grave. There followed the customary nine days of mourning, with at least a few women appearing every afternoon for the prayers and staying through the night. Don Silahyn's daughter-in-law arrived during the mourning period, but his friends and neighbors already had everything in hand. And since 1974, they have been visiting his grave and bringing little gifts of flowers.

Contrast of Zapotec and Mexican Styles

Two celebrations in Juchitán epitomize Zapotec and Mexican styles. The Vela Cinco de Septiembre dramatizes Zapotec identity, while La Noche Mexicana fulfils the same function for the Mexican. The Vela Cinco commemorates the defeat of the French army and its regiment of Tehuano traitors. Unlike most *velas* (all-night dances with associated features such as parades, daytime parties, and masses), which are sponsored by private individuals and societies, the municipal government gives the Vela Cinco and refers to it as being *de carácter cívico heroico* ("of civic, heroic nature") (Lopez Chinas 1969:83).

Celebrations associated with the Vela Cinco begin on September 1 and include bicycle races (appropriately named "Heroes Juchitecos"), boxing matches, baseball games, and evening concerts. On the morning of September 5, large crowds gather at the monument to the heroes of the battle and overflow into the streets and front yards. The municipal government awards trophies to the winners of the various sports events, bands play traditional Zapotec music, and local intellectuals and students recite Zapotec poetry and give speeches recounting the history of the famous battle. Sometimes these speeches take a conciliatory line, urging harmony between Juchitecos and Tehuanos, but, at the same time, they faithfully document the infamous betrayal of Mexico by the Tehuano Remigio Toledo. When the morning's entertainment is over, the crowd departs, its faith renewed in the truth of the old saying *Tehuano traidor* ("Tehuantepec traitor").

In the evening, a dance is held in the main street between avenues Efrain R. Gomez and Hidalgo. The women are expected to wear the local variant of the regional costume, and, indeed, only a few come in Western dress. Those who are not dressed in Zapotec fashion must sit in the back rows of the chairs surrounding the dance area. The women and young girls in the front rows present an unbroken line of brilliantly colored *enaguas* (long, full, gathered skirts) with freshly laundered *olanes* (traditional starched flounces of white Swiss lace). Heavy gold jewelry reflects the light of the mercury street lamps, and rainbow-hued hibiscus adorn the dark heads of the younger girls. From 8 P.M. until past midnight, several bands alternate between playing *sones* (Zapotec dance music consisting of alternate fast and slow sections) and *piezas* (Mexican popular dance music). As is customary, only women wearing *enaguas* perform the *sones*, but dress does not determine who will dance the *piezas*. Shyness and lack of expertise prevent many lower-class girls from dancing the *sones* even though they may be properly attired (Royce 1974). People begin to drift homeward in the early morning hours, having celebrated the most-important local holiday and reaffirmed the superiority of Juchiteco custom.

La Noche Mexicana celebrates Mexico's declaration of independence from Spain, which occurred on September 15, 1810. On the night of the 15th, the *grito* (cry of independence) of Father Hidalgo is reenacted, and an enormous *castillo* (arrangement of fireworks on a bamboo frame) is burned in front of the municipal palace. Parallel celebrations take place throughout Mexico on this night and on the following day. Just as September 5 is the most-important date in Juchiteco history, so is September 16 for the Mexican nation.

The party, which begins at 8 P.M. on the evening of the 16th, is held at the Casino Juchiteco, a modern, one-story building with a large inner patio. The capacity of the Casino is much less than that of the Vela Cinco enclosure. Also, unlike the Vela Cinco, which all social classes attend, the Noche Mexicana is attended almost exclusively by members of the middle and upper classes. The sponsors urge people to come in "typical Mexican costumes," and the most-frequent costumes are the china poblana for women and the charro for men (both of these costumes epitomize Mexicans within Mexico as well as in other countries). Although other Mexican Indian dress is worn, one never sees the Isthmus Zapotec represented. Most of the women who attend wear some form of contemporary evening dress—miniskirted afternoon dresses, elaborate pants suits, or floor-length dresses. Western style music is played by one of the bigger local bands, and, recently, rock and roll groups have been hired to alternate with the local band. The party begins to break up about 1 or 2 A.M.

Effectiveness of Zapotec Style as a Strategy

The most effective strategy the Zapotec have developed in order to maintain economic, political, and social control of the city of Juchitán involves wielding Zapotec style. In any threat from without, the outsiders are frozen out because they are not Zapotec. That can only be effective if the Zapotec have a united front backed by material resources and the outsiders are unable to mount a unified opposition. This, in fact, is the case in Juchitán.

The inability of the outside group to mobilize as a unit stems from the following structural properties: they are divided into a number of ethnic categories; they have come from many different states within Mexico and therefore have different regional outlooks and loyalties; classes are endogamous so that there is no kinship linkage between them; the outside upper class seldom marries into other upper-class families, preferring to look for spouses outside the city itself, usually from the home state or region. All these factors mean that the outsiders cannot generate an effective opposition. Even the emphasis placed by all of them on Mexican national values is not strong enough to override the divisions.

While adherents of the two styles typically interact in terms of stereotypes of each other because of imcomplete knowledge and under-standing, the social system itself has a built-in flexibility. The upwardly mobile Zapotec have the option of utilizing both styles as a way of maximizing their opportunities for advancement in the social hierarchy. This combining of styles both neutralizes potentially disruptive ele-ments and introduces aspects of Mexican national culture in a gradual and nonthreatening manner. By remaining in Juchitán rather than leav-ing and by incorporating both styles, these upwardly mobile Zapotec serve as models. Those who are unsuccessful serve as object lessons for those Zapotec who would think of abandoning Zapotec style. The suc-cessful ones have two effects: they are imitated by other ambitious Zapotec who might otherwise seek their fortunes outside Juchitán, and they are conduits of Mexican national style into Zapotec society, which can then adopt and modify those elements that are desirable. In this way, the Zapotec of Juchitán partake of the national culture, but at the same time they can stand apart and derive prestige and satisfaction from their own unique Zapotec style.

The differences and conflicts within the Zapotec group are always ignored when the group feels threatened from the outside. The desire to act as a unified group is not enough; there must also be the means. These the Zapotec have. Although upper-class and upper middle-class Zapotec families are the most-important promoters of Zapotec identity and power, they rely on extensive networks among the middle and lower classes for support. The Zapotec "family" taken in the broadest sense may be composed of 100 or more members, who represent all social classes. The wealthier members provide the social and political leadership, holding political offices and positions within social clubs. They use their offices to take care of the less-fortunate family members, finding them patronage jobs and feasting them at fiestas. The social network is extended beyond family boundaries by means of fictive kin-ship and friendship, which also cut across class lines. The Zapotec who reside outside Juchitán actively maintain their ties with the city, thereby making it possible to mobilize their loyalties. Underlying these connec-tions is a sense of a common territory and a common past. Since its founding, Juchitán has been a city on the same land. It has never fallen into outside hands, unlike the land held by most Indian groups. The Zapotec share the many battles fought throughout their history in de-fense of the land and the integrity of Juchitán.

Conclusion

How is it, one might ask, that the Zapotec of Juchitán have chosen to use their Zapotec identity as a weapon of opposition? Why did they not follow the general pattern for Indians of Mexico and adopt national style?

Part of the answer is that Zapotec style can compete successfully with Mexican national style within the local community. Because it is Indian in its associations and has ties with traditional forms and kin relations, any lower-class Zapotec can identify with it.

Initially, outside opposition came from Tehuantepec or Oaxaca City or the nation. Then, as the Isthmus became more prosperous, outsiders began to settle in Juchitán itself, and the threat came closer to home. From this point, in addition to Indian social classes, there developed outside, non-Indian classes, resulting in the division of Juchitán society into six social categories. They are parallel social hierarchies based on economic position and life style within the various ethnic affiliations; as these categories became fully defined and articulated, the elaborate Isthmus Zapotec style became more and more important as a social criterion in distinguishing between those whose power and influence derived from the local community and those whose power depended on outside forces.

In Juchitán one can, indeed, have it both ways if one is Zapotec, but outsiders are at a disadvantage. Short of marrying into an important Zapotec family, there is no way to enter the group that runs the city. The ultimate test of legitimate access to local power is whether or not one is a true Juchiteco, that is, a Zapotec born in Juchitán.

Juchitán has succeeded in maintaining its integrity as a Zapotec city while at the same time taking advantage of opportunities presented by the world outside. The key to this success lies in the nature of Zapotec style and in the way it is manipulated by Zapotec middle and upper classes in order to preserve their dominance. Significant features of Juchitán that allow this use of style are its size and density which permit the maintenance of internal standards, preservation of the speech community, and a self-contained economy.

Tactics of Choice

7

THE THESIS OF THIS BOOK is that ethnic identity goes far beyond simple either/or ascription. The ethnic group is a reference group *invoked* by people who *identify themselves* and are identified by others as sharing a common historical style. Our discussion of ethnic groups within colonies and nations emphasizes the changing image of ethnicity and the strategies devised to use it. In the chapter on immigration the complexity of ethnic identification is again illustrated, this time in relating the experiences of different immigrant populations who "melted" or not, depending on the circumstances. In the examination of symbols and stereotypes the nuances of ethnic identity are made visible especially through the discussion of differing perceptions of in-group and out-group.

Assumption or admission of an ethnic identity is at its foundation a negotiation within constraints. This is not to say that the element of ascription is not important in many instances. Being born and socialized into an ethnic group is ascriptive. Perhaps the most affectively satisfying ethnic identities are those that can demonstrate this kind of ascription into a group. Two conditions exist, however, that detract from the universality and importance of ascription as it applies to ethnic groups. One concerns those who are able to manufacture an identity for themselves successfully without the validation of birthright. The other concerns the many persons who disclaim, set aside, or reject an identity that is theirs by virtue of birth.

Ethnic Identity as an Achieved Status

Even for individuals who have a legitimate claim to the ethnic identity on the basis of which they are willing to be classified, some effort must be directed toward making that identity viable. Birth and a lengthy period of socialization into an ethnic heritage provide a person with a minimal competency in the identity. Moving logically from Barth's notion that affirming and reaffirming boundaries is necessary for those boundaries to remain salient, we may say that individuals must affirm and reaffirm their identity in order for it to remain a salient feature of their personalities. At the level of the individual, ethnic identity is both a mental state and a possible strategy but only if it can be activated. In a very real sense, ethnic identity is an acquired and used feature of human identity, subject to display, avoidance, manipulation, and exploitation (Lyman and Douglass 1973:350).

Double Boundaries

Let us return for a moment to the idea of double boundaries. Adequate performance in an identity is much more rigorously judged within a group than it is by outsiders. For the latter, a few tokens of the identity are usually sufficient—feathers and beadwork for Native Americans, sombreros and sarapes for Mexicans, ear locks and black coats for Orthodox Jews. In some instances, outsiders may demand more evidence of an identity, as in the case of the Lumbee of North Carolina. Their claims to Native American status would be recognized much more quickly if they could present a satisfactory inventory of features—language, tribal land, a common past as a tribe, Indian phenotypes, and ceremonies to name the traits that have been singled out as missing. In the Lumbee case, the "outsiders" are other Native Americans and the United States government. The reasons for the demand for an adequate performance are the competition for scarce resources and Native Americans' concern with being able to demonstrate a clearly separate identity in the larger society. The scarce resources are the monies available from the federal government to recognized groups of Native Americans. Unless there is an expansion of funds, the more groups competing for support the less there will be for each individual group.

Concern with an unmistakeable Indian identity is as real as the economic competition. Phenotypically, the majority of the Lumbee are not recognizably Indian. Many are classified as Black. Admitting ambiguous cases such as the Lumbee would dilute the power of native Americans both as an interest group and as symbols (cf. Blu 1980).

Except where special circumstances obtain, as in the case of the Lumbee, intragroup categorization on the basis of ethnic identity occurs at the level of caricature and stereotype. Such is not the case within groups where more-intimate knowledge of group culture allows more-exacting standards of judgment. The Zapotec of the Isthmus of Tehuantepec in southern Mexico have a well-defined aesthetic about what an adequate Zapotec performance is and judge their fellow Zapotec accordingly. For example, it is not enough to be able to converse in Zapotec; one must be able to make speeches in it, incorporate references to famous Zapotec of the past, and have a keen ear for puns.

The complexity of judging performance and of separating in-group and out-group stereotypes is well illustrated by the selection of a candidate for Princess of the Guelaguetza in 1972. The Guelaguetza is an annual festival of song and dance held in the capital of the state of Oaxaca at which various indigenous groups within the state are represented. Each delegation nominates one of its members to run for the title of Princess. The Zapotec delegation from Juchitán was in a quandary over whether to select someone who "looked Indian" or someone who was a good Zapotec. There was an advantage to the first since the judges were biased in this regard, and the delegation considered the possibility of finding someone who fit the stereotype (dark skin; high cheekbones; thick, dark, braided hair). A number of women were suggested, all of whom incidentally lived in the rural area surrounding the city, the area "where the Indians lived." All were rejected because they did not know how to dance Zapotec *sones*, did not own suitably fine festive costumes and respectable quantities of gold jewelry to go with them, did not know enough Zapotec history to be able to respond to the judges' questions and could not speak Zapotec well enough. In sum, none were good Zapotec, although they all satisfied the stereotype of Indian-ness. Ultimately, one of the upper-class members of the delegation who satisfied all the criteria for Zapotecness was chosen to represent the group. Although she was the darkest-skinned of the lot, she was not very dark, nor did she "look Indian." She did not win the contest for Princess.

Periodic Display of Ethnic Identity to Reaffirm Ties

In intergroup interactions, some kind of achieved adequacy is necessary for the periodic displays of identity that maintain or intensify bonds between individual group members. These displays are not required by the structure of the group by virtue of its position within society, nor are they necessarily programmed to occur on a regular basis. There seem to be circumstances, however, that call them forth rather predictably. Any stressful or ambiguous situation is likely to produce such displays. Disagreements between acquaintances or the establishment of new relationships are typical stressful or ambiguous situations.

Leonard Plotnikov and M. Silverman, in an article on Jewish ethnic signaling (1978), discuss displays designed to ease the strain. Ethnic signaling is a deliberate advertisement of one's ethnic identity. Informants in the authors' sample reported that they habitually used it and were very sensitive to its use by others. They frequently used discrete signaling when making a new acquaintance, primarily to establish the ethnic identity of the other person but also to signal in an ambiguous way their own identity. A woman who introduced herself as Mrs. Skolnick was asked if she were related to the "show biz personality." The question was an oblique reference to Menashe Skulnik, a Yiddish comedian well known to some American Jews but not to others. It was phrased in a way that allowed the questioner to pretend that someone else was meant if the interaction were to go in a certain way. As it happened, Mrs. Skolnick responded that she was not related to "Menashe," thereby reciprocating the signal.

Some degree of sophistication in an identity is necessary to participate successfully in this kind of signaling. An individual who is unable to do so may be relegated to the periphery of the group or even be discounted as a group member. It is difficult to maintain close relationships when one is ignorant of a whole body of cultural features and cues that figure prominently at crucial times in group interaction. In this sense, cultural illiteracy is as crippling as illiteracy in a language. And, if at the same time, the individual is assigned to that group by the larger society, his or her position is even more difficult.

Acquiring or Losing an Identity

Clearly, special ability is essential in acquiring or shedding an identity. Knowledge of the identity in question as well as an understanding
of identities related to it in the larger social context will enable the actor
to move into or out of the identity. In the first case, one must cultivate
the attributes of the new identity in order to be accepted by members of
the group, or, at the very least, so that the larger society will recognize
one's claim to group membership. In the second case, one has to know
the cues and attributes in order to avoid them. Both processes require a
considerable degree of self- and other-perception and the ability to
assess the relative importance of symbols and values.

Native ability and intelligence are necessary but not sufficient. Access
to group members and to occasions where one can observe ethnic behavior is crucial if one is to learn ethnic cues and appropriate behavior.
For adults this process is laden with stress. The risk of misreading cues
and behaving inappropriately is very high, and the responses range
from mild embarrassment to ostracism. No adult likes to be put in the
position of being a child again, yet this is essentially what is
required—one has to learn a "culture" from the very basics. Although
the adult is as ignorant as a child, he or she will not be afforded the
comforting indulgence that is shown to children whose behavior is culturally wrong. The adult learner also does not enjoy the same long and
leisurely time frame for acquiring cultural knowledge. He or she can
easily be discouraged unless the rewards are sufficiently tempting or the
first identity is particularly negative.

"Vulnerable" is perhaps the best word to describe an individual who
is acquiring or losing an identity. As with a snake shedding its skin, for
some period of time one is anomalous and therefore vulnerable. There
is real danger that one may be left in an uncomfortable middle ground
between identities, as was an unfortunate Zapotec of Juchitán.

Switching identities is sometimes employed by upwardly mobile
Zapotec as a way of improving their class status. One such lower
middle-class Zapotec, a doctor and a schoolteacher, attempted to improve his lot by acquiring characteristics of Mexican national style and
avoiding the symbols and values representative of Zapotec identity. But
his strategy was unsuccessful, and both groups rejected him. The repre-

sentatives of Mexican national identity regarded him as an Indian who did not know his place (he happened to be very dark-skinned, and he was not wealthy enough to be useful to the Mexican middle and upper classes). The Zapotec resented him for being a climber, for not fulfilling his social obligations to Zapotec society, and for implicitly casting Zapotec values and symbols in a negative light.

Other individuals engage in short-term identity switching. Many of the requirements for success are the same as for long-term switching, but some of the constraints and possibilities for strategy are different. Short-term switching will be discussed later in this chapter in relation to situational use of ethnic identity.

Constraints on the Tactics of Ethnicity

Physical Constraints

Physical constraints on the strategies of ethnicity are in some respects the bottom line. They may be so visible and permanent that they limit flexibility, regardless of favorable sociological and psychological factors. We can posit a continuum of ethnic groups on the basis of physical cues. At one end would fall the groups that are the most visible by virtue of their skin color. Next would come those characterized by distinctive body shapes and facial features. Somewhat further along would come characteristic hair types. At the other end of the scale we would find the groups that occupy the middle of every category. Of course the larger social context plays a vital role in determining the relative flexibility of any group.

Even individuals who have distinctive and immutable physical characteristics still have some room to maneuver. An American Black told me that he will often deny his nationality in favor of a more exotic background because in most situations a foreign identity is granted more status than the homegrown one.

Within certain limits, one can also alter physical features—by nose jobs, hair straightening or frizzing, protecting one's skin from the sun or overexposing it, contact lenses to change eye color, dressing to change body type. One cue that is often forgotten but which is an important factor in categorization is movement style. Individuals who may be totally bilingual or at home in a number of languages frequently fail to change their nonverbal repertoire to match the message being communicated by their choice of language.

Research conducted among English/German bilinguals by Irmgard Bartenieff (personal communication) indicates that the nonverbal patterns are more ingrained and more tenacious. Some people in her sample were unable to change their nonverbal codes at all; and even with those who could, there was a time lag during which the language had changed but the gestural system had not. Some people are much better movement mimics than others. Just as some individuals are tone-deaf, there are those who are movement-blind.

Sociological Constraints

Barth (1969) lists a number of constraints that derive from the structure of society as a whole. Three merit discussion. The first has to do with the images of particular ethnic groups as they fit into the larger society. Within the system of social stratification the different strata carry positive or negative weights. An ethnic actor has to know the ranking of the various groups if he or she is to incorporate ethnicity successfully into strategies for improvement.

Second, in complex societies role differentiation and specialization make it common for individuals to hold a variety of ideas and behaviors about ethnic identities that change according to role and situation. Such specialization produces what appear to be inconsistencies and makes it difficult for people to anticipate correct behavior. Lyman and Douglass offer the following example of specificity in complex societies:

> In the context of American race relations, a particular white might reside in a neighborhood opposed to equal housing for blacks, attend a church in which black participation is welcomed, belong to a labor union with covert discriminatory practices, and yet work for an equal opportunity employer. In each of these contexts the use of ethnic identity and identity saliencies will likely be conditioned by the structural considerations of specific role requirements. [1973:352]

Rapid social change aggravates this kind of situation even further because the lack of situational consensus normal to complex societies becomes more apparent. The same categories have different meanings to different individuals, and so any specific situation is subject to different interpretations. Tension and lack of fit between one's inner impulse and the overt action allowed by society characterize interactions. Individuals confronted by such inconsistencies are more reluctant to risk negotiating situations on the basis of ethnic identity than they would be in situations they perceived as being predictable.

Third, the use of ethnicity as a strategy is constrained by the amount of knowledge available to the various groups within plural societies. In most societies the dominant culture pattern is set by the most-powerful group. Members of the other groups may find themselves at a disadvantage because they do not have an insider's knowledge of the rules, roles, and relationships pertinent to the dominant group (Lyman and Douglass 1973:352). They are also forced to acknowledge tacitly the rules of the game set by the dominant group and may resent the state of affairs that requires them to do so. Their frustration and resentment are increased by their being treated by members of the dominant group in stereotypic terms. The frequent resort to stereotypes by the dominant group is symptomatic of its lack of knowledge of the cultural rules and practices of subordinate groups. Because the dominant group makes the rules for the society as a whole, it does not *have* to know details of groups under its control. Interestingly, that puts dominant culture members at a disadvantage in certain kinds of interactions because they never have to practice the kind of social manipulation that subordinate groups use constantly as a matter of survival.[1]

Incomplete knowledge of one another on the part of subordinate ethnic groups may lead them to resort to the dominant group's stereotypes in shaping their interactions. This tendency has been used effectively to prevent ethnic coalitions. In the Poor People's March, white stereotypes of Blacks accepted by Native Americans made it difficult to sustain cooperative efforts. Similar difficulties have plagued interactions between Mexican-Americans, Blacks, and Native Americans.

---

1. There is an interesting cultural difference in the value placed on social manipulation by Mexican society and by American society. The former stresses social manipulation as a tactic to improve one's status or, on occasion, simply to get one's way. Mexican children, if they are skilled enough, can always avoid punishment; in fact, this ability is valued and encouraged. By contrast, American children are taught from an early age that if they break the rules they will be punished, and attempts to manipulate their parents may result in further punishment.

Psychological Constraints

Some people are better than others at manipulating ethnic identities in the long term or situationally. Success or failure is influenced by both physical cues and sociological constraints, and equally compelling are factors that might be called psychological. One needs nerve, the willingness to risk embarrassment or ostracism, or the desire to repeat the euphoric experience of a successful image projection (Lyman and Douglass 1973:353). What kinds of persons can fulfil these requirements? We can speak of three types, and these cateogries are not mutually exclusive: those who perceive an advantage that outweighs the risk of failure; those who are confident of at least one identity; those who are timid and introverted.

Type 1

The first type can be either positively or negatively motivated. It includes persons who have been successful at identity manipulation and enjoy it for the power it bestows or for the sheer intellectual challenge it presents. Gerald Berreman (1975:85) presents the example of the *bahurupiya* ("one of many disguises"), a figure common to the Indian landscape, who makes a living by impersonating members of other castes. He will come into a city and go from one merchant to another, each time in a different identity. If his false identity is accepted, he will return to the gullible merchants in his own identity and ask for payment for a good performance. His is merely an institutionalized version of what many individuals do more informally. For example, when Isthmus Zapotec go to Mexico City to see that their children are accepted by the university or an advanced technical school, they will dress in an affluent Mexican national style and speak Spanish. They know from experience that in this context a Zapotec identity is not strategically wise.

Individuals who switch identities or have a whole repertoire of alter egos just for the sake of enjoyment are more numerous than one might think. Often they feel that their own identity is rather dull, and so they create other more-exotic or -exciting identities. They usually know the languages associated with those identities. The occasions that are likely to prompt this kind of switching are those where one can count on a certain degree of anonymity, such as a concert or a shopping expedition; and urban, cosmopolitan areas are more likely than small towns to facilitate this kind of behavioι.

There is always the danger of being exposed: Your assumed identity could be challenged by the person who legitimately holds that identity. If you fail the test of language, gesture, or knowledge of relevant people and places, your claim will not be accepted. Or, you may meet some- one familiar with one of your identities in a context where you have assumed another. Spies, like Berreman's *bahurupiya*, are another in- stitutionalized form of this kind of identity manipulation.

People who might not change identities under normal circumstances will do so if their situation is desperate. If their group is viewed as subhuman or as having certain negative traits, if they are subjected to constant humiliation, if their performance is utterly inadequate com- pared to other groups (Barth 1969:25), or if they perceive no possibility of improving their status without changing, then they will risk failure because their state cannot be worse. This phenomenon has been com- mon among the Indians of highland Chiapas in southern Mexico for a number of years. For some, the stigma of being an Indian in a ladino (or Mexican) dominated society has always been insupportable, but the number of persons who have attempted to "pass" has increased in re- cent times. The increase is partly due to more-frequent interactions be- tween Indians and ladinos, which means that for many there are almost daily reminders of their status. It is also a result of a rapidly growing Indian population in circumstances where everything from land to op- portunities to participate in ritual is limited. It has become more and more difficult for Indians to make decent lives for themselves within their own communities.

Type 2

In order to manipulate identities successfully, one must have some confidence in at least one identity, a kind of base from which one goes out and to which one returns. Knowing one identity intimately and being able to reflect on it objectively gives one a basis for comparison. One knows what one is not and which features are distinctive. But there is a large mental component as well. Confidence in being an adequate performer of one identity provides the psychological impetus for attempting others. A friend and colleague remarked that manipulat- ing totally manufactured identities would be difficult for her because she had three identities available. By birth and early socialization she was Russian. When she was eight her family moved to France, and she was educated in French schools. She later moved to England, where she spent much of her adult life. Now she lives in the United States. Sorting out her identities is made more difficult by the fact that, while she spoke Russian, she had not been educated in it; French was the language in which she was first literate, but she did not speak it as a native from birth; and her English was acquired mainly in the context of occupation and raising a family.

Type 3

Little cross-cultural research exists as documentation for the type of identity manipulator who takes on other identities as a way of compensating for shyness or an introverted personality. Intuitively, this category would seem to be a significant one. Such individuals have much to gain from expanding their repertoire of persona. It is a way of presenting a self which if rejected is not a rejection of one's real self. This protective strategy can be important for those with fragile egos. One may try out techniques that one might not risk if one's own ego were at stake. Presenting another self to the world is a way of keeping one's real self inviolate. The need for this kind of personal and psychological privacy is very common, and having a stock of false fronts is one good way of ensuring that privacy. By trying out new ways of interacting and signaling, one becomes more skilled and therefore eventually more confident.

The Structure of Situations

Strategies for using ethnic identity have to be planned and perhaps modified in accord with the structure of the situation and with people's perception of the structure. Restrictions and modifications brought about by structure are distinct from those we have spoken about earlier in the context of physical, sociological and psychological constraints. The difference has to do primarily with an individual's awareness of the constraining factors and, in a sense, the abstract versus concrete nature of the constraint itself. Limitations arising from the structure of situations tend to be more abstract, and individuals are frequently unaware of them except in some vague way.

Structure: Proportions

Proportions, that is, *relative* numbers of socially and culturally different people in a group are . . . critical in shaping interaction dynamics.
[Kanter 1977:965]

Rosabeth Kanter presents a compelling argument that the kind of interaction possible between socially and culturally different members of a
group is determined by the proportion each type constitutes and that
certain interactive patterns are inevitable given certain proportions. Her
article was based on a field study of a large industrial corporation that
employed saleswomen for the first time in 1972. Until then the sales
force had been exclusively male.

Kanter identifies four kinds of groups based on proportions but focuses on one of them, the skewed group. Its distribution is such that the
predominant type accounts for up to 85% of the total. She refers to the
numerically dominant type as the "dominants" and the others as the
"tokens." The term "token" was chosen for specific reasons. Individuals who are few in number are often treated as symbols, as representatives of their category rather than as individuals. Moreover,

Tokens are not merely deviants or people who differ from other
group members along any one dimension. They are people identified
by ascribed characteristics (master statuses such as sex, race, religion,
ethnic group, age, etc.) or other characteristics that carry with them a
set of assumptions about culture, status, and behavior highly salient
for majority category members. [Ibid.:968]

Three perceptual characteristics are associated with the proportional
rarity of tokens: visibility, polarization, and assimilation.

Visibility

Because tokens are so few in number they receive much more attention than members of the dominant group. That has several implications for social situations. (1) Whatever they do is in a sense a public
performance. Even when tokens make efforts to go unnoticed they suffer from "over-observation" (ibid.:973). Anonymity is a luxury they
cannot expect. (2) They are visible as representatives of their category,
and so whatever they do takes on additional symbolic meaning. Their
behavior is seen as predictive of what every other member of their cate-

gory will do. The group of women Kanter studied were always evaluated in two ways: how, as women, they performed as salespersons; and how, as salespersons, they performed as women (ibid.). (3) Tokens are visible and evaluated most often on the basis of characteristics associated with the master status — ethnic identity or sex, for example, rather than on the basis of the characteristics relevant to the particular environment. Again, in Kanter's study, women reported that they had no difficulty in getting attention but that they experienced great difficulty in having their technical abilities or their sales performance noticed and evaluated. They found themselves working twice as hard as the men to prove their competence. (4) The high visibility of tokens makes them afraid of retaliation if they make the dominants look bad. When a token does well, the dominant who is being judged comparatively suffers a public loss of face.

Kanter recorded two responses to the pressures brought about by the high visibility of tokens. One was to overachieve in an attempt to be recognized for one's performance in the sales role rather than for the token's master status. This response made anxiety levels of the dominants shoot up, and the tokens were described as overly ambitious and unaware of their "place." The commoner response was to try to achieve invisibility — wearing clothes that approximated the style of the dominants, avoiding public occasions, not speaking up at meetings, minimizing one's accomplishment. By keeping a low profile, the tokens hoped to avoid the disapproval of the dominants, which was certain to be engendered by visible overachievement.

Examples of both types of responses abound in the area of ethnic identity. Jews are continually being singled out and criticized for their "overachievement" in the areas of science, music, and business. "Disloyal" (in the sense of not being team players) is an adjective frequently applied to Jews who excel, and this labeling is typical no matter what the token ethnic group happens to be. The low-profile response occurs with painful consequences among second-generation immigrants. Children of immigrants who suffer humiliation and antagonism at the hands of their peers because they are different adapt very quickly by trying to blend in with their social environment. The shame and hostility that this strategy creates in the relationship between "Old Country" parents and their Americanizing children is painful for all parties and difficult to resolve.

Polarization

Polarization results from a heightening of the token's attributes in contrast to those of the dominants. Not only are tokens highly visible but the characteristics that make them distinctive are exaggerated. That brings the dominants together under the banner of commonality. Individual differences are forgotten in the face of the perceived threat to which all are exposed by the "different" tokens. The slogan of commonality becomes more than empty words as dominants exaggerate their common culture, especially those aspects that the tokens do not share. In Kanter's study the men in the sales force acted more male, exaggerating their male qualities and displaying aggression and potency. The saleswomen were their audience. Kanter describes a particularly revealing incident during the training period, when individuals were asked to create and act out examples of sales situations.

> In every case involving a woman, men played the primary, effective roles, and women were objects of sexual attention. In one, a woman was introduced as president of a company selling robots; she turned out to be one of the female robots, run by the male company manager. [Ibid.:976]

Exaggeration of the dominant culture also occurs when ethnic identity is the relevant master status. In the Isthmus Zapotec wedding (see chapter 6), since the bride was an outsider, the entire event was an exaggeration of Zapotec style. The purpose was to impress the outsiders, in this case certainly tokens, with the elegance of Zapotec custom and at the same time to heighten the boundaries between the two groups.

Differences are magnified by insuring that the tokens are responsible for interruptions in the flow of events: "Dominants preface acts with apologies or questions about appropriateness directed at the token; they then invariably go ahead with the act, having placed the token in the position of interruptor or interloper" (ibid.:977). The tokens are made to feel uncomfortable, like intruders. They are forced to acknowledge that the interaction will proceed by the rules of the dominants, otherwise it will be "unnatural." Finally, these interruptions signal to the tokens that their appropriate role is as audience rather than as participant. I have seen this tactic used in multi-ethnic situations in the United States. It has been used successfully by the Zapotec when non-Zapotec are in the token category. In fact, as an anthropologist I was automatically a token, and from time to time I was the occasion for just such interruptions as Kanter discusses. It was in this context that I discovered an additional twist to the strategy: I could be used to articulate unpleasantnesses that a Zapotec might wish to communicate but could not because of Zapotec cultural conventions.

I was chatting one morning with R as she finished sewing a cassock for the local priest. She complained bitterly about the poor quality of the material, saying that it would wrinkle, that it was hot, that it would not stand up to repeated washings. When she finished, she asked me to accompany her when she delivered the cassock. The priest told R how nice the cassock looked and what a good job she had done. R responded with, "Yes, but Anya says that the material is terrible; it will be too hot, it will wrinkle, and it won't wash well." She put her feelings into my mouth because it would have been inappropriate for her to say them!

At first I was puzzled by the fact that R would put me in this position, since we were like mother and daughter, and she had defended me on other occasions. Then I realized that, from her perspective, she had not endangered my friendship with the priest. My "lapse" of manners was perfectly explainable by my not being a Zapotec; and since I had been in Juchitán only nine months and would be leaving in another three, my relationships with Juchitecos were necessarily shallower and less hedged about by conventions. One additional note: As my commitment to Juchitán and my love for the Juchitecos becomes more obvious to them, I am less-often used in this way. Or, in Kanter's terms, I have become a dominant and only for rare strategic purposes am I regarded as a token.

Another mechanism associated with polarization is isolation. From time to time dominants will isolate tokens because they do not wish something discussed in their presence. They keep tokens from having access to aspects of the dominant culture they wish to keep secret by carrying out those activities when tokens are absent. This tactic is well known to students who have finally succeeded in gaining positions on faculty committees, only to find that no real business is discussed in front of them. It is also familiar to anthropologists who are kept from certain aspects of a society's culture by a variety of means — they are not told of an important event; they are given the wrong date or time; or women/men are not allowed in certain contexts.

In spite of the fact that tokens are viewed as deviant in the larger situation, they are expected to demonstrate their loyalty to the dominant group (ibid.:978). Tests of loyalty often require a token to turn against other tokens. Travelers outside their homeland experience conversations in which their own country is the subject of criticism. If one is going to be part of the group for any length of time, one feels compelled, if not to join in the criticism, at least to remain silent. The latter strategy is not often the luxury of the token, however, because he or she will be forced to contribute to the conversation. Tokens in multi-ethnic situations are subject to loyalty tests in which they acknowledge that they are the exception, that in reality all the dominants' negative stereotypes about their group are correct. Many upwardly mobile immigrants to the United States demonstrated their loyalty to and their fundamental acceptance of the dominant culture. Blacks who are in token situations face constant demands of this sort.

In addition to turning against one's category, one can also demonstrate loyalty by allowing oneself to be a source of humor. Witness the innumerable southern Blacks who shuffle through the pages of moonlight and magnolia novels, performing caricatures of themselves, or the countless Polish Americans who listen to and even tell Polish jokes. This way of forcing tokens to acknowledge the superior power of the dominant group also carries the seeds of self-hatred. One may find oneself believing the dominant group's stereotype or one may continue to perform in order to be allowed to remain on the periphery of the dominant group.

Assimilation or Role Entrapment

This third feature of token-dominant interaction closely resembles the perception of individuals in terms of stereotypes. In role entrapment the token's status is brought into line with the status of the token's category in the population at large. A stranger seeing a Mexican-American businessman in an area where most Mexican-Americans are itinerant farm workers, would assume he was a farm worker. Similarly, it is assumed that Chinese-Americans own laundries, Japanese-Americans make good gardeners, and the Zapotec are the Jews of the Isthmus.

The negative implications of status leveling and role entrapment are various and almost impossible to avoid. If one accepts the labeling, then one's options for maneuvering advantageously are drastically reduced as one's range of expression is limited. It is often easier to accept the false classification than to insist on being recognized as an individual with many aspects. Fighting role entrapment elicits anger and resentment on the part of dominant group members. No one likes having to revise categories or relinquish beliefs, and no one appreciates being put in the awkward position of being wrong or appearing to be a bigot. Finally, the dominant who is challenged in this way might easily resolve the dilemma by saying that the token is "uppity" and "doesn't know his/her place."

Proportion and Interaction: Summary

Kanter has documented for a male-female situation the effect of group proportions on interaction. Specifically, she dealt with skewed groups, where tokens made up 20% or less and dominants constituted 80% or more. Interactions in such skewed groups tend to be characterized by visibility, polarization, and assimilation or role entrapment. Tokens cannot escape notice, being viewed as symbols of their category. By virtue of being outside the dominant culture, tokens reinforce the sense of shared values among dominants even where there is ordinarily a diversity of value systems. Tokens are expected to behave in accordance with the stereotypes of their category held by the dominants. The result is that tokens suffer from pressures not faced by dominants — overachieve, underachieve, be "one of the guys" by laughing at oneself and one's category, inhibit one's expression, endure social isolation and caricature. Until group proportions are changed, it is difficult to change these patterns of interaction or the way in which ethnic identity is perceived and manipulated.

Structure: Folk Nomenclature for Ethnic Labeling

Michael Moerman (1965) was one of the first to propose and illustrate in a systematic fashion that every group has its own taxonomy of ethnic labels. Within these systems individuals assign labels to others in response to cues they have learned as diagnostic. Moerman suggests that it would be fruitful to compare the structure of folk systems with the prevailing institutional structure (such as state relations). Although labels and taxonomic levels arise out of the interaction of human beings with their social environment, once designated they act independently of human beings and affect people's perceptions and behavior. Folk nomenclatures are no different in this respect from institutional structures. They are different in that they give greater relevance to the situational use of ethnicity. Part of their situational importance derives from the fact that any folk nomenclature will have more labels than most institutional structures. Moreover, these labels change more quickly than do labels designating categories within institutional structures.

Partial Taxonomy of Ethnic Terms in Ban Ping

A	Chinese	Thai						Hill
B	Northern*							Central
C	North Country (in origin)*							
D	Yang Shan	Lue*				Yuan	Lao	
E		Phong*			La			
F		Thu-mawk	Ping*	Ch.Ban				

[After Moerman 1965:1224]

The multi-labeling phenomenon and the situational nature of folk taxonomies are illustrated in one of the taxonomic tables from Moerman's article on the Lue of Thailand. The asterisks in the table designate all the possible responses a Lue from the village of Ban Ping might give to the question "What kind of Thai are you?" The particular response a villager chooses depends on his or her perception of the level of contrast appropriate to the status of the questioner and the situation. In a more familiar example, an American traveling abroad will respond to the question "Where are you from?" with "the United States." If asked that question in the United States, the same person might reply "the West Coast," "California," "Northern California," "the San Francisco Bay Area," "the East Bay," "Berkeley," "the Berkeley Hills," "Panoramic Way." The answer would depend on how familiar the questioner is with the region.

In ethnic interactions, one may use the taxonomic structure to improve one's position and limit the maneuverability of others. The levels of ethnic labels allow the actor to control the amount of information given out about himself, thereby controlling the intimacy of the interaction. The hierarchical nature of the terminology also facilitates uniting interest groups in the most-efficient way when there is an outside threat. In Moerman's table, if the threat comes from the Thai La (on level E), the Thumawk, the Ping, and the Ch. Ban might all act together as Phong in order to meet a common threat. In the event of a threat from the Yuan or the Lao, however, one would see the La siding with the Phong.

Constraints: Summary

Individuals do not enjoy total freedom to manipulate identities. They operate within a system of constraints that includes physical, sociological, and psychological influences, and they are constrained as well by the structure of society and subcategories within it. All these constraining factors are relevant at two levels: that of their own physical reality; and that of the individual's perception of them, which may or may not correspond to the physical reality. Changes in the physical reality and in people's perceptions add to the complexity of the situation. Change and the perception of it may not be synchronized. On the one hand, people are frequently slow to notice change and continue to behave on the basis of a past reality. On the other, change may be brought about because it is perceived as already having happened. Perception is not uniform either. Individuals involved in an interaction perceive it and the larger context into which it fits in different ways. None of these constraints or the complexity introduced by individual perception make strategic manipulation of ethnic identity impossible, they simply make modifications and concessions necessary.

Situational Ethnicity

Definitions

"Situational ethnicity" implies the strategic use of an ethnic identity to fit particular situations. Let us first define "situation." In an analytical definition a social situation is "a temporally and spatially bounded series of events abstracted by the observer from the on-going flow of social life" (Garbett 1970:215). This definition is sensible in the abstract but it must be interpreted with care, as must all definitions, when it is applied to real-life events. The problem of folk versus analytical perceptions of the world is ever present. In the case of situations, the analyst must take care to carve out the same-sized unit as the people involved in the event. It is just as bad to focus on a smaller unit as to designate a larger one. It may often seem to the observer that what the "folk" interpret as part of an event is really a whole event in its own right, especially if the criterion of temporal and spatial boundedness is used.

For example, the time frame that defines the *vela* for the Zapotec of Juchitán is the 365-day year, during which a number of "events" occur: the choosing of the new sponsors, the handing over of the ritual paraphernalia ("la entrega de la cera"), the distribution of the invitational bread ("el repartido de pan"), the sending out of the meal to the *vela* society members, the parade, the all-night dance, the church mass, and the daytime party for the society members and their guests ("la lavada de olla"). Spatially and temporally these events are all separate. In G. Kingsley Garbett's definition, each is a social situation. To the Zapotec, however, they make up one logical unit rather than many discrete ones. What happens in one part has definite repercussions in other parts, and people's behavior is affected by their interpretation of the whole event or *vela*.

The Vela Pineda (*vela* of the Pineda families) in 1974 illustrates the inseparability of the parts. The date of the celebration is always the same, September 3. In August 1974, Porfirio Pineda, one of the patriarchs of the family, died. The 40-day mourning period, during which no festivities would normally be scheduled, was still in effect on September 3. The *vela* was given, however, because the invitational bread had already been distributed. This is a clear case of the unity of the *vela* as an event.

It may well be useful for the observer to take smaller parts as analytical units, but it is imperative to remember that there is a functional interdependence and unity in the minds of the people involved in the event itself, and that colors their behavior at each stage.

Kinds of Interactional Situations

The way people perceive an interaction influences the way they use ethnicity as a strategy, if, indeed, they use it at all. The parties involved in interactions range from close-knit members of the same group. to groups who are rivals but who share more or less equal status and are linked by some kind of exchange, to groups of unequal status and with no connecting links.

Close-knit groups are usually but not always ethnically homogeneous. Group closeness may be based on ties other than a common ethnic identity. Whether ethnically homogeneous or heterogeneous, however, close-knit groups always demonstrate a higher tolerance for deviance than do loosely connected groups. The more closely knit a group is the more different kinds of ties there are that link its members. With a greater number and variety of ties, deviant behavior can be more easily controlled, and it is unnecessary for the full panoply of ethnic symbolism to be displayed constantly.

Rival but equal groups neither share the same cultural conception nor have ready-made mechanisms for reconciling conflicts raised by lack of knowledge. Simply put, there is more potential for misunderstandings and fewer means for resolving them. Interactions assume the qualities of a performance as people begin behaving in conformity with the stereotypes of themselves. In Mitchell's (1969) terms, the interactions occur at the categorical level, that is, roles and relationships are determined by categorical affiliations. The demand for conformity to the symbols that are shared by all is high, and the symbols derive from one's categorical assignment vis-à-vis others.

Groups that believe each other to be unequal in status and that have few or no connecting links use their ethnic identity in the most stereotypic fashion. Because of the distance between such groups, conflicts arise less frequently. When they do, it is less vital that they be resolved because such resolution is not necessary for the survival of the groups. They may exist in a state of hostility for long periods with no damage to the integrity of either group. Such hostility may in fact be the kind of opposition needed to maintain a sense of uniqueness and identity (Spicer 1971).

The different kinds of interactive situations may be seen among the Zapotec. When the upper classes interact on social occasions they behave almost like families. There is no division into public and backstage behavior (Goffman 1959:238). It is permissible and common for individuals to display behaviors and material items associated with the Mexican national culture, which on other occasions is "the enemy." It is even common to argue over different interpretations of Zapotec history or style elements.

When the occasion is made more "formal" by the presence of Zapotec not so closely tied to the upper class, less disagreement is tolerated. Upper-class Zapotec interacting with lower-class Zapotec with whom they have neither kinship nor patron-client ties tend to display more of the stereotyped elements of Zapotec style and to separate public and backstage behaviors. Their neighbors the Lebanese fall into the same category of "other" when a situation is perceived as threatening, as occurred at a rehearsal for a performance of dance at an annual festival in the state capital (for a detailed description see Royce 1977:28–31).

The rehearsal had qualities of the first and second type of interaction. Three of the six women participants had very close ties of ethnicity, kinship, and school experience. They were all members of the same powerful Zapotec family and were first cousins to each other. Two other women were not of that family but were allied to them by patron-client ties. The last woman belonged to a rival upper-class family on her mother's side and to a wealthy Lebanese family on her father's. Interactions with her were always potentially threatening since she was not privy to the intimate knowledge shared by the other women. The six male partners were not members of either group, their ties being those of casual friendship. Moreover, they were further isolated by virtue of their sex.

A disagreement over the correct way of performing one of the dances activated the rivalry between the two families (let us call the Zapotec family the Gomez and the Zapotec-Lebanese the Martinez). One Gomez woman and the Martinez woman were performing a version of the *fandango* that was different from what the others were doing. In the discussion that ensued, two of the Gomez women and their two clients presented a united front to the Martinez dancer. The youngest Gomez, who had been performing the deviant version, refused to acknowledge that she was wrong. Continued refusal on her part led the rest of the Gomez to remove the argument from a setting that was threatening — that is, where there were persons who did not belong to their close-knit group — to one where only Gomez were present. In that "safe" setting, the recalcitrant Gomez was gently pressured into changing her position by reminders of her obligations of kinship to the Gomez name, of the rivalry with the Martinez, and that this particular Martinez was half Lebanese. When she still refused, the rehearsal was deferred to another day while the Gomez took the argument to one of the Gomez matriarchs for resolution. By virtue of her age and status she persuaded her stubborn granddaughter that her older cousins were correct. Again the argument was based on the right of the Gomez to be the arbiters of Zapotec tradition since they were one of the oldest Zapotec families. This right has not always been articulated so clearly, but in this case the right was being challenged by a rival Martinez and a half Lebanese at that.

An ironic postscript to this episode occurred at a party a month later when I was dancing the *fandango* with a Gomez woman. I was confident that I was dancing it correctly because I was doing the version that had the blessing of the Gomez matriarch. I was completely surprised when my partner informed me that I was doing it incorrectly. After many questions and much observation it became clear that there are a number of versions of the *fandango*, all of which are "correct." It is only when there are individuals present who belong to rival but equal groups that it is important to maintain the image of unity. The choice of the version supported by the matriarch illustrates even further the care with which symbol selection proceeds. The preferred Gomez version for potentially threatening situations is the most difficult one, and only very good (Gomez) dancers do it well.

To observe the third kind of interactive situation, that between groups with no ties and a perceived inequality, let us follow the group of twelve dancers to the performance at the festival. At the state capital, the Zapotec group was a very small island in a sea of non-Zapotec, most of whom regarded the Zapotec as "Indian" and therefore, quaint, provincial, and rather low in status. Whatever individual differences may have existed within the Zapotec group temporarily disappeared when outsiders viewed them all in terms of the same stereotype.

Time and Situational Ethnicity

Time is another significant influence on the strategic use of ethnicity. Ethnicity may be used as a short-term strategy or in a long-term way to improve one's status. Obviously these two strategies are not separable, since what one does from day to day ultimately affects what happens to one in the context of a lifetime. Conversely, long-range plans may well influence what one does on a daily basis.

Expediency and Situational Ethnicity

Expediency, or the prospect of immediate advantage, is a powerful motivator. Individuals will select an ethnic group as the appropriate reference on particular occasions if they see an advantage to be gained. In a classic article on situational ethnicity, Judith Nagata furnishes an excellent example of the mutability of ethnic identification depending on the situation. An urban *kampong* (residential unit) in George Town, Penang, is multi-ethnic, but when it felt itself threatened by alien land developers, it became monolithically Malay. The Malay Chamber of Commerce was suspected of profiting from the land deal, and so they were described as proud and self-interested Arabs who were exploiting the poor Malays. In another dispute, when the *kampong* was threatened by the Chinese, all the "Arabs" became Malay once again (1974:40). Some Chinese, in turn, converted to Islam in order to get taxi licenses, which are normally reserved for Malays (ibid.:45).

Lyman and Douglass illustrate what they call "ethnic impression management" with the example of an individual who was born in Puerto Rico, was educated in Europe, and happens to be of Vizcayan Basque ancestry. He may be a Vizcayan, a Spanish Basque, a Basque, and additionally

> a continental gentlemen when functioning in American high society, a fellow Latin American when dealing with an intellectual from any Latin American country, and a Puerto Rican when dealing with U. S. Consular officials (Puerto Ricans are, if they accuse officials of discrimination, more likely to receive preferential treatment in U. S. embassies than other bearers of U. S. passports). [1973:355]

Long-Range Strategies

Long-range goals are usually articulated in the idiom of upward mobility. Most "passing" occurs in situations where the social strata are well defined and, while not rigid, are fixed enough to allow individuals to make long-range plans on the basis of them. Many colonial situations inspired this kind of behavior. Colonial rule frequently interjected the stability and predictability that had been lacking in the pre-colonial situation. Moreover, colonial governments often redefined the social hierarchy and, in so doing, created social competition where it had not existed before or where competition had previously taken other forms.

John Chance (1978) documents just such a case for Mexico under Spanish colonial rule. The Spaniards, with their passion for racial classifications, invented innumerable schemes for handling the populations of the New World. As the colonial period progressed, the number of categories increased as the mixing of the various people became more and more frequent. The more distinctions that were made, the easier it became for persons of any kind of blood mixture to claim *mestizo* status (mixture of Indian and European). Being a *mestizo* was infinitely superior to being a *zambo* (Black and Indian), a *negro*, or an *indio* or a *natural*. The category was sufficiently broad that individuals of the other three backgrounds could often make others recognize their claim to *mestizo* status. The categories of *criollo* (person born in the New World of European parents) and *gachupine* (European born in Europe) were beyond the grasp of most aspiring mixed-bloods. Colonial census records list many more *mestizos* than could be expected from the number of Indians and Spaniards who would have produced offspring. The figures indicate that a large number of people were "passing" successfully as *mestizos*.

The Waswahili of East Africa also have long-range views of upward mobility (see Arens 1975 and chapter 3 of this volume). They used the colonial laissez-faire attitude toward and lack of knowledge of the complex mix of tribal peoples, ex-slaves, East Indians, and Arabs in the East African colonies. If a Waswahili could convince a census taker that he had at least one Arab parent, he was assured of being classified as an Arab. The Waswahili status was clearly undesirable, and soon the censuses showed almost no Waswahili, but a great increase in Arabs. Waswahili status remained undesirable until nationalism became a fact. Then it was associated with forward thinking, progressive attitudes, and cosmopolitanism as contrasted with the insularity and provincialism of the tribal peoples, and there was a corresponding burgeoning of the Waswahili in the census.

Switching an identity is sometimes a two-generation process. In many parts of Latin America, an Indian who wants to move up in the social hierarchy often struggles to get an education, find a better job, move out of the Indian community, and perhaps marry a non-Indian. He reaches the end of his life with only the consolation that his children have achieved a better status. At this point, the changing of an identity is a shift from a birth-ascribed status to another, achieved status, and the change is permanent. The strategies are of necessity different from those involved in situational switching.

Negotiation, Impression Management, and Alter Casting

One of the basic tenets of assimilationist theory was that individuals who clung to their ethnic identity and those who emphasized one or another identity according to the demands of the situation suffered neuroses and feelings of marginality. Both of these behaviors were regarded as maladaptive but, of the two, identity switching had perhaps the worse connotation, both for theorists and for those who considered themselves non-ethnics. Both felt that there was just the slightest hint of dishonesty about the process of switching. After all, one could not straddle two or more identities at the same time. One either was an X or one was not; one could not be an X some of the time and a Y the rest of the time. It just was not in the American tradition to resort to such subterfuges.

It is more difficult to maintain such theories now, as evidence accumulates of groups and individuals who switch identities as a matter of practical necessity and who are neither marginal (at least not on the basis of their identity switching) nor neurotic. It is significant that in addition to "situational identity" we now have "impression management" and "alter casting." The addition of these terms acknowledges that people recognize the advantages of having more than one identity and being flexible enough to choose the one appropriate to the occasion. It also acknowledges that some individuals and groups actively use their identity and are not just passively cast into a category.

Negotiation

> Since every social relationship ultimately turns on the identities of the actors involved, every relationship includes this implicit or explicit negotiation of identities. . . . Ethnic identities in a plural society are thus part of a repertory in the drama of everyday encounters and crucial situations. [Lyman and Douglass 1973:360]

Individuals and, for that matter, groups do not simply accept the world as a given but rather engage in a continuous process of manipulating and constructing social reality. In plural societies, ethnic identity is one of the building blocks of social reality, and, in every ethnically plural interaction, the relevant identities are displayed, hidden, switched, or negotiated until the actors are satisfied with the interpretation of the scene or, if not satisfied, at least agree on a mutually comprehensible version. Other reference groups or statuses, such as class, age, or sex, are rarely absent; often the first step in negotiation is to determine which referent will be the primary one.

Impression Management

Impression management, or the selective display of symbols of one's identity or status, takes place at both the group level and the individual level. For ethnic groups occupying subordinate or token positions in the larger society, certain strategies of impression management are common. They include limiting public displays of ethnic culture to those items acceptable to the larger society. The "cafeteria culture" nature of American taste in food makes for the proliferation of so-called ethnic food places, such as taco stands, soul-food restaurants, Chinese restaurants, pizzerias, and Greek cafes. Americans will also tolerate ethnic displays in costume and dance but are far less accepting of the other elements that constitute the culture of any group, and so those become the areas that are restricted to private display (ibid.:348).

A second strategy of subordinate ethnic groups is to put the dominant group in a role that will benefit the subordinate group. In the past, a common tactic was to arouse sympathy for the group. In chapter 6 we saw that a group was more likely to generate feelings of sympathy if it was perceived as subordinate and nonthreatening. The dominant group could then indulge its feelings of paternalism toward a group it could regard as inferior and dependent. This tactic has lost its appeal for many ethnic groups in today's world. For the sake of group pride it is preferable to cast the dominant group in the position of oppressor and to play on feelings of guilt. This strategy was adopted by both Native Americans and Black Americans.

These two strategies are also incorporated at the individual level, where, if anything, a greater degree of flexibility is possible because individuals are not necessarily bound to a public group policy. At times it is advantageous to play upon the difference between an aggressive group strategy and a more "passive" individual one. The message being sent by the individual belonging to the subordinate group might read, "Yes, most X (Blacks, Native Americans, Chicanos, etc.) would like to take back forcibly what they think has been stolen from them, but I am a reasonable person." This kind of strategy subtly reminds the other participant that the use of force is a real option and draws attention to the individual as a reasonable person who does not always behave in the stereotypic way of the group. The possibilities for manipulation increase dramatically with each additional potential reference group. Individuals will play off one group against another in an attempt to turn the situation to their own advantage or to avoid being trapped by a negative image. This ploy is analogous to the old "good guy/bad guy" routine employed by detectives and police in works of fiction.

Alter Casting

Impression management is the manipulation of identity to an individual's advantage, while alter casting is the manipulation of an interaction. If, for example, you hold the dominant status in terms of social class but not ethnic group, it is to your advantage to recognize the other person in terms of his or her class rather than ethnic group. Obviously, persons with a large repertoire of statuses will have an advantage over those with more-limited repertoires:

> The man who can successfully impose a single identity on another can usually extract considerable compliance from him as well; the man who maintains a multiplicity of roles can usually escape the onerous burden of any one of them by adopting another. [Ibid.:359]

Because all the participants in an interaction are engaged in negotiation at some level, no single person can define the situation unless all the others abdicate their rights. Most interactions involve some degree of compromise and bargaining. Even the most subordinate of groups implicitly has the power to change the course of an interaction because its mere presence is a reminder of the larger context (in the same sense that Kanter 1977 describes what happens in the presence of tokens).

Ethnic Cues and Clues

Ethnic cues and clues form the basis from which identities are negotiated. Cues are the features over which the individual has little or no control—skin color, hair type, body shape, and any other physical characteristic that can be used to categorize a person. Clues, in contrast, are identifying marks that people reveal during the course of an interaction in order to establish a specific identity. They may include language, dialect, origin, patterns of nonverbal communication, and in-group knowledge. Cues establish the fabric of the interaction, and clues embroider upon it.

Interactive skills become crucial in the manipulation of ethnic clues. One must know one's own background and limits and be able to make lightning assessments of the other participants. One must be able to rank the range of clues so that one begins with clues that are revealing; yet ambiguous enough to allow for retreat, as in the example of Jewish ethnic signaling cited earlier in this chapter. Some clues will elicit information about the other participants' identities or perceptions of the situation.

> Ideally the situation amounts to reciprocally escalating presentation of relevant information by which one actor enhances the risk of ethnically labeling himself in order to ascertain the acceptability of the label to another. [Lyman and Douglass 1973:362]

Manipulation and Long-Term Change

Ethnicity may be manipulated as a matter of expediency, or it may be managed so as to bring about a permanent change of status. Let us now examine the relationship between these strategies. The possible combinations are the two strategies existing side by side, in a mutually exclusive relationship, or, more rarely, in alternation.

A member of the Zapotec lower middle class who wants to move up in the class hierarchy may plan a long-term strategy that involves switching to a Mexican identity. To do so, he must not only acquire all the elements of a Mexican identity—language, dress, life-style, value system—but also convince Mexicans of his sincerity and worth by abandoning all his Zapotec traits. Neither the acquisition nor the disposition is an overnight process, and there are many problems in achieving the latter. Fundamental to all the symbols and forms of Zapotec style is friendship based on lifetime reciprocity. The many complex ties between individuals are essential for survival in an environment that is sometimes harsh socially and physically. An individual who fails in his reciprocal obligations can no longer expect support from friends and kinsmen. Only a person who is financially self-sufficient and can withstand ostracism can afford to make a permanent change without resort to situational identity management.

More commonly, a Zapotec with this strategy in mind will work toward long-term change by acquiring an education that will allow him to hold a job appropriate to the desired status, by gradually building up a network of Mexican friends and supporters, and by marrying his children into Mexican families. At the same time, he will maintain his Zapotec network at a reasonable level. To do so successfully requires situational manipulation of the two identities while working toward the long-term change.

In a kind of reversal of the usual "passing," the Yaqui have steadfastly worked toward a permanent Yaqui identity while at the same time manipulating aspects of Mexican identity when it is to their advantage to do so. For both the individual Zapotec who wants to become a Mexican and the Yaqui, who as a group are reinforcing and elaborating their Yaqui identity, the best strategy is one that recognizes the necessity of situational identity manipulation as well as a plan for long-term change.

Two contexts promote the use of situational manipulation of ethnicity to the exclusion of long-term change. The first is a rigid and closed caste society. The second, more-insidious, context is the existence of a unique history and culture that lulls a people into a sense of well-being.

Berreman speaks of the first context:

> Despite ethnic heterogeneity, impersonal interaction, the dependence of ethnic ascription and response on the specific context, and the prevalence of impression management, urban residents of Dehra Dun cannot, and do not for the most part, change their ethnic identity. [1975:93]

He argues that ethnic identity based on caste, religion, region of origin, and language is a matter of birth and early socialization. But that is also the case in other societies where one does see permanent change of identity. The difference lies in the lack of ambiguity in a closed caste society. There is no room for permanent identity change because the categories are too rigidly defined. Because of the emphasis on belonging to one category or another, day-to-day interaction is characterized by a concern for manipulating these categories, for managing the impression one conveys:

> Although changes in identity are difficult and unusual, it is usual and
> expectable that people will be called upon to make choices among
> alternative and complementary statuses in various circumstances, es-
> pecially where status summation is imperfect. [Ibid.:94]

In one sense, it is as though situational manipulation were filling the
need for flexibility in a context where there is no flexibility over the
long term.

In the second context, situational or expedient manipulation of an
ethnic identity becomes an end in itself and seduces individuals with its
offer of a safe, nondemanding haven. Because individuals can be comfortable in their context of ethnic chauvinism, they do not feel the need
to make long-term changes in their position within the larger society.
As stated so well by Irving Howe, "The ethnic impulse necessarily carries with it dangers of parochialism. . . . The ethnic community too
often shuts its eyes or buries its head while clinging anxiously to re-
ceived customs" (1978:197). Movements for large-scale social change
require a vision that transcends the boundaries of individual ethnic
groups. Adherence to ethnic identity can incapacitate individuals by its
forced inward focus. The lack of success of the Poor People's March on
Washington is a perfect example of this kind of debilitating
parochialism. If individuals can feel rewarded by their pride in an ethnic
past, why should they bother with long-term change? The problem is
that there is no way of estimating how long the current "fashionable-
ness" of an ethnic heritage is going to last. How long will ethnic groups
continue to be able to use their heritage as a bargaining point? When the
fashion passes, will any permanent changes have been realized?

Conclusion

Ethnic identity at its core involves negotiation within constraints.
Ascription is only a small part of the claim to an ethnic identity.
Further, achieved qualities are essential if an ethnic identity is to be
maintained successfully. The constraints on the tactical use of ethnic
identity arise from a variety of causes: physical, sociological, psychological, and structural. The relative importance of the cause varies from
context to context and over time.

The cause and function of situational ethnicity as well as its behavioral requirements are part of the strategy in the choice of an ethnic identity in preference to other possible reference groups. Situational ethnicity is heavily involved in the relationship between ethnicity and long-term permanent change of status.

Changing Images

PART FOUR

Myth and Reality

8

ETHNIC IDENTITY AND ETHNICITY assume and are ascribed such an infinity of guises and motives that separating the myth from the reality seems a hopeless task. Some scholars are now adopting ethnic group and ethnic identity as replacements for tribe and tribal identity respectively, while an equal number are arguing just as firmly that today's New Ethnicity is radically different from yesterday's tribalism (see Stein and Hill 1977). Michael Novak (1971) regards ethnic identity as the salvation of the future, but Orlando Patterson (1975) sees it as the enemy of individualism, and Irving Howe (1978) claims ethnicity lulls people into complacency and parochialism. Finally, how are we to evaluate such happenings as white parents claiming Black identity in order to register their children in the school of their choice; women, veterans, senior citizens, and homosexuals all using the imagery of ethnicity; and dogged determination to cling to stereotyped images of certain ethnic groups when statistics prove them patently false?

One truth that emerges from the confusion is that there are no neutral feelings where ethnicity is concerned. This is true of scholars viewing the scene and of individuals and groups actively involved in ethnic interactions. The vocabulary of ethnicity is the property of everyone, although there is a bewildering array of dialects.

Contemporary Ethnicity—A New Phenomenon?

The vocabulary used to describe ethnic groups has undergone a subtle euphemization. We seldom speak today of minorities, marginal groups that have been unable or unwilling to assimilate, and the neurosis of switching identities. In today's world, an ethnic identity can be a weapon, a tool for improving one's status. We surely have seen the power invested in ethnicity in the United States when to be lacking in an ethnic background is to be culturally disadvantaged. Moreover, when groups engage in what Weston LaBarre has called a "perverse one-downmanship" that makes "minority into superiority solely because it is not a majority" (in Stein and Hill 1977:x), that is a commentary on the significance of ethnicity.

As the language has changed so has the reality of the situation. Walker Connor (1977) points out that in the last twenty years nearly half the independent nations of the world have suffered from dissonance that is rooted in ethnicity. He argues convincingly that even if the origins and the causes are similar to those in the past, the intensity and the scale of contemporary conflicts are quite different. Part of the explanation lies with the expansion of the international system of communication, as we saw in the discussion of nationalism. Because of jet travel, newspapers, radio, and satellite television, no part of the world is isolated from events anywhere. A budding ethnic separatist movement in Canada is fueled by events in Northern Ireland or Belgium. The insularity of Chinese in Malaysia is affected by the repression of Chinese in Africa. Not only do ethnic successes or persecutions in other parts of the world have a morale-building effect on other ethnic movements but also strategies are borrowed.

An argument can be made that the hostilities in Northern Ireland go back to the twelfth century or that the Walloons and the Flemings have long been antagonistic in Belgium. The difference is that the focus of today's conflicts is not religion or language or any single feature. The conflicts are frequently based on ethnic groups' acting as interest groups, broadly defined. Then, even if cultural differences become minimal, the ethnic group can still be used as a vehicle for mobilizing individuals to act in the group's interests. Ethnic groups are more and more often the basis of mobilization. Ethnic conflicts have become one form in which interest conflicts within and between states are pursued (Glazer and Moynihan 1975:7).

Detractors as well as supporters of the New Ethnicity agree that the contemporary manipulation of cultural differences is unlike anything that has preceded it:

> The New Ethnicity is a "revitalization movement," a "nativistic movement," . . . ; it is *something new* and clearly distinguishable from what scholars see as time-honored or timeless cultural units. . . . [it] is a new identity that selectively incorporates cultural content from the past. The key to such use is not the past, however, but current needs. The New Ethnicity offers a sense of descent and of affiliation that confers the illusion of continuity with the chosen past. [Stein and Hill 1977:2]

In other words, the past is important not for its own sake, but for the sense of tradition that it confers on contemporary groups, which may, in turn, be used to gain both material and spiritual advantages over other groups. Further, not all of the past is reconstructed as part of current symbol systems, only the "useful" aspects. An analogous case are family genealogies that conveniently omit the proverbial horse thief.

In fact, it is when the undiscriminated past is dwelt upon that ethnicity becomes crippling. Reminiscing about the way it used to be prevents people from attending to contemporary problems. When critics of the New Ethnicity focus on this aspect they are correct in their attacks. To cast all instances of ethnicity into this category, however, is misleading. We have enough examples of the active selection of ethnic identity symbols to indicate that a positive benefit is possible.

Factors Contributing to Contemporary Ethnicity

Martin Kilsen (1975) argues that the Black movement in the United States initiated the recent period of neo-ethnicity. He limits his argument to the influence on United States groups, but Glazer and Moynihan see an even wider sphere of influence: "a black power" movement in the West Indies, a "civil rights" movement in Northern Ireland, "black panthers" in Israel, and some French Canadians who claimed they were "white niggers" (1975:21). They conclude that each group using the idiom of the Black movement was well aware of its situation and its reason to feel aggrieved, and that the worldwide mass media simply exposed each group to the example of another movement.

Increased Heterogeneity of States

Along with the expansion of communication, ease of travel has been contributing to the heterogeneity of countries. In the great wave of immigration in the nineteenth century, which was prompted by the international economic situation, masses of laborers were moved around the world. The transfer of cheap labor has not yet ceased. In northern Europe, for example, there is a continual influx of labor from the south. Common Market regulations allow laborers from any participating country to work in any other member country, and many emigrate illegally in search of a better living. In sum, the heterogeneity begun by nineteenth-century emigration is still being advanced by today's movement of peoples, many of whom are prompted by the same desires as their nineteenth-century counterparts.

Rise of the Welfare and Socialist States

Ethnic groups become convenient foci when welfare and socialist states must confront the realities of maintaining their citizens' loyalites. According to Glazer and Moynihan, governments that "do things" for large and amorphous groups squander their resources and get nothing in return. A better strategy is

> to make claims for groups small enough to make significant concessions possible and, equally, small enough to produce some gain from the concessions made. . . . A British prime minister who does "something for the workers" probably doesn't do much. . . . Doing something for the Scots, however, becomes an increasingly attractive and real option for Westminster. [1975:9]

To a certain extent, this kind of ethnic patronage has always existed, but with the rise of a positive image for ethnicity, the practice has expanded to unbelievable proportions. This is especially ironic in light of the various civil rights acts of the 1960s, which prohibit any categorization based on race, color, or national origin, among other statuses (ibid.:10). In order to dole out the government largesse equitably and correct past patterns of discrimination, however, the government had to be able to pinpoint certain groups. Boxes for race, color, and national origin began to appear on application forms, and since it was to their benefit (as was sometimes indicated explicitly) to do so, members of subordinate groups checked the boxes. This practice was an expansion of one well known to Native Americans, who for years preceding the civil rights movement, had had to prove that they were enrolled members of recognized tribal groups in order to receive benefits from the government.

Inequality

Inequality strengthens boundaries between social categories in two situations: (1) Everyone shares the same norms, and groups and individuals are variously successful in meeting them. Most cases of class stratification fit this description. (2) Each group has a different set of norms. Ethnic group plurality is such a situation. Competition between groups in both cases generates boundary-maintaining behaviors, but cultural pluralism may ultimately be the more devisive of the two. Glazer and Moynihan (1975) and many others have recognized that the rallying power of ethnicity lies in its combination of interest and affect. As Shils and Janowitz indicated in their study of the Wehrmacht (1948), primary group ties, of which ethnicity is one, become the irreducible allegiance when other ties are shattered by circumstance. Moreover, ethnic interests do not have to accept a common set of norms, as do social classes. When various ethnic groups occupy unequal positions, one finds, in addition to boundary maintenance, competition for a larger share of the available resources.

Primordial Sentiments

A final factor that has influenced the contemporary significance of ethnic identity has been the appeal of primary, affective ties in a world where much interaction is between persons occupying institutionalized roles, where the importance of the individual is often subverted to some vague notion of social good, where the future is uncertain. The ethnic group has many of the same qualities as the family. An individual may claim membership by ascription often without demonstrating any achieved characteristics. In that sense, it is a ready-made support group but with some important differences.

> The ethnic group differs from the kinship community precisely in being a group (which believes in its common descent) but not a community, unlike the kinship group which is characterized by actual communal action. In our present sense, the ethnic community itself is not a community; it only facilitates communal relationships. [Weber 1947:306]

Weber highlighted the differences that make ethnic groups more functional than kinship groups in many modern contexts. The ethnic group is there to facilitate relationships, but it does not have a corporate existence as a community to which members owe daily allegiance. When ethnic group membership is inconvenient, the individual may choose to ignore it. Further, the ethnic group is a larger category than the family or lineage, so that an individual ethnic has the backing of a larger community when it is necessary. This feature is especially important in a mobile society. It is much easier to find an ethnic community than one based on actual kinship. An ethnic connection may provide material benefits as well as help one avoid feelings of anonymity, disorientation, or not belonging. Much intangible good derives from familiar food, music, language, and social forms.

Why Ethnicity?

If we accept contemporary ethnicity as a new and significant phenomenon, then we are bound to ask the crucial question, why is ethnicity used, rather than some other strategy of association? Weber wonders whether the actual content of communal action based on ethnicity is any different from that based on any other body of custom:

> There is no difference between the ethnically relevant customs and customs in general, as far as their effect is concerned. The belief in affiliation of descent [*Abstammungsverwandtschaft*], in combination with a similarity of customs, is likely to promote the diffusion of communal action among those allied by ethnic ties, because "imitation" is generally encouraged by the consciousness of community. . . .The content of communal action that is possible on an ethnic basis remains indefinite. [1947:308]

In our original definition, ethnic group was described as a reference group. To explain the popularity of the ethnic group, we must consider two other possible reference groups, social class and religion.

Social Class

We have noted at various points the prediction that social class would soon make ethnicity obsolete. Attached to this notion was the belief in the basic conservative and devisive nature of ethnicity as a point of reference. In 1853 Karl Marx made this point succinctly as he explained how British rule came to be established in India:

> The paramount power of the Great Mogul was broken by the Mogul Viceroys. The power of the Viceroys was broken by the Mahrattas. The power of the Mahrattas was broken by the Afghans, and while all were struggling against all, the Briton rushed in and was enabled to subdue them all. A country not only divided between Mohammed-an and Hindoo, but between tribe and tribe, between caste and caste; a society whose framework was based on a sort of equilibrium, re-sulting from a general repulsion and constitutional exclusiveness be-tween all its members. Such a country and such a society, were they not the predestined prey of conquest? [In Stone 1977:5]

If one holds Marx's view, it is then natural to believe that as a country, state, or nation progresses, it will gradually slough off ways that are antithetical to modernity and replace them with more-adaptive re-sponses. Scholars, politicians, and political thinkers agreed that class would be the most effective organizing principle for modern nations, but it has not succeeded in replacing ethnicity even where a social class structure has followed on the heels of independence. Not only has ethnic identity been no handicap but it has been the vanguard of a number of nationalistic movements.

Religious Movements

The relationship between religious movements and ethnicity as strat-egies is interesting and complex. We can point to many instances where ethnic groups have used a primarily religious idiom to voice their in-terests. For other groups, such as the Jews, the religious component is seemingly inseparable. Still other groups have shifted between ethnicity and religion as points of reference.

As Van den Berghe (1976) has argued for class, religious movements and ethnicity seem to be alternate choices, rarely existing at the same time. Stating it in another way, when access to political activity is avail-able, ethnicity appears to be the usual choice of strategy. When political activity is stifled, punished, or nonexistent, people's energies find an outlet in revitalization movements, millenarianism, or religious cults.

In the example of the Yaqui and their neighbors, the Mayo, the former were successful in maintaining their identity through a combi-nation of resources: relative isolation, early prosperity, and opposition.

They were willing to fight for their identity, and they had the resources to do so successfully. The Mayo in contrast, lacked all the strategic resources necessary for their survival. They did not enjoy the protection of nearby mountains; they did not have the strong organization into towns that the Yaqui had; and they suffered drastic reductions in their population from epidemics. They had none of the means with which to forge a political organization that would be effective against outside opposition. Mayo history has been characterized by a series of revitalization movements, especially in the last fifteen years. They feature voices of the Virgin and Jesus telling selected Mayo, who then pass along the message, that they are being punished for their lack of attention to Mayo tradition. Each time a vision appears there is a revival of the culture, but it gradually diminishes until it is renewed by another voice. The energy generated by the voices and visions is turned back on itself in the form of the elaboration of ritual. With limited energies, little if any effort is directed to Mayo identity in the political sense. It is all dissipated and defused by religious movements.

Two observations by different writers based on data from different areas support the hypothesis that ethnicity and religiously based movements are mutually exclusive. Basil Davidson (1955) commented on the relationship between tribal politics and religious movements in Africa:

> It cannot be an accident that these "dissident religions," these strange Biblical forms of subversion should be peaceful in territories, such as the Gold Coast or the French Sudan, where Africans have a legitimate political outlet, and the reverse of peaceful in the Belgian Congo, where Africans have none. There are close analogies in Kenya and South Africa. Wherever Africans are balked in every means of political advance, they tend to take their own way out. [Cited in Emerson 1960:66]

"A legitimate political outlet" means that the Africans invest their energies in governmental activities and are not reduced to channeling their desires for recognition into religious movements of a violent sort.

Kilsen (1975) offers additional support in his observations on the American Black movement. He maintains that in movements for ethnic legitimization, two components must characterize each successful movement—psychological/cultural (particularistic) processes and political (universal) processes. He cites many instances of Black leaders who thought they could succeed on the particularistic component alone and did not need to make the compromises required of them by the political process. Kilsen disagrees: "No such movement can approximate its particularistic or identity focused goals without the aid of the substantive benefits derived from politics and power" (ibid.:251). Without the latter, the particularistic aspects of the movement turn in on themselves; they become ritualistically self-indulgent, messianic, and millenarian.

It is too soon to reach any conclusions about the relationship between ethnicity and millenarianism or to make any value judgments about their relative merits. It may be that religious movements are a way of keeping alive ethnic sentiments when there are no other means. They would function then as one sphere of interaction. Spicer (1971) had suggested that there were three such spheres necessary for the continuance of persistent identity systems—the moral, the political, and that of a common language. On the other hand, it may be that such violent movements are dysfunctional over the longer time span. They may use up the "moral credit" of a group in the eyes of the larger society, which may take measures to control both the group and its religious beliefs. Such was the effect of the Ghost Dance on Plains Indian groups in the late nineteenth century and the Cult of the Speaking Cross among the Maya, which led to the Caste War of Yucatan. Alternatively, a group may become so engrossed in the religious sphere that it gradually forgets any idea of political activity.

In the case of the Sephardic Jews, religion and religious oppression have been credited with preventing assimilation. Seymour B. Liebman argues, following Henry C. Lea, that "if Spain had decreed complete religious equality and freedom for all Jews within their realm, within fifty years, the Jews would have assimilated and abandoned Judaism" (1978:103). In this case the group perceived itself as identical in terms of nationality with the larger entity but forced to maintain a separate identity because of religious persecution.

Concerning the advantages of one of these reference points over another, I would agree with writers such as Kilsen, who argue that the religious component of any movement for ethnic revitalization can only have a harmful effect if it becomes the sole basis of the movement and an end in itself. The combination of the two, however, leads to undeniably powerful positions based on affect and institutional clout.

Pros and Cons

"Ethnicity," "ethnic identity," "ethnic group"—all these words are capable of provoking the strongest passions. The scholar, the politician, and the person on the street have opinions about the value or the evil influence of ethnic identity. Sometimes their opinions are justified by sociological arguments surrounding the nature of society and human groups; sometimes false statistics and stereotypes are proffered; and sometimes simple expediency holds sway. The last is true of both supporters and detractors, and the ultimate expediency can be practiced by either: "It is one of the more ghastly paradoxes of modern times that it has become a simpler matter to exterminate a population than to change its habits" (Diringer 1962:89). The fact that this kind of "solution" is possible in today's world makes the subject of ethnic differences all the more explosive. It is a mandate for us to explore carefully the arguments on both sides.

Arguments for the Negative Impact of Ethnic Identity

Countering the argument that ethnic identity is contrary to individual fulfillment, supporters of ethnic identity argue that it is one of the few areas in which one *can* be an individual. Identification with an ethnic group requires some adherence to group norms, some participation in a group mind. To the extent that this identification becomes an individual's sole identity, it is dysfunctional. Such single-minded adherence occurs under certain circumstances: (1) Strong groups demand more conformity, and because they are strong, individuals feel that they will benefit by being conforming members. (2) Societies that have a large number of ethnic groups tend to foster greater intergroup cohesiveness because there are more groups competing for the same resources (Patterson 1975:11). (3) Weak or anomic individuals will cling to an ethnic identity because they lack other sources of identity.

Devereux makes a compelling argument for the potential of ethnic identity (or *any* group identity) to destroy the multidimensionality of human beings:

> [A]n insistent and even obsessive stressing of and clinging to one's ethnic (or any other "class") identity reveals a flaw in one's self-

conception as a unique multidimensional entity. . . . An overriding
emphasis on one of a person's several "class" identities . . . simply
seeks to shore up a flawed self and an uncertain awareness of one's
identity as a person. The current tendency to stress one's ethnic or
class identity, its use as a crutch, is *prima facie* evidence of the impend-
ing collapse of the only valid sense of identity: one's differentness.
[1975:67–68]

Patterson agrees with Devereux, most publicly in an article entitled
"Ethnicity and the Pluralist Fallacy." He asserts that ethnicity and "the
spurious social philosophy of pluralism that rationalizes it, are the new
dangers to individuality and personal autonomy" (1975:10). He is perfectly correct, of course, when he speaks of the "vulgar extremes" to
which ethnicity has sometimes gone; these are deplorable. He also criticizes the liberal defense of ethnic pluralism, which claims that diversity
is a desirable end in itself, that a heterogeneous society is a more vital
one. Given the conditions in which many ethnic groups live, it is hard
to condone the kind of attitude that would keep them as they are so that
our "cafeteria" society may enjoy them when it feels the need for a little
diversity. What these critics are saying is that ethnicity does not promote individual identity but is just the latest in a series of mechanisms
that submerge the individual in the group.

A second and equally serious criticism of today's ethnicity is that it
glorifies the past and so obstructs progress. Richard Sennett (1976), in
the *New York Times*, voices the opinions of many critics: "The virtues
of ethnic community in the past have become a yardstick to measure
present-day communal emptiness, and, not coincidentally, an ideological weapon to fight reforms like racial integration." For him, ethnic
identity is used to shore up the myth of decline, the idea that the present
is inferior to the past. He believes that nostalgia, especially as a part of
politics, is debilitating. The same concern is shown by Howe, the
author of a clear-eyed account of Jewish immigrants in the United
States, who fears that today's Jews will be lulled by a sentimentalism
that erases memories of ugliness and hatred (1978:195). And he sees the
dangers of the parochialism that accompany the ethnic impulse: "the
smugness of snug streets as against the perilous visions of large cities,
the indulgent celebration of habitual ways simply because they are
habitual" (ibid.:197). He fears the anaesthetizing process of retreat into
an all-absorbing, all-forgiving group identity.

Sennett, Howe, and others are protesting the crippling effect that mindless acceptance of an ethnic identity may have. Their fear is that potentially troublesome groups may be encouraged to spend their energies on Columbus Day parades, while the real political game is played elsewhere and by different rules.

Another criticism of ethnicity is that it can create division and a separatist ideology. This movement has a long history, and at its core is fear of the stranger. Every society that is composed of different ethnic groups is, at some time or another, suspicious of those groups, of their loyalty to the larger entity. The ethnonationalistic movements discussed in chapter 4 have done little to lay this suspicion to rest; on the contrary, they have exacerbated it. This strategy is very different from that used by previous ethnic groups that were trying to gain some control over their own destinies. The new strategy plays on the basic fear that dominant groups have of those subordinate to them. Will all this lead to what Stein and Hill (1977b) have called the "ideology of exclusivism" or a "Balkanization of American life"? It must be admitted that there is the potential for the abrogation of social conscience if one's highest allegiance is to one's ethnic group. To take one example, that of integration, Stein and Hill contend that separate but equal is the logical outcome of the New Pluralism. "Under the New Pluralism . . . no one need speak of racial segregation, but instead one can speak . . . of ethnic resegmentation in culturally homogeneous neighborhoods in which, surely, no outsider would wish to live" (ibid.:186–187).

Finally, there is the argument that ethnic identity is essentially a negative identity. It is a perverse clinging to an outmoded past. More than that, it has become today a deliberate choice of negative symbols: "The semantics and the symbolism of the movement celebrate emblems of identity that were only recently repressed and repudiated" (Stein and Hill 1977a:214). A negative imagery defines ethnic identity: "Others outside the ethnic boundary still define the New Ethnic's identity" (ibid.:215). The negativism can refer as well to the process of identification. George De Vos and L. Romanucci-Ross (1975) point out the possibility that defining oneself as an ethnic may have a hostile and paranoid component. Moving to sociological interpretations of the process, Sennett (1976) again refers to past-orientation: "the language of ethnic revivalists is like the language of museum curators, talk of conservatism, preservation, restoration. The ethnic revivalists speak as they do because they are obsessed with the idea that ethnicity is dying out."

Arguments for the Positive Influence of Ethnic Identity

Equally compelling arguments can be made in favor of ethnic iden-tity. One answer to the anti-individualism argument is the intermediate nature of the ethnic tie, which was discussed earlier in this chapter. It is larger than the family or kindred, yet requires less of a daily commit-ment. It satisfies the need for a flexible group bound by affective or primary ties beyond the family. It is flexible in that members may in-voke the ethnic tie when necessary or disregard it when it is a liability. Even in a crisis situation in which the group must present a united front in order to survive, the choice of belonging still resides with the indi-vidual member. Although larger than the family, the ethnic group is still smaller than most other social groupings and more distinctive. One has a more-distinct, more-individual identity as a member of an ethnic group than as a member of a social class, and the satisfaction of par-ticipating in an ethnic festival is missing from events connected with one's social class.

We find refutation of the argument that ethnicity is a strategy of the past, that it is conservative and opposed to progress, in the words of two of ethnicity's opponents, Stein and Hill (1977a,b). They see the New Ethnicity as actively editing the past so that it presents a better image. In other words, the past is not sacred; rather, it provides mate-rial for a contemporary scenario designed to benefit group members. When it is used this way, there is no obsessive clinging to history for its own sake. In defense of the past as a component of today's ethnicity, it must be argued that an historical element generally allows a group to muster a larger membership and present a stronger image to the world.

The third objection, that directed toward the tendency toward separatism, also has a positive side. As Geertz (1963) has stated, move-ments toward nationalism in Malaysia used ethnic blocs as the stepping stones to a state-level of organization. They were the one obvious way of organizing people politically that was indigenous to the country, and as such they proved their worth in post-independence politics. Many African nations have had the same experience. Ethnic segregation, whi has more frequently been self-imposed, is the opposite swing of the pendulum from a context in which ethnicity was not allowed. Given time, a balance should be struck.

The negative element in contemporary ethnic movements is easily explained if one looks at ethnicity as a recent reaction to previous anti-ethnic attitudes. Retaliation is an understandable emotion given the circumstances, hence the shame attached to being a non-ethnic; one has to have ethnic roots. Conversely, the ethnics, especially the so-called white ethnics, have frequently chosen to define themselves in terms of what non-ethnic America is not. This use of negative imagery is by no means new (the reader will recall the story of "Yankee Doodle"). It has been used successfully by some of our most-enduring cultural identity systems, the Jews, for example. Symbols are always built up out of interaction in any case, and one can only judge their positive or negative qualities over the long term.

We can do more than simply refute the arguments advanced by critics of ethnicity. We can offer some benefits. The most important is the flexibility that an additional identity provides for the individual in the constant give and take of interaction. Moreover, it is easier to claim an ethnic identity than any other. There are many more ethnic identities than religious ones. Further, one can be committed as much or as little as one chooses to an ethnic group. Unless the group is under extreme pressure from outside, relatively few demands are made of individual members to demonstrate their allegiance. In moving to a new location, one can choose to activate ethnic ties, as the Pakistanis do in London, or to ignore them, as the Maltese do in England.

The ethnic group provides an affective experience outside the nuclear family. As Shils and others have amply demonstrated, people search out affective ties, which are rare in today's society.

Lastly, the element of pride is not to be taken lightly. Today, ethnic identity is not a shameful thing; in fact, its absence is. Ethnic pride is not limited to the group itself; it is the heritage of each and every member. It is the savor and remembrance of the past. More important, it is the promise of the future.

References Cited

Albert, Ethel
  1960   Sociopolitical Organization and Receptivity to Change: Some
          Differences between Ruanda and Urundi. *Southwestern Journal of
          Anthropology* 16:46–74.
Ardener, Edwin
  1970   Witchcraft, Economics, and the Continuity of Belief. In *Witch-
          craft: Confessions and Accusations*, edited by Mary Douglas. Lon-
          don: Tavistock.
Arens, William
  1975   The Waswahili: The Social History of an Ethnic Group. *Africa*
          45:426–438.
Balandier, George
  1951   The Colonial Situation: A Theoretical Approach. In *Social
          Change: The Colonial Situation*, edited by Immanuel Wallerstein.
          New York: John Wiley & Sons, 1966.
Barnes, J.A.
  1960   Indigenous Politics and Colonial Administration. *Comparative
          Studies in Society and History* 2(2):133–149.
Barth, Fredrik
  1969   *Ethnic Groups and Boundaries.* Boston: Little, Brown and Co.
Berreman, Gerald
  1975   Bazar Behavior: Social Identity and Social Interaction in Urban
          India. In *Ethnic Identity: Cultural Continuities and Change*, edited by
          George De Vos and L. Romanucci-Ross. Palo Alto: Mayfield
          Publishing.
Beuf, Ann H.
  1977   *Red Children in White America.* Philadelphia: University of Penn-
          sylvania Press.
Bittle, William
  1962   The Manatidie: A Focus on Kiowa Tribal Identity. *Plains An-
          thropologist* 7:152–163.

233

Blu, Karen
    1980   The Lumbee Problem: The Making of an American Indian People.
            Cambridge: Cambridge University Press.
Borgese, G. Ant.
    1934   Romanticism. In Encyclopedia of the Social Sciences, vol. 13, edited
            by Edwin Seligman. New York: Macmillan. Pp. 426–434.
Breton, Raymond and M. Pinard
    1960   Group Formation among Immigrants: Criteria and Processes.
            Canadian Journal of Economics and Political Science 26:465–477.
Brettell, Caroline B.
    1977   Ethnicity and Entrepreneurs: Portuguese Immigrants in a Cana-
            dian City. In Ethnic Encounters: Identities and Contexts, edited by
            George Hicks and P. Leis. North Scituate, MA: Duxbury Press.
Chance, John
    1978   Race and Class in Colonial Oaxaca. Stanford: Stanford University
            Press.
Charsley, S.R.
    1974   The Formation of Ethnic Groups. In Urban Ethnicity, edited by
            Abner Cohen. London: Tavistock.
Cohen, Abner
    1969   Custom and Politics in Urban Africa. Berkeley: University of
            California Press.
    1974   Two-Dimensional Man. Berkeley: University of California Press.
Cohen, Abner, ed.
    1974   Urban Ethnicity. London: Tavistock.
Coleman, Terry
    1973   Going to America. New York: Anchor Books.
Collier, George A.
    1976   Fields of the Tzotzil: The Ecological Bases of Tradition in Highland
            Chiapas. Austin: University of Texas Press.
Colson, Elizabeth
    1953   The Makah Indians: A Study of an Indian Tribe in Modern American
            Society. Minneapolis: University of Minnesota Press.
    1968   Contemporary Tribes and The Development of Nationalism. In
            Essays on the Problems of Tribe, edited by J. Helm. Seattle and Lon-
            don: University of Washington Press. Proceedings of the 1967
            Annual Spring Meeting of the American Ethnological Society.
            Pp. 201–208.
Connor, Walker
    1977   Nation-Building or Nation-Destroying. In Race, Ethnicity, and
            Social Change, edited by John Stone. North Scituate, MA: Dux-
            bury Press.
Coser, Lewis
    1956   The Functions of Social Conflict. Glencoe, IL: Free Press.
Covarrubias, Miguel
    1946   Mexico South: The Isthmus of Tehuantepec. New York: Alfred
            Knopf.
Crumrine, Ross
    1964   The House Cross of the Mayo Indians of Sonora, Mexico. The An-
            thropological Papers # 8. Tuscon: University of Arizona Press.

Curtin, Philip D., ed.
  1972   Africa and the West: Intellectual Responses to European Culture. Madison: University of Wisconsin Press.

Dahya, Badr
  1974   The Nature of Pakistani Ethnicity in Industrial Cities in Britain. In Urban Ethnicity, edited by Abner Cohen. London: Tavistock.

Davidson, Basil
  1955   Enlightened Colonialism. The Reporter January 27:34–39.

Dench, Geoff
  1975   Maltese in London: A Case Study in the Erosion of Ethnic Consciousness. London: Routledge & Kegan Paul.

Deutsch, Karl
  1966   Nationalism and Social Communication: An Inquiry into the Foundations of Nationality, 2d ed. Cambridge: MIT Press.

Deutsch, Karl and W.J. Flotz, eds.
  1963   Nation Building. New York: Atherton Press.

Devereux, George
  1975   Ethnic Identity: Its Logical Foundations and its Dysfunctions. In Ethnic Identity: Cultural Continuities and Change, edited by George De Vos and L. Romanucci-Ross. Palo Alto: Mayfield Publishing.

De Vos, George
  1975   Ethnic Pluralism: Conflict and Accomodation. In Ethnic Identity: Cultural Continuities and Change, edited by George De Vos and L. Romanucci-Ross. Palo Alto: Mayfield Publishing.

De Vos, George and L. Romanucci-Ross, eds.
  1975   Ethnic Identity: Cultural Continuities and Change. Palo Alto: Mayfield Publishing.

Diringer, David
  1962   Writing. New York: Frederick A. Praeger.

Dixon, Joseph K.
  1913   The Vanishing Race: The Last Great Indian Council. New York: Bonanza Books.

Doornbos, Martin
  1972   Some Conceptual Problems Concerning Ethnicity in Integration Analysis. Civilisations XXII, 1(1972):263–284.

Ekvall, Robert B.
  1939   Cultural Relations on the Kansu-Tibetan Border. Chicago: University of Chicago Press.

Emerson, Rupert
  1960   From Empire to Nation: The Rise to Self-Assertion of Asian and African Peoples. Cambridge: Harvard University Press.

Epstein, A.L.
  1958   Politics in an Urban African Community. Manchester: Manchester University Press.

Fichte, Johann Gottlieb
  1968   Addresses to the German Nation, edited with an introduction by George A. Kelly. (Originally published in 1896 in German.) New York: Harper & Row.

Fortes, Meyer
 1945 *The Dynamics of Clanship among the Tallensi*. London: Oxford University Press.

Francis, Emerich K.
 1976 *Interethnic Relations: An Essay in Sociological Theory*. New York: Elsevier.

Gambino, Richard
 1975 *Blood of my Blood: The Dilemma of the Italian-Americans*. New York: Anchor Books.

Garbett, G. Kingsley
 1970 The Analysis of Social Situations. *Man* 5:214–227.

Gearing, Frederick
 1970 *The Face of the Fox*. Chicago: Aldine/Atherton.

Geertz, Clifford
 1963 Primordial Sentiments and Civil Polities in New States. In *Old Societies and New States*, edited by Clifford Geertz. New York: Free Press.

Gelfand, Donald E.
 1973 Ethnic Relations and Social Research: A Reevaluation. In *Ethnic Conflicts and Power: A Cross-National Perspective*, edited by Donald Gelfand and R.D. Lee. New York: John Wiley & Sons.

Glazer, Nathan and Daniel P. Moynihan
 1963 *Beyond the Melting Pot: The Negroes, Puerto Ricans, Jews, Italians, and Irish of New York*. Cambridge: MIT and Harvard University presses.

Glazer, Nathan and Daniel P. Moynihan, eds.
 1975 *Ethnicity: Theory and Experience*. Cambridge: Harvard University Press.

Gluckman, Max
 1949 *An Analysis of the Sociological Theories of Bronislaw Malinowski*. The Rhodes Livingstone Papers #16. London: Oxford University Press.

Goffman, Erving
 1959 *The Presentation of Self in Everyday Life*. New York: Doubleday Anchor Books.

Gordon, Milton
 1964 *Assimilation in American Life: The Role of Race, Religion, and National Origins*. New York: Oxford University Press.

Gorer, Geoffrey
 1975 English Identity over Time and Empire. In *Ethnic Identity: Cultural Continuities and Change*, edited by George De Vos and L. Romanucci-Ross. Palo Alto: Mayfield Publishing.

Hall, Jacqueline D.
 1977 Women and Lynching. *Southern Exposure* 4:53–55.

Hansen, Marcus Lee
 1948 *The Immigrant in American History*. Cambridge: Harvard University Press.

Hechter, Michael
 1971 Towards a Theory of Ethnic Change. *Politics and Society* 2:21–45.

Hicks, George and Philip Leis, eds.
  1977   Ethnic Encounters: Identities and Contexts. North Scituate, MA:
          Duxbury.

Howe, Irving
  1978   The Limits of Ethnicity. In Ethnic America, edited by M. Weiser.
          New York: The H.W. Wilson Co.

Hudson, Charles M., ed.
  1971   Red, White, and Black: Symposium on Indians in the Old South. Pro-
          ceedings of the Southern Anthropological Society, #5. Athens:
          University of Georgia Press.

Ianni, Francis
  1974   Black Mafia: Ethnic Succession in Organized Crime. New York:
          Simon & Schuster.

Isaacs, Harold R.
  1975   Idols of the Tribe: Group Identity and Political Change. New York:
          Harper & Row.

Isajiw, Wsevolod
  1974   Definitions of Ethnicity. Ethnicity 1:111–124.

Kanter, Rosabeth M.
  1977   Some Effects of Proportions on Group Life: Skewed Sex Ratios
          and Responses to Token Women. American Journal of Sociology
          82:965–990.

Kilsen, Martin
  1975   Blacks and Neo-Ethnicity in American Political Life. In Ethnicity:
          Theory and Experience, edited by Nathan Glaser and Daniel P.
          Moynihan. Cambridge: Harvard University Press.

Klaff, Vivian
  1977   Residence and Integration in Israel: A Mosaic of Segregated
          Peoples. Ethnicity 4:103–121.

Kohn, Hans
  1944   The Idea of Nationalism: A Study of Its Origins and Backgrounds.
          New York: Macmillan.
  1946   Prophets and Peoples. New York: Macmillan.
  1953   Pan-Slavism: Its History and Ideology. New York: Vintage Books.
  1968   Nationalism. In International Encyclopedia of the Social Sciences, vol.
          11.

Kroeber, Alfred L.
  1963   Style and Civilization. Berkeley: University of California Press.

Ladd, John
  1975   Conceptual Problems Relating to the Comparative Study of Art.
          In The Traditional Artist in African Societies, edited by Warren
          d'Azevedo. Bloomington: Indiana University Press.

Lantz, Herman
  1958   People of Coal Town. New York: Columbia University Press.

Lattimore, Owen
  1940   Inner Asian Frontiers of China. New York: American Geographical
          Society.

Leach, Maria and J. Fried, eds.
    1949   Standard Dictionary of Folklore, Mythology, and Legend, vol. 2. New
              York: Funk & Wagnall's.
Lemarchand, René
    1966   Social Change and Political Modernization in Burundi. Journal of
              Modern African Studies 4:401–434.
    1975   Ethnic Genocide. Society 12:50–60.
Levy, Sydelle
    1975   Shifting Patterns of Ethnic Identification among the Hassidim. In
              The New Ethnicity: Perspectives from Ethnology, edited by John
              Bennett. St. Paul: West Publishing Co.
Lieberson, Stanley
    1961   A Societal Theory of Race and Ethnic Relations. American
              Sociological Review 26:902–910.
Liebman, Seymour B.
    1978   Jews as an Ethnic Group in the Americas. In Community, Self, and
              Identity, edited by Bhabagrahi Misra and J. Preston. The Hague:
              Mouton.
Light, Ivan H.
    1972   Ethnic Enterprise in America: Business and Welfare among Chinese,
              Japanese, and Blacks. Berkeley: University of California Press.
Lindgren, Ethel
    1938   An Example of Culture Contact without Conflict. American An-
              thropologist 40:605–621.
Lipset, Seymour M. and Stein Rokkan, eds.
    1967   Party Systems and Voter Alignments: Cross-National Perspectives.
              New York: Free Press.
Lopez Chiñas, Gabriel
    1969   Juchitan. Mexico, D.F.: Vinnigulasa.
Lyman, Stanford M. and William A. Douglass
    1973   Ethnicity: Strategies of Collective and Individual Impression
              Management. Social Research 40:344–365.
MacGaffey, Wyatt
    1972   The West in Congolese Experience. In Africa and the West: Intellec-
              tual Responses to European Culture, edited by Philip D. Curtin.
              Madison: University of Wisconsin Press.
Malinowski, Bronislaw
    1945   Theories of Culture Change. In Social Change: The Colonial Situa-
              tion, edited by Immanuel Wallerstein. New York: John Wiley &
              Sons, 1966.
Mannoni, Dominique
    1956   Prospero and Caliban: The Psychology of Colonization, translated by
              Pamela Powesland. London: Methuen and Co. Ltd.
Marx, Karl
    1977   The Future Results of British Rule in India (originally published
              in 1853). In Race, Ethnicity, and Social Change, edited by John
              Stone. North Scituate, MA: Duxbury Press.
Mead, George Herbert
    1934   Mind, Self, and Society. Chicago: University of Chicago Press.

Metzger, Paul
    1971   American Sociology and Black Assimilation. *American Journal of Sociology* 76.
Mitchell, J.C.
    1956   *The Kalela Dance: Aspects of Social Relationships among Urban Africans in Northern Rhodesia.* Rhodes Livingstone Papers #27.
Mitchell, J.C., ed.
    1969   *Social Networks in Urban Situations.* Manchester: Manchester University Press.
Moerman, Michael
    1965   Ethnic Identification in a Complex Civilization. *American Anthropologist* 67:1215–1230.
Mussolini, Benito
    1964   The Doctrine of Fascism (orginally published 1938). In *Dynamics of Nationalism*, edited by Louis Snyder. Princeton, N.J.: Van Nostrand.
Nagata, Judith
    1974   What Is a Malay? Situational Selection of Ethnic Identity in a Plural Society. *American Ethnologist* 1:331–350.
Novak, Michael
    1971   *The Rise of the Unmeltable Ethnics.* New York: Macmillan & Co.
Parsons, Talcott, ed.
    1961   *Theories of Society.* New York: The Free Press.
Patterson, Orlando
    1975   Ethnicity and the Pluralist Fallacy. *Change: The Magazine of Higher Learning* 7 (2).
Plotnikov, Leonard and M. Silverman
    1978   Jewish Ethnic Signalling: Social Bonding in Contemporary American Society. *Ethnology* 17:407–423.
Redfield, Robert
    1941   *The Folk Culture of Yucatan.* Chicago: University of Chicago Press.
Ronen, Dov
    1979   *The Quest for Self-Determination.* New Haven: Yale University Press.
Royce, Anya Peterson
    1974   Dance as an Indicator of Social Class and Identity in Juchitán, Oaxaca. In *New Dimensions in Dance Research: Anthropology and Dance (The American Indian)*, edited by Tamara Comstock. New York: Committee on Research in Dance.
    1975   *Prestigio y Afiliacion en una Comunidad Urbana: Juchitán, Oaxaca.* Serie de Antropologia Social #37. Mexico, D.F.: SEP/Setentas.
    1977   *The Anthropology of Dance.* Bloomington: Indiana University Press.
Rudin, Harry R.
    1938   *Germans in the Cameroons, 1884–1914.* New Haven: Yale University Press.
Rustow, Dankwert A.
    1968   Nation. In *International Encyclopedia of the Social Sciences*, vol 11, edited by David Sills.

Said, Abdul and Luiz R. Simmons
    1975   The Ethnic Factor in World Politics. *Society* 12:65–74.
Saloutos, Theodore
    1956   *They Remember America.* Berkeley: University of California Press.
Schermerhorn, R.A.
    1974   Ethnicity in the Perspective of the Sociology of Knowledge.
            Ethnicity 1:1–14.
Sengstock, Mary C.
    1977   Social Change in the Country of Origin as a Factor in Immigrant
            Conceptions of Nationality. *Ethnicity* 4:54–70.
Sennett, Richard
    1976   Pure as the Driven Slush. *New York Times,* May 10.
Shibutani, Tamatsu and Kian M. Kwan
    1965   *Ethnic Stratification.* New York: Macmillan.
Shils, Edward
    1957   Primordial, Personal, Sacred, and Civil Ties. *British Journal of
            Sociology* 8:130–145.
Shils, Edward and M. Janowitz
    1948   Cohesion and Disintegration in the Wehrmacht in World War II.
            Public Opinion Quarterly 12:280–315.
Skinner, G. William
    1963   *The Thailand Chinese: Assimilation in a Changing Society.* New
            York: Asia Society.
Snyder, Louis, ed.
    1964   *The Dynamics of Nationalism.* Princeton, N.J.: Van Nostrand.
Social Science Research Council
    1974   Comparative Research on Ethnicity: A Conference Report, edited
            by Wendell Bell. *Items* 28, 4:61–64. New York: Social Science Re-
            search Council.
Spicer, Edward
    1962   *Cycles of Conquest.* Tucson: University of Arizona.
    1971   Persistent Identity Systems. *Science* (4011):795–800.
Spitzer, Leo
    1972   The Creoles of Sierra Leone. In *Africa and the West: Intellectual Re-
            sponses to European Contact,* edited by Philip D. Curtin. Madison:
            University of Wisconsin Press.
Stein, Howard and Robert Hill
    1977a   *The Ethnic Imperative: Examining the New White Ethnic Movement.*
            University Park: Pennsylvania State University Press.
    1977b   The Limits of Ethnicity. *The American Scholar,* Spring.
Stone, John, ed.
    1977   *Race, Ethnicity, and Social Change.* North Scituate, MA: Duxbury
            Press.
Szalay, Lorand B. and James E. Deese
    1978   *Subjective Meaning and Culture: An Assessment through Word Associa-
            tions.* New York: Halsted Press.
Taylor, William
    1969   *Cavalier and Yankee.* New York: Harper & Row.
Thompson, Hunter
    1967   *Hell's Angels.* New York: Ballantine Books.

Tonkinson, Robert
    1974   The Jigalong Mob: Aboriginal Victors of the Desert Crusade. Menlo
            Park, Cal: Cummings.
Trueblood, Marilyn A.
    1977   The Melting Pot and Ethnic Revitalization. In Ethnic Encounters:
            Identities and Contexts, edited by George Hicks and Philip Leis.
            North Scituate, MA: Duxbury Press. Pp. 153–168.
Turner, Frederick J.
    1893   The Significance of the Frontier in American History. American
            Historical Association, Annual Report for the Year 1893 (Wash-
            ington, DC:1894). Pp. 199–227.
Van Den Berghe, Pierre
    1976   Ethnic Pluralism in Industrial Societies: A Special Case? Ethnicity
            3:242–255.
Vysny, Paul
    1977   Neo-Slavism and the Czechs. Cambridge: Cambridge University
            Press.
Wallerstein, Immanuel, ed.
    1966   Social Change: The Colonial Situation. New York: John Wiley and
            Sons, Inc.
Walsh, James P.
    n.d.   The Ethnic, Political History of San Francisco 1890–1932. Cited in
            American Philosophical Report of Committee on Research 1975.
Weber, Max
    1947   Ethnic Groups. In Theories of Society, edited by T. Parsons. New
            York: The Free Press, 1961.
    1977   On Nationalism, Ethnicity, and Race. In Race, Ethnicity, and Social
            Change, edited by John Stone. North Scituate, MA: Duxbury
            Press. Pp. 18–25.
Webster's Seventh New Collegiate Dictionary, 1963. Springfield, MA: G. and C.
            Merriam & Co.
Whitten, Norman E.
    1976   Sacha Runa: Ethnicity and Adaptation of Ecuadorian Jungle Quichua.
            Urbana: University of Illinois Press.
Willis, William S.
    1971   Divide and Rule: Red, White and Black in the Southeast. In Red,
            White, and Black, edited by C. Hudson. Proceedings of the
            Southern Anthropological Society, #5. Athens: University of
            Georgia Press.
Wirth, Louis
    1944   The Problems of Minority Groups. In The Science of Man in the
            World Crisis, edited by R. Linton. New York: Columbia Univer-
            sity Press. Pp. 347–72.
Wolff, Richard D.
    1974   The Economics of Colonialism: Britain and Kenya 1870–1930. New
            Haven: Yale University Press.
Woodham Smith, Cecil Blanche
    1962   The Great Hunger: Ireland 1845–1849. New York: Harper & Row.
Zangwill, Israel
    1909   The Melting Pot: Drama in Four Acts. New York: Macmillan Co.

Index